AF614075

HIGHWAYS AND BYWAYS

A EUROPEAN PILGRIMAGE

HIGHWAYS AND BYWAYS

A European Pilgrimage

Nicholas Schofield

GRACEWING

First published in England in 2024
by
Gracewing
2 Southern Avenue
Leominster
Herefordshire HR6 0QF
United Kingdom
www.gracewing.co.uk

ISBN 978 085244 571 6

Cover image
Mont St Michel, France

Cover design by Bernardita Peña Hurtado

Typeset by Word and Page, Chester, UK

CONTENTS

Western Europe

Central Europe

Eastern Europe

Northern Europe

INTRODUCTION

Hilaire Belloc famously said that 'the Faith is Europe and Europe is the Faith'. In the globalised world of the twenty-first century this may sound smugly Euro-centric yet there is an important truth here. Without the perspective of the Christian Faith, a traveller in Europe will miss out on many nuances and depths. A historic church is more than just a building, with a tower so many feet (or metres) high and paintings by such-and-such an artist. A pilgrimage site more than just the gawdy shops and devout crowds. A religious festival more than just an exotic expression of local custom and folklore.

This volume is a companion to *Highways and Byways: Discovering Catholic England* (Gracewing, 2023), though it stands alone. Like the previous title, it is based on articles written for my 'Nova et Vetera' column in the *Catholic Times* between 2010 and 2020, with a few pieces written more recently. They reflect the various places I had the privilege of visiting during that decade—before a combination of Brexit, Covid-19 and the Russo-Ukrainian War made travel more complex and expensive (hopefully only in the short term!).

Of course, there is no claim to be a comprehensive guide and the omissions are too numerous to mention. Although some major shrines and cities have been included—Fatima, Lourdes, Paris, Santiago de Compostela, and, of course, Rome (which I felt deserved a separate section)—the focus is on the byways, the surprises, the hidden treasures of Europe that deepen and enrich our appreciation of the Faith. The book is best to be dipped into rather than read from cover to cover, and there are inevitable similarities between successive tales of heroism and sanctity, of apparitions and miraculous images, hidden and then rediscovered. As with the previous volume, I have unashamedly included popular traditions and legends, which not only add colour but (often) deepen our understanding of these holy sites. And there is frequent mention of British and Irish connections—of missionaries, recusants and Jacobites! After all, our islands remain a vital part of the story of European Christianity.

As I put this collection together, I think of all those I have shared these journeys with. This book is dedicated to them all. My late parents, Edward and Clare Schofield, who gave me my first taste of overseas travel. Angela Atkins, the late Frances Atkins, Mikey Atkins, and Dr Samuel Seddon, with whom I have shared many happy adventures in Donegal, Saxony, Portugal and elsewhere. My Finnish cousins—Pastor Chris, Päivi, Julius and Suvi Montgomery for some memorable times in Helsinki. My seminary chums, Fr Marcus Holden, Fr Mark Vickers and Fr Richard Whinder, who have indulged me in some ambitious and rewarding itineraries over the years. The late Mick How and Rick Jackson who introduced me to the battlefields of France and Flanders. Fliss, Grahame and Marcus Davenport, who suggested a day trip to Paris as this book was being completed. Jan Grensemann, who drove me round numerous German pilgrimage churches in his Jaguar. Georgina and the late Seamus McMorrow, who took me to Lucca and San Pellegrino. Fr John Berg who hosted me in Switzerland, the canons of Klosterneuburg for their generosity in Vienna, and Arno Hommel and all at the Dutch Zouavenmuseum. Parish groups from Our Lady of Willesden, Harlesden (with Sr Sheila Gosney RJM), and Our Lady of Lourdes and St Michael, Uxbridge, on pilgrimages organised variously through Tours for Churches, Pax Travel, Kensington Travel and St Peter's Pilgrimages. And, of course, to Tom Longford and all at Gracewing for their support and advice over the years and for bringing another publication to fruition.

Nicholas Schofield

ROME

THE ETERNAL CITY

SANTO SPIRITO IN SASSIA

All Roads Lead to Rome

The wonderful thing about the Eternal City, even for first-time visitors, is that everybody feels at home: 'all roads lead to Rome', as they say. Walking along the streets, half-remembered history lessons come to life, connections between historic events and characters are made, and there is an ever-present realisation that this is the cradle of Western civilisation and faith.

Moreover, as the British pilgrim stands at the airport check-in, there is a sense that many others have made this journey; that the queue actually stretches across the centuries. We do not know who the first pilgrim from these lands was. There was certainly much to-ing and fro-ing between Rome and the local churches, even in the early centuries, and the journey from Britain to Rome was made for a combination of business, pleasure and devotion. St Wilfrid's visit of around 653 is one of the first recorded, while his fellow Northumbrian St Benedict Biscop came no less than five times.

The journey was full of dangers. These included attacks from Saracens, Alpine snowstorms (which killed Archbishop Ælfsige of Canterbury as he made his way to Rome to collect the pallium in 959) and outbreaks of plague (claiming the life of another unlucky Archbishop, Wighard, in 668). Nevertheless, the pilgrims kept on coming. St Bede indicates that their number was already numerous by the late seventh century.

They included royalty. Several kings, such as the powerful rulers of Wessex Cædwalla and Ine, ended their days in Rome and were buried in the old St Peter's. Cœnred of Mercia arrived around 709, having resigned his crown, and was promptly tonsured by the pope. The future Alfred the Great visited in 853 and had the privilege of the pontiff standing as his confirmation sponsor. The Tuscan town of Lucca still venerates St Richard, 'King of Wessex', who died there *en route* for Rome.

Bernini's famous colonnade in St Peter's Square is supposed to resemble two outstretched arms, embracing the world and welcoming the crowds of pilgrims. However, there are several particular places where British visitors feel especially welcome. When the young Nicholas Wiseman, later to become first Archbishop of Westminster, arrived at the Venerable English College in 1818, as it re-opening after the Napoleonic Wars, he wrote: 'one felt at once at home … it was English ground'.

Just around the corner from the Vatican there is a reminder that there was an English institution in the city, the predecessor of the English College, from a very early date. The clues are in the name: the Renaissance church of Santo Spirito in Sassia and the street running alongside the Tiber, the Lungotevere in Sassia. This was once the Saxon Quarter, the Burgus Saxonum, and it is said that King Ine founded a *schola* or hospice there. Its origins are obscure but there was undoubtedly an 'English colony' in the locality, dating from the eighth century, where Anglo-Saxon pilgrims could find hospitality. The church of Santo Spirito still treasures an image of Our Lady, reputedly given to the church that once stood there by Ine, and if you are brave enough to get into the sacristy, you will see paintings of the king founding the Schola (with the help of Gregory II) and Offa, the great King of Mercia, adding to it in 794. It is said that this latter ruler donated one silver penny to the Schola for every yeoman family in his territory. No wonder there is a tradition that these early Saxon monarchs instituted 'Peter's Pence' as a sign of their devotion to the successor of St Peter—a collection revived in the nineteenth century, at a time of papal peril, and continuing to this day.

The Schola seems to have survived for nearly 500 years, though it faced many challenges. In the early ninth century, a disastrous fire destroyed much of the Burgus Saxonum, 'through the carelessness of some men of English race', but Pope Paschal I helped in its rebuilding. By the time of the Norman Conquest, the Schola was experiencing some decline, caused by travel restrictions in England, disputes with the emperor in Rome and the distraction of the 'armed pilgrimages' that we call the Crusades. Rome itself was often a violent, unstable place. About 1162 St Thomas of Canterbury reported that the Schola had dwindled to a few clerics, so it was little surprise that in 1201 Innocent III, the great reforming pontiff, turned the Schola into the Ospedale di Santo Spirito, which stands there to this day.

VENERABLE ENGLISH COLLEGE

The Cultural World of the English College

Rome is a city of seminaries, the United Kingdom alone being represented by the Beda, Irish, Scots and Venerable English Colleges. The last of these happens to be my own *alma mater*. It glories in the memory of its Forty-Four Martyrs and many other distinguished alumni. Yet, it is more than just a seminary. Since its foundation in 1362 as a hospice for English pilgrims and its transformation in 1579 into a seminary, it has been an important centre for the English in Rome, acting on occasion almost like an unofficial embassy.

We should not merely think of the College as a little piece of Rome that will be forever England. There were close interactions with the society and culture that surrounded it. The College came to be a not insignificant property owner. In the neighbouring streets the eagle-eyed can still spot small plaques with the words 'Coll. Ang.' (*Collegium Anglorum*). There was a summer villa in Monte Porzio (later replaced by Palazzola), a house at La Magliana for days-off and a vineyard on the Palatine, overlooking the Circus Maximus.

During the sixteenth and seventeenth centuries, the College enjoyed a lively cultural life, earning it a place amid the splendours of Baroque Rome. In the 1580s, for example, the College commissioned some of the leading Roman artists of the day to provide paintings for the church. The famous 'Martyrs' Picture', which still stands majestically above the main altar in the chapel, was painted by Durante Alberti, who later served as one of the *principi* of the Accademia di San Luca, the leading society for artists in Rome. On the feast of the College Martyrs (1 December) students gather to sing the *Te Deum* in front of the painting, just as their forebears did whenever news reached the College of a martyrdom.

Shortly after the 'Martyrs' Picture' was placed in the chapel, another important artist, Niccolò Circignani (known as 'Pomerancio') painted a series of frescoes depicting in sometimes gory detail the British Martyrs, from the beginnings of the Church up until the reign of Elizabeth I. He produced a similar set of martyrdom frescoes for the ancient church of Santo Stefano al Monte Celio, which belonged to the German and Hungarian College.

A century later, one of the most inventive of Roman artists was working in the English College: Andrea Pozzo. As early as 1581 a Sodality of the Blessed Virgin Mary was founded, as was common practice at many of the institutions run by the Jesuits. When the College building was remodelled in the 1680s, it gained a splendid new chapel for the use of the Sodality, now known as the 'Martyrs' Chapel'. In my time, this was used for Morning Prayer, private meditation and the 'visit' after dinner. Overhead is Pozzo's stunning ceiling fresco of the Assumption. Two years later this Jesuit lay brother would begin his masterpiece on the ceiling of Sant' Ignazio, which included, in the absence of an actual dome, a brilliant *trompe l'œil* substitute. Alberti, Pomerancio and Pozzo were all in the artistic 'premier league' of their generation.

The English College had a similarly impressive musical tradition. Felice Anerio was briefly *maestro di cappella* at the College from 1584 to 1585, giving an idea of the magnificence of its liturgical celebrations. Anerio's *Requiem* is still used by choirs today. However, having a salaried musical director seems not to have been the norm; musicians were typically hired for special occasions and composers commissioned to produce pieces. Rome, however, was an important city of music and those employed were often of the highest quality. The great Giovanni Pierluigi da Palestrina may have been commissioned to write a motet, *Posuisti, Domine,* for the feast of the College patron, St Thomas of Canterbury. A further connection is provided by his famous contemporary, Tomás Luis de Victoria, who was ordained subdeacon, deacon and priest in the chapel in August 1575. The medieval hospice had not yet made the transition to a seminary but the officiating bishop was the last of old English hierarchy, Thomas Goldwell, formerly Bishop of St Asaph.

The College was, as we have already mentioned, directed by the Jesuits, from shortly after its foundation until the Society's suppression in 1773. Drama played an important part in the Jesuit *Ratio Studiorum* (programme of studies), ticking a number of boxes. It played an important educational role in training the memory, developing eloquence, assisting deportment and increasing self-confidence. For lay students, drama taught the 'gentlemanly' arts of music, singing and dancing and might even attract patronage. Theatre also provided an excellent opportunity for public relations, catechesis and propaganda. The plays invariably had a religious or moral theme, such the lives of martyr saints (St Thomas of Canterbury or St Thomas More, for instance). There was often political commentary, such as that found in *Hierarchomachia or Antibishop,* which satirised the early-seventeenth-century controversy surrounding the appointment of an archpriest to govern the English secular clergy. The discovery in 2014 of a First

Folio of Shakespeare that had formerly belonged to the Jesuit English College at St Omer suggests that his plays may have been performed in Rome too.

The College productions necessitated elaborate costumes, staging and special effects; indeed, it was Jesuit ingenuity that invented the theatrical 'trap door'! After the departure of the Jesuits, drama continued to play an important part in the life of the College. When the seminarians had to flee Rome in May 1940 they discarded their normal cassocks and wore clothes provided by the theatrical department. One wonders whether they all looked equally *incognito*.

The Venerable English College is the oldest overseas British institution still in existence. More than just a Tridentine seminary, it had a surprisingly rich cultural life that made the most of the artists and musicians working in Rome, as well as the creative aspects of the Jesuit curriculum. The English Colleges on the continent were thus able to participate in the Catholic culture of Europe and hold liturgical and theatrical celebrations that would have been banned back home.

PIAZZA PASQUINO

Talking Statues

It is easy to walk past poor old Pasquino. Situated on a small square just beside the famous Piazza Navone, his battered statue consists of a flattened head and twisted torso. But, especially in the past, he played an important role, venting the frustration of Romans against the pope or political leaders. He was one of several 'talking statues' around which anonymous placards were placed and from his name derives the English term 'pasquinade', meaning 'a satire or lampoon, originally one displayed or delivered in a public place'.

Pasquino's statue is normally identified as King Menelaus, husband of Helen of Troy, whose face launched a thousand ships. It once formed part of a more elaborate composition depicting Menelaus lifting up the body of Patrocius, possibly dating to the third century BC. It was evidently buried in the vicinity and discovered during building work in the fifteenth century. The statue was named after Pasquino the tailor who once lived and worked in the area. His shop, claimed one nineteenth-century writer, 'was made the common resort for lovers of gossip and scandal in consequence of the peculiar talent possessed by its proprietor of writing lampoons upon his neighbours'. It is easy to see how the tradition of a 'talking statue' gradually arose.

On 25 April, the Feast of St Mark, Pasquino was the focus of a festival of poetry, often under the patronage of a cardinal. The statue was temporarily restored with *papier mâché* limbs and mythological costume. However, for much of the year Pasquino was a figure of protest, with popes coming under attack for their wars, taxes and nepotism, especially at the time of their election or death. At the death of Sixtus V in 1590, for example, Pasquino commented: 'Thefts, duties, taxes, hatreds, predations, bulls, reforms, *bandi*, assaults and tortures, though the death of Sixtus V they will end'.

It was said at the demise of Urban VIII, half a century later, that 'never has Pasquino prattled so much than for the death of this pope'. Urban's war against the Farnese Duke of Parma, for example, led to taxes on wine, salt, meat and bread. 'He stirred up cruel war', chafed Pasquino, 'he filled the world with his wicked fame that invented fifty taxes'. During his lifetime this Barberini pope was much criticised for removing the ancient bronze from the portico of the Pantheon in order to provide materials for Bernini's great *baldacchino* over the high altar of

St Peter's. This led to one of the most famous of all pasquinades, even though it was actually attached to the columns of the Pantheon rather than the statue of Pasquino himself. The anonymous writer wrote: *Quod non fecerunt barbari, fecerunt Barberini*, 'What the barbarians did not destroy, the Barberini did'. A similar satire claimed: 'Urban robs Flavius to pay for Peter', while when a tax on wine was proposed in order to build the Trevi Fountain, Pasquino ranted: 'Urban taxes our wine, then seeks to amuse us with water'.

Urban's successor, Innocent X, similarly fell victim to Pasquino's jibes. He commissioned Bernini to erect the celebrated Fountain of the Four Rivers in the Piazza Navona, incorporating an ancient obelisk that had been brought to Rome by the Emperor Domitian. Erected at considerable expense, Pasquino was highly critical of his neighbour: 'Innocent consecrated this obelisk to eternity, erected at expense of us innocents'. While the fountain was being built, placards appeared on the blocks of stone with the words: 'We do not want Obelisks and Fountains, it is bread that we want. Bread, Bread, Bread!' Slurs were also made against the pope's influential sister-in-law, Donna Olimpia Pamphili: *Olim-pia, Nunc impia* ('Once pious, now impious').

It is little surprise that successive popes tried to silence Pasquino. Adrian VI, the last non-Italian to be elected until St John Paul II, is said to have considered throwing the statue into the Tiber, until he was warned that, like a frog, he would only croak louder in water. Paul IV started a successful campaign against the pasquinade writers, with the result that the statue became particularly vocal at his death, while St Pius V issued a bull against them and had some arrested.

It was not only popes who were victims of Pasquino's tongue. During the French occupation, the letters of Napoleon's name were taken to form the following acrostic: ***N**on **A**mat **P**opulos **O**mnes **L**eges **E**vertit **O**mna **N**ostra **E**ripit* (loosely translated as 'He doesn't love the people, he overturns all the laws, he steals everything we have').

Pasquino was not the only 'talking statue' in Rome. Indeed, he would often enter into dialogue with his five colleagues across the city. These were mostly antique in origin: 'Marforio', the recumbent statue of a river god on the Capitoline; the 'Abate Luigi', now beside Sant' Andrea della Valle; 'Madama Lucrezia', a large Roman bust near the Basilica of San Marco; and a deformed Roman sculpture known as 'Il Babuino' (baboon). The last of the 'talking statues' was of more recent origin: 'Il Facchino', a Renaissance statue of a man holding a barrel, now on via Lata. The city thus became an open-air theatre of political comment and the pasquinades, which were written in Latin or Roman dialect, were much talked about, copied and sold, and even alluded to in operas. They performed much the same functions that blogs and social media do today.

The fall of the Papal States saw the close of Pasquino's golden age but he never completely retired. When Hitler visited Mussolini in 1938, this message appeared: 'My poor Rome, made of travertine, you've dressed up in cardboard to show off for a dauber [i.e. a crude painter] who thinks he owns you!' Posters and placards can still be seen around the bashed statue to this day.

The Papal States are often dismissed as being corrupt and tyrannical. However, at the death of the much-vilified Urban VIII, one commentator marvelled that 'the city speaks, writes and curses without respect and without fear'. The tradition of Pasquino and the other 'talking statues' of Rome shows that a degree of free speech and public debate existed that would have been the envy of many contemporaries.

TOR DE' SPECCHI

Francesca Romana

Despite falling within Lent, 9 March is regarded as a red-letter day in the Eternal City the feast of St Frances of Rome. Her magnificent convent of Tor de' Specchi ('Tower of Mirrors'), situated close to the large 'wedding cake' memorial to the first modern King of Italy, is open all day and crowded with Romans, pilgrims and (in my experience) seminarians skipping lectures. There are many opportunities to venerate the saint as they visit her rooms, admire the series of fifteenth-century frescoes depicting her life and miracles, and walk around the airy cloister. Many collect bottles of holy oil and leaves from a tree which the saint is believed to have planted.

'Francesca Romana', like Bridget of Sweden, was a married woman and a mother. She was in charge of a large household and, despite being attracted to a life of devotion and rigorous penance, once remarked that 'it is most laudable in a married woman to be devout but she must never forget that she is a housewife. Sometimes she must leave God at the altar, to serve Him in her housekeeping'. Let it be noted that housekeeping in her case meant not so much dusting and washing but the administration of the estate and managing a substantial staff.

St Frances suffered many trials, not least of which were the sufferings of her family due to the unstable political conditions of Rome at the time. Her husband, Lorenzo, was severely injured in one skirmish (in which he fought for the cause of the pope) and her son, Giovanni Battista, was taken hostage. She also had to cope with the deaths of another son and a daughter, the former dying from the plague when he was just nine years old.

Yet St Frances became known for her works of charity, her efforts to promote peace and her many miracles. She founded a community of women, the Oblates of the Tor de' Specchi, with whom she spent her final years after being widowed. Starting as a group of like-minded women who lived with their families while following a simple rule and helping the sick and poor, they adopted the communal life in 1433 and moved into the Tor de' Specchi. It was a surprisingly informal, 'open' convent, mixing monastic ideals with lay spirituality. The fact that no public vows were taken proved to be an advantage in the second half of the nineteenth century, when the property of so many religious houses was seized by the state. It was successfully argued that the Oblates lived in a free religious association and their property could therefore not be categorised as that of a religious order. It survived intact.

Since the death of St Frances in 1440, her convent has remained one of the spiritual hubs of the city. By the seventeenth century there were, at one stage, 138 Oblates, including members of the Colonna, Massimi, Orsini, Pamphili and other prominent Roman families. The jumbled assembly of medieval buildings was gradually replaced by a splendid new convent, boosted by the foundress' canonisation in 1608. Saints such as Philip Neri, Francis de Sales and John Bosco were closely associated with the community, and Pius IX's niece, Maria Pia, was a member. Today, though the Oblates dwindle in number, the influence of their Mother is still felt.

St Frances was granted the privilege of having the visible presence of her guardian angel by day and by night, which later became her iconographic symbol—normally shown as a youth dressed in a dalmatic or tunicle. When she committed a sin, the angel would hide until the saint made an act of contrition; in the midst of trials the celestial guide gave her comfort. It is because of this special protection and her ability to see in the dark (thanks to the angel's light) that Francesca Romana is regarded as the patron of motorists and is undoubtedly kept busy on the streets of the Eternal City. No wonder the crowds flock to her convent on her feast day!

SANTA MARIA IN VALLICELLA

The Saint of Cheerfulness and Kindness

St Philip Neri is surely one of the most attractive of saints—and one of the most unusual. Originally from Florence, he came to Rome as a layman and lived a life of deep prayer. He would often visit the catacombs for this purpose and at Pentecost 1544 experienced a globe of fire which descended from heaven and penetrated his heart, filling him with God's love. After his death, it was found that his heart was abnormally large and had even forced two ribs apart.

St Philip lived at a time of great reformers, and though, in so many ways, he is one of them, he also stands apart. As a layman he did much to catechise, to organise works of charity and to promote the Forty Hours' Devotion (designed as an alternative to the carnival celebrations). After being (somewhat reluctantly) ordained a priest at what was then the very mature age of 36, he organised gatherings in his room for prayer and instruction. They eventually had to move to a larger space, a chapel that they called the 'Oratory', and its influence soon spread across the Eternal City. Eventually these informal gatherings became formalised as the Secular Oratory (consisting of devout laymen) and the Congregation of the Oratory, a community of priests and brothers. This was approved by the Holy See in 1575 and by the time of St Philip's death twenty years later, a splendid new church (the Chiesa Nuova—Santa Maria in Vallicella) was being erected in Rome for the Oratorian community.

St Philip was not chiefly concerned with any 'specialised' work or grand strategy, but rather focussed on the priestly apostolate *per se*, based around celebrating the sacraments and preaching the Gospel. He was not primarily concerned with education or missionary evangelisation, as his friend St Ignatius was. He produced no learned tomes, like St Robert Bellarmine, and followed no system of Church reform, like St Charles Borromeo; he did not devote himself to the sick in the same way as St Camillus de Lellis, nor immure himself within a cloister, like his fellow Florentine, St Catherine dei Ricci. St Philip rather led by example; his words were inscribed on the hearts of his penitents; he reformed Church and society through his ministry in the confessional. He achieved all this with a spirit of joy, good humour and gentleness.

At the very heart of St Philip's charism was the Mass. It is, indeed, appropriate that the majority of paintings of the saint depict him in priestly vestments. His disciple and biographer, Antonio Gallonio, writes that during Mass 'he would suddenly be so filled with the Holy Spirit that he could hardly pour the wine and water into the chalice in the usual way; his hands would be raised up so that he looked as if he were dancing or jumping up'. Throughout his life, we are told, St Philip continued 'to receive those assaults of divine love' so that he elevated the Host and Chalice quickly for fear that he might never be able to lower his arms and, to distract himself, he would sometimes walk the length of the altar, talk to people around him, and make comments to the server about the quality of the light. As he vested in the sacristy, he would listen to amusing poems or play with little dogs. If it had been any other priest, these actions would have seemed irreverent; but they were manifestations of his sanctity that are uniquely his own and can never be imitated.

For over three decades St Philip lived at San Girolamo della Carità, situated opposite the English College. He must have known many of the seminarians and, knowing that they faced martyrdom back home, greeted them in the street with the words *Salvete, Flores Martyrum!* (Hail, Flower of the Martyrs!). Indeed, it became their custom to obtain his blessing before they returned to England. Fast forward 250 years and the most famous of the Oxford converts, St John Henry Newman, regarded this quintessentially Roman institution, founded at the height of the Catholic Reformation, as being ideally suited for Protestant England. Oratories were founded at Birmingham and London (the latter under another notable convert, Frederick Faber).

It is easy to see why Newman found the Oratory so attractive. He thought 'the nearest approximation in fact to an Oratorian Congregation' was an Oxford College—'take such a College ... change the religion from Protestant to Catholic, and give the Head and Fellows missionary and pastoral work, and you have a Congregation of St Philip before your eyes'. What he had done at Oriel and Littlemore could clearly be continued under the watchful eye of St Philip. The Exercises of the Oratory, for example, not only included prayer but talks and discussions 'dealing at times with the same matter, scientific or literary, as those lectures in the Mechanics' Institutes' or apologetic topics. It could serve very well the evangelisation of industrial Britain and resembled, in part, a spiritual tutorial.

Moreover, St Philip was well known for his liberty of spirit, which well suited the English temperament. The Oratorians are bound not by vows but by mutual charity; there is no reliance on a long list of rules and regulations. Newman wrote that words such as 'austerity' or 'sternness' are 'unknown in an Oratorian House'. Indeed, 'it was

St Philip's object, instead of imposing laws on his disciples, to mould them, as far as might be into living laws, or, in the words of Scripture, to write the law on their hearts'. And so the saint's influence continues to this day.

SAN MARCELLO AL CORSO

San Marcello and its Crucifix

Amidst the anxiety and suffering of Covid-19, two Roman images stick in my mind. Firstly, that of Pope Francis walking along the Via del Corso. This narrow street is normally full of shoppers but on this occasion it was deserted. The pope walked alone, accompanied only by his security, and made a surprise visit to the church of San Marcello al Corso to pray in front of the miraculous crucifix for an end to the pandemic, for the sick and all healthcare workers.

The crucifix was later brought to a similarly empty St Peter's Square for an extraordinary Urbi et Orbi blessing—empty but watched by millions worldwide. It was moving to watch the Vicar of Christ carry the monstrance alone to the entrance of the basilica and bless the city and the world.

At the centre of both these poignant moments was a large fifteenth-century crucifix. The church where it is kept is not particularly well known, though it is frequented by students of the nearby the Gregorian University, especially during the stresses of 'examtide'.

Despite its baroque façade, San Marcello is one of the Eternal City's oldest parishes, tracing its origins to around 308 when it was the house of a devout lady called Lucina, wife of Pinianus. The sacred mysteries were secretly celebrated there and it was closely associated with the pope of the time, St Marcellus, who is most famous for dividing Rome into twenty-four parishes or *tituli*. Within a few years the oratory was closed during the persecution of Maxentius. The buildings were used as stables for the public carriers (*catabulenses*)—essentially the postal service—and, according to one tradition, the pope himself was condemned to stable work, 'wretchedly clad and wearing a hair-shirt' as he 'worked in the vile service of the animals'. He eventually died as a result of his treatment and was buried in the cemetery of St Priscilla; in the fifth century, however, his remains were translated to the church that now stood on the site of Lucina's house.

The church was rebuilt several times and given to the Servite Order in 1375. In 1519 it was destroyed by a fire and all that remained was a large crucifix, which emerged out of the ruins intact, still with a small oil lamp burning in front of it. It soon gained a reputation for being miraculous, especially in 1522 when Rome was hit by the plague. The crucifix was carried in procession to St Peter's, despite the restrictions placed by the authorities. The procession took some sixteen days since the crucifix was taken to each region of the city and the people flocked to pray in front of it. Gradually, the plague lessened in its intensity and each neighbourhood was eager to keep the crucifix for as long as possible. By the time the crucifix returned to San Marcello, the plague was over. These events led to the foundation of an Archconfraternity of the Most Holy Crucifix in 1526 and the completion of a separate confraternity chapel, the Oratorio del Santissimo Crocifisso, in 1568. The tradition began of taking the crucifix to St Peter's each Holy Year and in times of crisis; many will remember the moving scenes of St John Paul II embracing it in 2000 while repenting of the various sins committed by members of the Church.

After the fire of 1519, funds were collected to rebuild San Marcello and designs produced by Jacopo Sansovino. However, the money was used to bribe the mercenaries of the Emperor Charles V so that the complex was preserved during the Sack of Rome in 1527. The present façade only dates from the seventeenth century.

As with so many Roman churches, there is an interesting English connection at San Marcello: go to the third chapel on the right-hand side, next to the chapel of the crucifix, and you will find the tomb of Cardinal Thomas Weld, who died in 1837—one of two widower English cardinals in the nineteenth century (the other one being Manning). The Weld family was based in Lulworth Castle in Dorset. Thomas married Lucy Clifford, by whom he had a daughter, and became Squire of Lulworth in 1810, but was widowed five years later. Once his daughter was grown up and herself married, Thomas entered the ecclesiastical state; he was ordained a priest in 1821 and a bishop five years later. The original plan was that he would work as a coadjutor bishop in Canada but poor health meant that he never crossed the Atlantic. He resided in Rome and was made a cardinal in 1830, a mark of recognition to England in the year following Catholic Emancipation. Cardinal Weld's titular church was San Marcello al Corso and his apartments at the Palazzo Odescalchi became a major magnet for the English Catholic community. Weld was able to work for British interests in Rome.

The most distinctive thing about Cardinal Weld was that he was often seen in company of his grandchildren, raising many a Roman eyebrow. On one occasion, it is recounted, he was caught in a violent storm while driving through the streets and raised his ceremonial umbrella (found in all cardinal's carriages) to shelter his grandchildren. He was known as the 'Cardinal of the Seven Sacraments'.

Cardinal Weld died unexpectedly on 19 April 1837 and was buried at his titular church, alongside his daughter and son-in-law. Of his grandchildren, William became Bishop of Clifton, Henry was awarded the Victoria Cross at Inkerman (during the Crimean War) and Mary Constantia helped recruit for the regiment of the Pontifical Zouaves to defend the pope's temporal sovereignty in the 1860s.

Not far from Cardinal Weld lies another eminent member of the Sacred College, Ercole Consalvi, Secretary of State under Pius VII and a protégé of the Cardinal Duke of York. His portrait can be found in the Waterloo Chamber at Windsor Castle, in recognition of his contribution to restoring peace and stability to post-Napoleonic Europe. Together they await the Day of Resurrection, gathered round the Cross, in which they placed their hope and to which we also turn in our hour of need.

SANTA MARIA DEGLI ANGELI

The Meridian in the Basilica

On a visit to Rome we made our way to Termini station to catch a train to Frascati, a favourite spot for an excursion. However, since the next train was nearly two hours away, we decided to tour some of the churches in that part of the Eternal City and so found ourselves, within five minutes, at the Basilica of Santa Maria degli Angeli e dei Martiri.

At first sight the church looks very ancient. And it is. The building was cleverly designed by Michelangelo to use the surviving walls of the Baths of Diocletian, so that the facade is a hotchpotch of Roman ruin and Renaissance structure. The baths were huge, the largest in Imperial Rome, and the basilica was built on the *frigidarium*, the cold room; a nearby church also takes its name from them: Santo Bernardo alle Terme (St Bernard at the Baths).

Although the property had been given to the Carthusians in the eleventh century, no church or monastery was built there until the sixteenth century. Perhaps the profane baths were thought a rather unsuitable location for a consecrated church. It is said that St Philip Neri once passed the spot and saw an evil spirit in the form of a man whose face changed quickly from youth to old age. The saint made the sign of the cross and the spirit fled.

However, it also seemed most appropriate to build a church there. Diocletian had, of course, been a notable persecutor of Christians. Indeed, an old tradition said that over ten thousand Christian slaves were condemned to hard labour in erecting the baths and that, after the project was completed, they were put to death and later venerated as 'St Zeno and his Companions'. A church using the walls of the Baths was thus a fitting memorial to the martyrs and a sign of the triumph of Christianity over paganism. As an inscription on the church walls read: 'What was an idol is now a temple of the Virgin ... Demons begone!'

Today the basilica is perhaps best known for an unusual feature in one of its transepts: a meridian line on the marble floor commissioned by Clement XI in 1702. As the science of astronomy advanced, it was found that churches, with their high walls and darkened spaces, made ideal observatories. Much information could be gained from a beam of sunlight passing through a carefully made hole in the church wall and moving across the floor. The idea was that at noon it would pass the meridian line and the length of the solar year could be calculated. The church effectively became a pinhole camera, a solar observatory.

Meridians can be found in various churches around the world—St Sulpice in Paris, San Petronio in Bolgna, St Peter's in Rome and elsewhere. This was a result not only of the Church's patronage of science but the need to date Easter precisely. The Council of Nicaea had decreed that Easter should be celebrated on the Sunday following the first full moon after the vernal equinox and, in order for it to be kept on the same day around the Church Universal, it was calculated in advance. The need for accuracy led to a new calendar being introduced by Pope Gregory XIII in 1582—this removed ten days from the calendar and thus corrected a discrepancy that had been building up.

Meridians continued to be built to check the accuracy of the calendar and Clement XI thought Santa Maria degli Angeli an appropriate place for a number of reasons. The ancient walls were stable and had long stopped settling into the ground. The structure was vast and orientated towards the south, thus receiving much exposure from the sun. Moreover, the use of a Roman building for this purpose symbolised the old (pagan) Julian calendar being replaced by the (Christian) Gregorian one.

The meridian also brought prestige to Rome—if Bologna had a well-known meridian, designed by Giovanni Domenico Cassini (the discoverer of four of Saturn's moons) in 1655, then so should papal Rome! Built by Francesco Bianchini, the new meridian not only allowed observation of the sun but also the stars Polaris, Arcturus and Sirius.

Easily missed is a fascinating oval plaque in the floor, a few feet away from the meridian. Around the edge is the name *Iacobus III D.G. Magnae Britanniae etc Rex* ('James III, by the grace of God, King of Great Britain')—referring, of course, to the exiled son of James II. In the centre are the words: *Felix Temporum Reparatio* ('Happy Restoration of the Times'). This has a double meaning. It refers to James's official recognition of the Gregorian calendar in 1721—somewhat belatedly, for most European countries had accepted the Gregorian reforms long before, but ahead of Protestant Britain, which only adopted the calendar in 1752. It was a bold step, distancing himself from the British way of dating and showing his close connections with Catholic Europe. But, of course, there is also reference to the long-desired restoration of James to the Throne of Great Britain. The previous year his wife had given birth to 'Bonnie Prince Charlie' and the Stuart succession seemed assured.

Most importantly, the meridian reminds us of an important truth that is frequently overlooked. As J. L. Heilbron wrote in his illuminating study on the subject, *The Sun in the Church: Cathedrals as Solar Observatories*, 'the Roman Catholic Church gave more financial and social support to the study of astronomy for over six centuries, from the recovery of ancient learning during the late Middle Ages into the Enlightenment, than any other, and, probably, all other, institutions'. Forget the black legend of Galileo; the Church loved to gaze at the stars.

SANTISSIMO REDENTORE E SANT'ALFONSO

Our Lady of Perpetual Succour

The church of Santissimo Redentore e Sant'Alfonso in Via Merulana, the titular church of Cardinal Vincent Nichols, is not one of the ancient basilicas to which pilgrims flock. It is slightly off the beaten track, on the street that links St John Lateran to St Mary Major, not far from Termini station. Yet it is a fascinating place with a surprisingly little-known story full of British connections.

Sant'Alfonso all'Esquilino, as it is often called, houses a famous image of Our Lady, one which most readers will recognise: Our Lady of Perpetual Succour (or Perpetual Help), reproduced widely and the focus in many places of a popular Novena. In the picture, the Christ Child holds His Mother's hand as He gazes at angels holding the instruments of His future Passion. Mary, meanwhile, looks down at Him with an expression of deep compassion and love. This beautiful icon was first venerated in Crete, where it probably originated, but in the 1490s was obtained by an Italian merchant who transported it to Rome. Some people say he stole it; others that he purchased it or brought it to safety for fear of the Turks. Whatever the motive, he kept it in his house until he became seriously ill and, on his deathbed, asked that it be venerated by the faithful. On 27 March 1499 the icon was taken in procession to the nearby church of San Matteo on the Via Merulana. During the procession, a paralytic was cured. This brought the image much fame and over the centuries numerous favours were attributed to Our Lady of Perpetual Help.

San Matteo, which for a time was cared for by the Irish Augustinians, was destroyed during the Napoleonic occupation of Rome. Fortunately, the wonder-working image was saved and hung in several churches. The Redemptorists moved to a property near the original site of San Matteo and permission was granted to bring the icon to their new church of Sant'Alfonso in 1866. As in 1499, miracles were reported, including a young girl who regained use of a paralysed leg. Soon afterwards the image was solemnly crowned by the Vatican Chapter and the devotion was rekindled and spread across the world by the Redemptorists. She has even been named Patroness of Haiti.

Sant'Alfonso claims to be the last church to have been built in the Eternal City before the fall of the Papal States. It is in the gothic style and was designed by an Englishman, George Wigley, who was also helped bring the Society of St Vincent de Paul to Great Britain. The church was built at the expense of one of the early Oxford converts, the Redemptorist Fr Edward Douglas (1819–98). Though little known today, he is a most intriguing figure. Descended from the earls of Douglas and Mar and related to the Marquess of Queensberry, he was educated at Eton and Christ Church, Oxford. At university he was influenced by Newman's sermons and numbered among his friends Charles Scott Murray and William Lockhart, who would both convert to Rome and play an influential role in the Church. Douglas himself led the way, being received into the Church during a visit to the Eternal City in 1842.

It is said that he had gone to Rome with Scott-Murray and queued up to witness the papal ceremonies for the Feast of the Chair of St Peter. Being British, Scott-Murray had brought his umbrella but was not allowed to bring it into the ticketed area—and so he deposited it in the nearest confessional, opposite the tomb of Benedict XIV. He was later unable to retrieve it and sent Douglas to pursue the matter. The conversations that he had with the Carmelite friar in whose confessional the umbrella had been found were crucial in his path to conversion.

Thanks to his inheritance of a large sum of money, Douglas was able to travel extensively and three years after his conversion made a memorable trip to the Holy Land, which formed the basis of a book published later in life. His initial desire was to become a Franciscan and it was with them that he was ordained in 1848. However, poor health required him to look elsewhere and so, we read, 'he found a second St Francis in St Alphonsus de Liguori, the founder of the Redemptorists'.

Working for a while in Ireland and London (where he partly paid for the erection of St Mary's, Clapham), he was called to Rome in 1853. Here, once again using his family fortune, he purchased the Villa Caserta on the Via Merulana, to serve as the General House, and built the adjoining church of Sant' Alfonso. It reminds us that the converts of the nineteenth century brought not only spiritual but sizeable financial benefits, without which the 'Second Spring' would have been impossible.

Fr Douglas remained at Sant'Alfonso as rector for forty years. When papal Rome fell and the Italian government began confiscating ecclesiastical property, he declared that the Villa Caserta was his own personal property and exempt from the legislation. He even boldly hoisted the Union Jack and sent his documents to the British ambassador for his assistance, although when the matter was referred to London orders were given that the flag must be taken down.

Fr Douglas also held important posts within the Redemptorists—including (on three occasions) Roman Provincial—and seems to have been well known among the British community in Rome, with an extensive network of friends and contacts. He made many converts, included David Hunter-Blair (the writer and Abbot of Fort Augustus), and after his death there was even talk of a cause for his beatification.

SANTA MARIA IN ARA COELI

Sibyls and Bambinos

One of my favourite Roman churches is that of the Ara Coeli, run by the Franciscans, tucked behind the Victor Emmanuel monument and accessed via a steep staircase of 124 steps. It contains many interesting features, including an ancient icon of Our Lady, giving its name to the church, and the tomb of St Helena, mother of Constantine and, according to some, the daughter of 'Old King Cole'.

According to legend, the church was built on the site of an altar erected by the Emperor Augustus, with the inscription *Haec ara Filii Dei est* ('This is the altar of the Son of God'). It was here that he had consulted the Tiburtine Sibyl (normally associated with Tivoli) about his successor. She saw a golden ring appear around the sun, in the middle of which stood a beautiful Virgin holding a child. A voice was heard: 'This woman is the Altar of Heaven (Ara Coeli)!', and the Sibyl told the emperor: 'This Child will be greater than you'.

In times past, the Jewish prophets were counterbalanced by pagan sibyls, prophetesses who were honoured by the ancient Greeks and Romans. Heraclitus was the first to mention a sybil as early as the sixth century BC. Their number tended to fluctuate between nine and twelve and they were normally identified by the place where they lived, such as the 'Delphic Sybil' or 'Cumaean Sybil'. In later centuries their prophecies were given a Christian interpretation and they came to be represented in Catholic art, drama and music. Indeed, the opening of the *Dies irae* (traditionally used at Requiem Masses) says: 'That day of wrath, that dreadful day/shall heaven and earth in ashes lay / as David and the Sybil say' (*Teste David cum Sibylla*).

The Ara Coeli reminds us of this ancient tradition, whereby the Gentile as well as the Hebrew world looked towards the coming of the Saviour. And the fulfilment of all these prophecies and hopes is neatly represented in a small chapel just beyond the sacristy, containing the miraculous *Santo Bambino,* dating from around the fifteenth century and carved, it is said, from an olive tree that stood in the Garden of Gethsemane. It narrowly escaped destruction during the French occupation of 1798, thanks to the foresight of a devotee who hid the image with the nuns of San Cosimato.

Sir George Head, a not entirely sympathetic visitor to Rome in the mid-nineteenth century, described the Bambino as 'about the size of a child of two years old, the cheeks remarkably full and round, painted red and white, like the cheeks of a doll' and 'enveloped in swaddling-clothes of scarlet and gold, that, after the Italian fashion, conceal the whole body like the cerements of a mummy'. The miraculous image was often taken to the homes of the seriously ill and, it was said, the fate of the patient was indicated by the colour of the Bambino's cheeks, 'which, in the event of a favourable termination, remain red … and where death is about to ensue, turn pale invariably'. The writer once 'chanced to meet the Bambino *in transitu* on one such occasion, on its way to the chamber of the afflicted person, whither it was conveyed in an ordinary hired carriage, covered with a scarlet cloth and resting on the knees of two Franciscan friars, who sat apart in each corner of the vehicle'.

It was at Christmas that the church of the Ara Coeli truly came alive, with the Bambino being placed in the crib. Head reported 'it is impossible to penetrate the compact mass of people gathered round about, or even catch a glimpse of the object without very considerable exertion' and 'the 124 steps leading to the entrance are all day crowded with a moving mass, ascending and descending, of women in white caps and red and yellow bodices, all with step as light and faces as smiling as if going to or coming from a theatre'. Moreover, stalls appeared 'where plain and coloured engravings of the Bambino are not only exposed for sale at various prices, but urged upon the public by the vendors with the same steady importunity as playbills in the neighbourhood of the Opera-house'.

Moreover, during Christmas time, local children would be brought to the church to deliver well-rehearsed 'sermons' in honour of the Christ Child. M. D. Stenson noted that 'their unaffected simplicity is very sweet, their bows and courtesies most natural and attractive; some of the small orators are so tiny that they have to be held by their mother or nurse whilst they pronounce their short discourse, gazing meantime with wide open eyes at the Royal Infant whom they are addressing'.

The original Bambino was unfortunately stolen in 1994 by, in the words of a recent guidebook, 'a blasphemous thief commissioned by someone who has removed it from worshippers and from everyone else, whether to destroy it, profane it or possibly enjoy it in evil and saddening secrecy (given that its fame prevents it from being sold)'. A replica was quickly commissioned, and blessed by St John Paul II. It is still the object of fervent devotion and I was present there one Epiphany when a cardinal took the Bambino in procession to the steps of the basilica and, surveying the fine cityscape, gave the divine Infant's blessing *Urbi et Orbi*.

ROME AT CHRISTMAS

The Music of the Pifferari

Christmas, more than any other feast, is closely associated with music. For many people it is the only time of year when they willingly listen to church choirs and put on the classical repertoire. My mother always thought Christmas began with listening to the 'Service of Nine Lessons and Carols' on the radio.

The traditional sounds of Christmas in Rome, at least in bygone days, were rather different from those heard in King's College: peasant musicians came down from the nearby mountains, armed with bagpipe (rather more primitive than the ones we know and love in Scotland) and a relation of the oboe called the *piffero*. These musicians were generally known as *pifferari* and for a period of about a fortnight after the Immaculate Conception they would walk through the streets of the Eternal City. If they passed a wayside Marian shrine—of which there are many—they would pause to play a serenade, heads uncovered.

Sometimes they were actually employed by the owners of a property with a sacred image to perform a novena; they also entered shops which had erected an impromptu shrine. 'Nothing seems more pleasing', wrote William Neligan in the 1850s, 'than the *coup d'œil* presented by the shops in Rome at this season of the year, when the Madonnas are illuminated, and the goods offered for sale artistically disposed on inclined planes, form a pyramid on which the painting of the Blessed Virgin rests, ornamented with flowers and lights.'

One observer recalled that 'it is a spectacle at once edifying and picturesque, to see a street in Rome brilliantly lighted by thousands of luminous specks [the lights before the street shrines], like the fireflies of Italy, and resounding with the rustic music of the *pifferari* of Calabria or the Abruzzi. At all times these mountain musicians assemble a great concourse of people at the foot of the Madonnas, especially in Advent; for they seem anxious to introduce by their rural airs the feast of the shepherds, the most holy night of Christmas.'

The composer Hector Berlioz wrote that the musicians 'usually wear broad coats of brown cloth, and the same pointed hats worn by brigands; their appearance has a kind of wild mysticism which is full of originality'. The music was certainly novel to most visitors; 'the bagpipe, supported by a large *piffero* which sounds the bass, plays a harmony of two or three notes, over which a medium length *piffero* performs the melody. Then on top of it all two small and very short *pifferi*, played by children of 12 to 15 years, rain down trills and cadences and bathe the rustic melody with a cascade of exotic ornaments'. Rather like the Highland pipes, 'heard at close quarters the sound is so loud as to be almost unbearable; but heard from a certain distance this strange orchestra has an impact which leaves few unmoved'. Such was their picturesque quality that *pifferari* became a popular subject with artists.

The Romans normally welcomed these visits; indeed, it was said that one year when they did not appear there was famine and flood. However, the *pifferari* could sometimes be a nuisance. Stendhal complained that they 'have been waking us up at 4 in the morning. It's enough to make a man hate music'. The more unscrupulous were locals who dressed up as Abruzzi peasants to please tourists, rather like the Roman legionaries posing for photos outside the Colosseum today. *Pifferari* were even known to introduce lyrics questioning the virtue of the wives of those who failed to give a donation! After Christmas some of these musicians could return to their homes, whether in the Abruzzi or nearer to Rome, having made a small fortune.

A great deal of Christmas music has a 'pastoral' flavour, calling to mind the intimate, rustic scene at the stable in Bethlehem. Some carols derive from folk tunes and dances, such as *Good King Wenceslas* or *Ding, dong merrily on high!* Composers often adapted such melodies in their Christmas pieces—one thinks of the soothing 'Sinfonia' found in both Bach's *Christmas Oratorio* and Handel's *Messiah*, which imitate the sounds of the bagpipe and *piffero*.

As a student in Rome, I encountered *pifferari* once or twice, but they were becoming a rare sight. This is a pity because they remind us of the meaning behind Christmas.

ROME IN LENT

Station Churches

One of the most distinctive Lenten customs is that of the station churches in Rome. Dating back to the late second or early third centuries, a church was allotted to each day of the season and to this day pilgrims continue to visit these stations.

Open up an older Missal and it is easy to find the names of the station churches. Some are well known—for instance, on the Fifth Sunday of Lent, as well as Easter Tuesday, we read: *Statio ad S. Petrum* and our minds and hearts are transported to the great Vatican basilica. On the Second Sunday of Lent, though, we are at one of Rome's hidden gems: Santa Maria in Domnica, situated on the Caelian Hill and boasting a celebrated ninth-century mosaic in the apse. For Catholics worldwide, the Lenten stations formed a tangible link with the Eternal City and with the customs of the early Christians.

Scholarly opinion is divided on the origin of the word *statio*. Some argue it comes from *stare*, to stand, calling to mind the long prayers during which the congregation stood. Others claim it originated as a military term, linked to a Roman soldier's guard duty, watching carefully for the enemy—an appropriate image for Lent as we do battle with sin, using the weapons of prayer, almsgiving and self-denial.

Whatever the exact origins, the word 'station' came to be used for the Masses that would be said each day during Lent (and other important seasons) in a different Roman church. The clergy and people would first gather in the afternoon at a church known, rather fittingly, as the *ecclesia collecta*. The pope or his representative would normally be there, together with the seven deacons assigned to each of the districts of Rome. Once all had gathered and a prayer was said, they would process to the station church or *statio* singing litanies. Mass would then be celebrated, after which the Lenten fast for that day would officially be over and some refreshment could be enjoyed.

The station churches eventually became fixed although over the years several disappeared and had to be replaced. Thus, the station of San Ciriaco, a church near the Baths of Diocletian, was transferred to Santa Maria in Via Lata because it had fallen into ruins. Today each *statio* has a solemn Mass, normally celebrated by a visiting cardinal and featuring a procession with litanies (though normally this is done round the church rather than from an *ecclesia collecta*).

The custom had fallen into decline and was revived over the last hundred years, with indulgences granted by Pius XI and Pius XII. In 1959 St John XXIII visited the station for Ash Wednesday, the Dominican church of Santa Sabina on the Aventine, where he received the ashes. His example has been followed regularly by the last three pontiffs. Another important catalyst has been the Masses organised at each station by the Pontifical North American College.

As a seminarian, I tried to attend some of these Masses. Twice I saw St John Paul II arrive at Santa Sabina and watched the procession of cardinals make their way from the nearby church of Sant'Anselmo. Then the following day, a Thursday (our day off), I would go to San Giorgio in Velabro, partly because of its English connections—it was Newman's titular church as cardinal. But soon, sad to say, my Lenten enthusiasm waned and the seminary timetable as well as the distance of some of the churches made further visits impractical. A special effort was made on the Tuesday of the Fourth week in Lent when the *statio* was just down the road from the College at our parish church, San Lorenzo in Damaso.

The focus of the station was not so much the building but the saint who gave the church its name and, in many cases, was buried there. The liturgist Pius Parsch wrote that this patron played an important part in the liturgy of the day: 'so vividly was the station saint before the minds of the assembled people that he seemed present in their very midst, spoke and worshipped with them'. Thus, with such saintly company, the pilgrimage through Lent continues.

ROME IN HOLY WEEK

The Miserere and the Veronica

One of the most famous pieces of sacred music is the sublime setting of the *Miserere* (Psalm 50) by Gregorio Allegri (1582–1652), who sang for many years in the Sistine Chapel. Even those who know little of choral music will probably recognise this piece, with its alternating chant and polyphony, and its soaring top C. Composed for the Sistine Chapel, it was sung each year at the Office of Tenebrae.

Until the Second Vatican Council, Tenebrae was one of the main services of Holy Week. It was essentially the combination of Matins and Lauds (Office of Readings and Morning Prayer in modern parlance) for the last three days of Holy Week. 'Tenebrae' means darkness or shadows and the ceremony involved the gradual extinguishing of fifteen candles on a special structure called a 'hearse' (a name which underlines the funereal feel of the service). While the Benedictus was sung, the final candle was removed to behind the altar, symbolising Christ's burial in the tomb. The chapel was in complete darkness and it was at this point that the *Miserere* would have been sung. Then the *strepitus* began—a noise made by the banging of books on the stalls. It called to mind the earthquake that took place on Good Friday and also constituted the Church's mourning and her prayer that Christ should return. The lone candle was finally brought back, placed on the hearse and all departed in silence.

No wonder Tenebrae at the Sistine Chapel was such a popular part of the Grand Tour—a combination of the dramatic ritual, the stunning location and, at its heart, the famous music. Writing in 1826, the Catholic author John Richard Digby Beste noted that 'tickets of admission were given to the ladies, and a part of the chapel is partitioned off for them. All the men got in as far as they could, while a space was set apart for those whom their dress entitled to such distinction. Here, during the whole of the office, I waited with impatience till the *Miserere mei, Deus* should commence. What had I not heard of this psalm! Of the gradual extinction of the tapers; of the figures of Michael Angelo's famous Last Judgment frowning from the walls, as the shades of night slowly overspread the sanctuary'. Such was his high expectation that he was ultimately disappointed by the Roman way of singing, disgusted by the presence of the *castrati* and felt drowsy when the lights were extinguished.

Never has a piece of music been such the stuff of legend. The Holy See realised that Allegri's *Miserere* was an exceptional composition and it is often claimed that it refused to allow any copy to leave the Sistine Chapel, under pain of excommunication. This is often presented as yet another example of the Church's secrecy and obscurantism. In actual fact, unofficial copies were widely available for sale and by the 1770s at least three copies were known to exist outside the Eternal City. One was held by Emperor Leopold I, another by the King of Portugal, and a third by Padre Martini, a Franciscan composer and musical scholar. The emperor was gravely disappointed when his choir performed the piece in Vienna and he complained to the pope that an inferior composition had been sent. It seems, however, that methods of performance differed in Rome and Vienna and the copy did not include the ornamentations that were the speciality of the Sistine Choir. As Cardinal Wiseman noted, 'the written notes are simple and unadorned; but tradition, under the guidance of long experience and of chastened taste, has interwoven many turns, dissonances and resolutions, which no written or published score has expressed'.

There is no evidence that the Papacy threatened excommunication for those who made unauthorised use of the *Miserere* though it is clear that it wanted to protect the piece. In the absence of copyright laws, music could very easily be copied, stolen or plagiarised. It was not uncommon to restrict the number of copies being made and to memorise the music, so that it was passed on orally—making the work of modern musicologists rather more complicated.

A further '*Miserere* legend' holds that when the fourteen-year-old Wolfgang Amadeus Mozart visited Rome in 1770, he heard the *Miserere* sung at Tenebrae on Holy Wednesday. Suffering from insomnia that night, he proceeded to write it out from memory. Returning to the Vatican on Good Friday, he was able to check the veracity of his version and only made a few minor corrections.

His father Leopold, a composer in his own right, wrote to his wife: 'You have often heard of the famous *Miserere* in Rome, which is so greatly prized that the performers are forbidden on pain of excommunication to take away a single part of it, copy it or to give it to anyone. But we have it already. Wolfgang has written it down and we would have sent it to Salzburg in this letter, if it were not necessary for us to be there to perform it. But the manner of performance contributes more to its effect than the composition itself. Moreover, as it is one of the secrets of Rome, we do not wish to let it fall into other hands.'

It seems that the Mozart showed off his achievement to his admirers, possibly including the English music historian, Charles Burney, who he met in Bologna. The following year Burney published the *Miserere* in London, leading some to assume that he obtained a copy from Mozart. Perhaps we will never know, for no original copies of Mozart's transcript survive, though Burney's edition is unadorned, while the performance enjoyed by the young composer would have been full of embellishment. Burney may have had access to the copy kept by Padre Martini.

The *Miserere* that sounds so familiar to us is the result of modern editors and musicologists, though attempts have been made by choirs like The Sixteen to rediscover Allegri's original sound. Whatever version we might listen to, though, the *Miserere* and the other musical classics of Holy Week are bound, in the words of Wiseman, to leave the listener 'in a state of subdued tenderness and solemnity of feeling, which can ill brook the jarring sounds of earth, and which make it sigh after the region of true and perfect harmony'.

*

The Stations of the Cross presents us with a series of moments in which Jesus received the compassion of others: He meets His mother, is helped by Simon of Cyrene and His face is wiped by Veronica—resulting in His image being imprinted on her cloth. The only one of these characters not to be mentioned in the Gospels is Veronica; it is the apocryphal *Acts of Pilate*, dating from the fourth or fifth century, that first alludes to her. Over the centuries, tradition has given her the names Berenice, Seraphia or Veronica, which comes from the Latin *vera* ('true') and the Greek *ikon* ('image').

The existence of the woman Veronica is closely linked to one of the most famous relics of Christendom: an image of Christ's face, 'not made by human hands', which is said to be her veil. First mentioned in the sixth century, it was carried into the battle of Solachon by the Byzantine forces as they faced the Persians in 586. Art historians have suggested that from the sixth century onwards depictions of Christ become remarkably similar, as if based on some authentic image that served as a model—perhaps the image on the veil or a similar image bearing the face of Christ, the 'Mandylion', which was supposedly sent to the King Abgar of Edessa by the Saviour.

Eventually the veil was brought from Constantinople to Rome and became known as 'the Veronica', one of the principle relics venerated by pilgrims. Some of the earliest references to it in the Eternal City are made by two separate English pilgrims in 1199: Gerald of Wales and Gervase of Tilbury. Indulgences were attached to the veil and badges of it were widely sold as souvenirs.

Then it mysteriously disappeared in the early sixteenth century, around the time that the new Basilica of St Peter's was being constructed and the city was sacked by German mercenaries (1517). Was it lost or stolen or hidden away? Some say it was taken to Manoppello, where there is an intriguing image of the *Volto Santo* that was first recorded around 1508. Similar objects can be found in Vienna, Alicante, Jaén and elsewhere. Were some of these early copies, or (as has been suggested) did they come from different folds of the original veil, or is one the actual Veronica itself?

At a later stage, a veil reappeared at St Peter's and even to this day it is shown on the Fifth Sunday of Lent. I remember once attending Vespers on this occasion and seeing three of the canons appearing on the balcony above Bernini's statue of Veronica beneath the dome. They were holding a frame which contained an image partly covered in metal; at a distance it almost looked like a large baking tray! Bells rang as they blessed the congregation with the relic.

In 1849, at a time when a Roman Republic had been declared and the pope had fled to Gaeta, the veil was solemnly exposed and the image seen to grow pale, seemingly reacting to the political turmoil. This led to a revival of devotion to the 'Holy Face', helped also by the visions of Sr Marie of St Peter, a Carmelite of Tours, who encouraged acts of reparation to wipe away, as it were, the dirt and spit that the nineteenth century had thrown at Christ's countenance. There was a boom in reproductions of images of the Veronica, authorised by the canons of St Peter's who had custody of the relic. They kept a careful eye on the propagation of the devotion. Indeed, in the Middle Ages if a monarch requested to privately venerate the veil he had first to be admitted to the Chapter of the basilica.

The existence of the relic purporting to be the veil is beyond doubt, but who was the woman Veronica, assuming, of course, that she actually existed? An early tradition identifies her as the woman with the haemorrhage who was healed by touching the garments of Jesus, as recounted in each of the synoptic gospels. There is some similarity between this gesture and that of Veronica wiping the face of Jesus. Perhaps in doing so Veronica was trying to give something back to the Lord who had healed her?

From at least the eleventh century it was suggested that Veronica had travelled to Rome with the veil. The Emperor Tiberius was cured of sickness through contact with it, before the precious relic was entrusted to Pope St Clement. Another legend claims that Veronica became a missionary disciple, bringing the good news to the western coast of France. She is depicted arriving in Bordeaux with St Martial and bringing with her relics of the Blessed Virgin and St John the Baptist. She lived to a ripe old age and was buried either at St Seurin, Bordeaux or Notre Dame de Fin des Terres ('Our Lady of Land's End'), in the nearby seaside resort of Soulac-sur-Mer—once an important part of the medieval English pilgrimage route to Santiago. This last church is interesting in that it was almost entirely covered by sand in the 1700s before being uncovered and restored at great expense. The ancient city of Noviomagnus that stood on the site and which presumably would have been known (possibly) by Veronica was itself lost to the Atlantic in the sixth century.

Another charming story has her marry Zacchaeus, the tax collector of Jericho who climbed up a sycamore tree in order to see Jesus. Together they came to France but whereas Veronica chose the active life, Zacchaeus became a contemplative. In the Middle Ages he was identified with St Amadour, who lived as a hermit and founded the sanctuary of Rocamadour, situated dramatically in a gorge off the river Alzou, north-east of Cahors.

At the end of the day, however, these biographical details do not really matter. The encounter of Jesus and Veronica is one of the most beautiful and tender moments on the Way of the Cross. It is, in many ways, a feminine counterpoint to the assistance given to Jesus by Simon of Cyrene, although it is interesting that Veronica is venerated as a saint while Simon is not. She becomes an urgent summons to us all not to turn away from the suffering around us.

CASTEL GANDOLFO

The Pope's Summer Playground

The Italians have the wonderful concept of *villeggiatura*: a summer break not in the sense of a package holiday or an exhausting tourist itinerary but rather a retreat to the country for a time of refreshment and repose, preferably at the family villa. This is not only a very healthy concept but also a practical necessity given the summer heat.

Traditionally most Roman seminaries and religious houses would have had a property outside the Eternal City to which an escape could be made during the harsh summer months. The English College is one of the few still to have one—the beautiful Villa Palazzola, perched on the edge of Lake Albano, south-east of Rome, and used today not only by seminarians but many groups of visitors.

The view is astonishing: over the raised garden wall are the densely wooded slopes leading down to the oval lake, situated in a volcanic crater; far in the distance is Rome, with the dome of St Peter's visible on a clear day, and the glistening Mediterranean; and straight ahead, on the other side of the lake, is Castel Gandolfo, with its papal summer palace, Bernini church and Vatican observatory. Here it is that the Roman pontiff traditionally withdrew for summer rest, prayer and study. It was never a complete holiday, of course: there were still meetings, audiences and appearances for the Sunday Angelus.

As a seminarian I often walked around the lakeside path to this peaceful oasis. Approaching 'Castel G' (as it was referred to), much-needed shade is provided by the large ilexes planted by Urban VIII (1623–44) and a sign announces that the town is twinned with Chateauneuf du Pape, which fulfilled a similar purpose when the popes resided in Avignon (France) and required a summer residence. It is a short walk into the main town square, dominated by the papal palace. The presence of Swiss Guards and the collection of vulgar souvenir stalls make the town a veritable 'little Vatican'. The 1929 Lateran Treaty officially declared the palace and its grounds as Vatican territory. Much of the land is used by the papal farm—milk, olive oil, honey and other products are sent to the Vatican. There are animals, too—including, at one stage, two gazelles given to Pius XI by the Apostolic Delegate in Egypt. The pope (who had established the farm) always visited them during his stays at the villa.

Castel Gandolfo could be said to be the only remnant of the old Pontifical States outside the Eternal City. The town's extra-territorial status meant that at least 12,000 sought refuge there during the Second World War, including many Jews. The papal apartments were even used as a maternity hospital. Sadly, the town did not escape bombardment by the Allies and 500 were killed or wounded on just one day (10 February 1944).

Not surprisingly, given the stunning location, there were many villas in the area during ancient times. Indeed, the ruins of Domitian's great villa can still be seen in the papal gardens. After passing through the hands of several powerful Roman families, the town finally became the pope's summer playground at the turn of the seventeenth century. Urban VIII was the first to spend his summers there and adapted an existing palace for papal use, with the help of the architect Carlo Maderno. Interestingly, the palace nearly became the Palazzo Stuart when, in 1718, Clement XI (1700–21) offered it to the exiled Stuarts. However, 'James III' turned the offer down since the property was considered rather too small and unsuitable in the winter, since there were no working fireplaces or chimneys (hardly a necessity for the popes in the Roman summer).

Trudging around the town, it is fun to imagine how popes occupied themselves while on holiday. Those who were aged and frail would have been unable to make the most of the surrounding countryside and several pontiffs seem not to have used the town as a summer residence. Innocent XII, for example, spent one night there but the visit coincided with such bad weather that he never returned. More recently, Pope Francis chose not to use the palace and opened it to the public.

Others came to love the spot. Benedict XIV, known for his witticisms, told his secretary when faced with numerous requests for audiences: 'I do not want to be bothered here; we have to put up with all these people when we return to Rome'. Alexander VII, whose family owned a magnificent property a few miles away at L'Arricia, was fond of walking under the ilexes and boating on the lake. Clement XIV would go riding and sometimes startled his attendants by galloping off into the distance for some peace and quiet. This eventually had to stop after several accidents. Gregory XVI seems to have enjoyed fishing on the lake, following to the letter the words of his divine Master: *Duc in altum* ('pull out into the deep').

The Victorian travel author, Augustus Hare, recorded that 'Pius IX spent part of each summer here before the invasion [of 1870]; and every afternoon saw him riding on his white mule in the old avenues or on the terraced paths above the lake, followed by his cardinals—a most picturesque and medieval scene'. He would walk around the town and visit houses, even those belonging to the poorest. If there was not enough food in the house he would give out generous gifts of money.

Let it not be forgot, however, that popes occasionally came here to die and pass into the eternal *villeggiatura,* most recently Pius XII (1958) and Paul VI (1978). The latter expressed his love for the spot during an Angelus address in August 1972: 'we too enjoy this God-given gift, by breathing the fresh air, admiring the beauty of our natural surroundings, appreciating the enchantment of its light and silence, and seeking here to restore our lack of energy, which is never enough and now even a little scarce'.

SOUTHERN EUROPE

Greece, Italy, Malta, Portugal,
San Marino, Spain, Turkey

ATHENS (GREECE)

St Paul in Athens

If Paris has the Eiffel Tower and Sydney its Opera House, the unmistakable icon of Athens (and indeed the whole of Greece) is the Parthenon. From the rooftop of our pilgrimage hotel, there was a fine view of it, perched on top of the majestic Acropolis and splendidly lit up at night. It formed the perfect backdrop to a glass or two of *ouzo*.

The Acropolis and the Parthenon, it should be noted, are not the same thing. Many ancient Greek cities were built around a raised area called an *acropolis*, which is derived from *akron* (high place) and *polis* (city). Here there would typically be a fortress, where the citizens could retreat in times of danger, and a series of religious buildings. The Parthenon in Athens was built on the Acropolis in the fifth century BC as a temple to the goddess Athene, celebrating a recent victory over the mighty Persian Empire. It is seen by many as a perfect and much-imitated example of classical architecture.

Of course, there is an ongoing debate about the sculpture that once decorated the building and is now displayed in several European museums—most notably the marbles 'rescued' by the seventh Earl of Elgin and deposited in the British Museum in 1817. Much ink has been spilt over whether this was an act of cultural vandalism or a far-sighted move that saved them for posterity.

Few remember that the Parthenon was a church for a large part of its existence. Turned into a place of Christian worship in the sixth century AD, it was dedicated to the Blessed Virgin Mary, thus replacing that other virgin, Athena. Although Christians are often accused of destroying much classical civilisation, the temples that have survived more or less intact were those that were transformed into churches. Think of the Roman Pantheon, which became the Basilica of St Mary of the Martyrs, or, elsewhere in Athens, the Theseum, a temple of the god Hephaistos that served as a church of St George in the Middle Ages. The Parthenon, then, does not only belong to ancient Greece; it was a place of Christian pilgrimage, with many precious relics, and, during the Latin occupation of Athens (1205–1458), when the city was ruled by French, Aragonese and Italian dukes, it was actually a Catholic church.

In the fifteenth century Byzantine rule was replaced by that of the Turks and the Parthenon became a mosque; its medieval bell-tower converted into a minaret. In 1682, George Wheler, an English visitor, wrote that 'the Roof over the Altar and Quire added to the temple by the Greeks, hath the picture of the Holy Virgin on it, of Mosaic Work, left yet by the Turks; because, as they say, a certain Turk having shot a Musquet at it, his hand presently withered'.

Its present ruinous state dates back to a Venetian attack in 1687, part of a Christian offensive against the Turks in the years following the Siege of Vienna (1683). As the Venetians besieged the city—which, by this stage, was a shadow of its former self—many of the population sheltered within the Parthenon, along with a store of gunpowder. It was hit by artillery and the resulting explosion destroyed the old temple and killed around 300 people; 'the bombs did their work so effectively', wrote one contemporary, 'that never in this world can the temple be replaced'.

Athens is, of course, closely connected to St Paul, who would have beheld much of the same Parthenon that we still see today. He came alone, waiting for his companions Silas and Timothy, and as he wandered about the streets was 'revolted at the sight of a city given over to idolatry'. The place was full of temples and statues; indeed, a proverb said that there were more gods in Athens than men! St Paul proclaimed the Gospel in the synagogue and in the *agora* or market place, where even Epicurean and Stoic philosophers argued with him. Having made quite a stir, he was summoned before the Areopagus council, a high court that considered (among other things) religious matters. It met on a rocky outcrop beside the Acropolis, which today has stunning views of the city and is occupied by tourists taking selfies or lying in the sun. Mounting the low summit is something of a challenge, especially if you use the rock-hewn steps, and it is hard to imagine what it looked like in St Paul's time and whether he was as unsteady and dishevelled as this writer as he made his ascent.

Yet it was here that he made his famous 'Sermon on the Unknown God': 'I noticed, as I strolled around admiring your sacred monuments, that you had an altar inscribed: To an Unknown God. Well, the God whom I proclaim is in fact the one whom you already worship without knowing it'. As a skilled evangelist, he managed to find a local point of connection and build on the religious longing that he witnessed around him.

St Paul did not stay in Athens long. He made at least two converts: a woman called Damaris, about whom we know next to nothing, and Dionysius the Areopagite, a member of the council before whom the apostle spoke. Local tradition says that St Paul had to hide after converting the councillor, taking refuge in what is still called 'St Paul's

Well'. Another tradition has St Dionysius, many years before, standing in the Parthenon on the day of Christ's crucifixion and scratching a cross on one of its pillars as he felt the resulting earthquake. In Byzantine times, the cross was proudly shown to pilgrims to the church.

Over the years St Dionysius came to gain several new identities. He was remembered as first Bishop of Athens and patron of the city. In the early sixth century, a series of mystical writings was wrongly ascribed to him, their author now called 'Pseudo-Dionysius the Areopagite'. He was also misidentified with St Denis, the bishop and martyr commemorated in Paris.

The nineteenth-century Catholic cathedral in Athens is dedicated to St Dionysius and remembers the legacy of the apostle. Although St Paul did not establish a church, as such, in the city and wrote no epistles to the Athenians, his brief visit was a landmark event: an early encounter between the Judaeo-Christian world and classical antiquity.

BARCELONA (SPAIN)

The Jewel of Barcelona

Looking at the skyline of Barcelona, it is remarkable that the most iconic landmark is surrounded by cranes, still (at the time of my visit) under construction—the Basilica of the Sagrada Familia. It must have been the case for many medieval towns as they raised their gothic cathedrals; but this is a church for the modern age, unlike any other ecclesiastical building in Europe.

Of course, there are other churches worthy of a visit. There is Santa Maria del Mar, as the name suggests situated near the sea, and the medieval cathedral dedicated to the Roman martyr, St Eulalia, whose torments included being rolled down a street in a barrel full of knives. The street can still be seen nearby, with a cruelly steep gradient: the Baixada de Santa Eulalia (the Descent of St Eulalia). The saint now lies at peace in the crypt and the thirteen raucous geese kept in the cloister are a tribute to the martyr's assumed age at the time of her passion. The church of Santa Maria del Pi (Our Lady of the Pine Tree) in the Gothic Quarter originated in a tradition that a statue of Our Lady was discovered inside the trunk of a pine tree near the city walls by a fisherman looking for wood to build a boat.

But it is to Sagrada Familia that the crowds flock. I was unsure how I would react to such a 'one off' church but, like so many visitors, I was overwhelmed by the colours, the complex vaulting, and the pillars which resemble trees. There may be echoes of Disneyland, sandcastles and a science fiction film set, but the building is solidly based on a coherent theological vision. Sagrada Familia truly is a sermon in stone; every detail has meaning.

The genius behind this was the architect Antoni Gaudi. Born in 1852 to a wealthy family, he studied architecture at Barcelona but, due to his unique artistic vision, got only a mediocre result—on being awarded his degree, the school's director is said to have commented: 'we have given this academic title either to a fool or a genius. Time will show'. Gaudi set himself up in offices in Barcelona and began to make a name for himself, especially after meeting Eusebi Guell, a wealthy industrialist with a love for the arts who would become his patron. Gaudi's buildings can be found throughout Barcelona (and beyond) and have become the city's 'brand'. It is the Sagrada Familia, though, that is seen as his masterpiece, even if left unfinished at his death.

The mid-nineteenth century was a difficult period for the Catholic Church. The pope in Rome faced losing his temporal sovereignty as a result of Italian unification. Spain had seen constant attacks on the Church, confiscations of property and the shutting of religious houses; and the worst was still to come. At the same time, Catholicism was experiencing a resurgence and there was a growth of lay associations, such as the Association of the Friends of St Joseph, led by a bookseller, Josep Maria Bocabella. By 1878 it boasted half a million members. The idea soon emerged of building an Expiatory Temple of the Holy Family as reparation for the sins of modernity. It is a great paradox that the great landmark of a city marked by long periods of anticlericalism and liberalism is a church built with such motives.

The Association bought a piece land outside the city centre, where flocks of goats could still be seen, and employed an architect by the name of Francisco de Paula del Villar. The foundation stone was laid on St Joseph's Day 1882 but he resigned the following year and Gaudi (still a young architect) was given the commission in his place. As time went on, the project became the principle focus of his life and in his last years he virtually lived on site.

The design showed the architect's strong faith—there would be a forest of spires, one for each of the twelve apostles and four evangelists, and for Our Lady and (tallest of all) Jesus, though His was slightly lower than Barcelona's Montjuïc hill as Gaudí believed that his creation should not surpass God's. As Pope Benedict said at the basilica's consecration in 2010, Gaudi 'brought together the reality of the world and the history of salvation, as recounted in the Bible and made present in the liturgy. He made stones, trees and human life part of the church so that all creation might come together in praise of God, but at the same time he brought the sacred images outside so as to place before the people the mystery of God revealed in the birth, passion, death and resurrection of Jesus Christ'.

Gaudi was not just an architectural genius with a well-developed theological understanding; he was also a man of God. In his youth he was something of a dandy and a gourmand, but he increasingly withdrew within himself as he got older. Though he could be bluff and opinionated, many remarked on his humility and ascetic lifestyle. He had a great love for the poor and built alongside the Sagrada Familia a school for the children of his workers. He lived like a hermit and his daily routine consisted of early morning Mass, many hours in the workshop, frugal meals and an evening walk to his Oratorian confessor.

It was while walking to the church of Sant Felipe Neri on the evening of 7 June 1926 that he was knocked down by a Number 30 tram. It seems that he often walked along oblivious of the world around him, deep in his thoughts, and that he also strongly believed in the rights of pedestrians over trams and cars. As he lay in the street, many assumed he was a drunken tramp. He had no papers of identification on him—only a copy of the Gospels and some nuts in his pocket, his underpants held together by safety pins. When his friends began searching for him, he was eventually found and soon bishops and artists lined the corridors of the Hospital de Santa Cruz. But it was too late; three days after the accident, the great architect was dead.

Gaudi's death did not mark an end to the Sagrada Familia—as he often said to his impatient colleagues, 'my client can wait'. Gaudi felt no hurry since his master was eternal and the principle concern was that the work was done for His glory, *ad majorem Dei gloriam.*

There were many challenges along the way. The basilica was, of course, a potent symbol of the Church and her opposition to revolutionary principles. In 1936, during the Spanish Civil War, the Communists raided the church, set fire to the crypt and destroyed many of Gaudi's plans and models. The tombs in the crypt were broken into, though it seems that Gaudi's remains were left in peace. Nevertheless, Salvador Dalí heard from the children of a friend that the architect's body was seen being dragged through the streets.

The basilica was not always as popular with locals as it is today. In the years following Gaudi's death, writes the historian of the city Robert Hughes, 'most workers in Barcelona regarded it with indifference or outright hostility as a gloomy, excessive symbol of the ideology of their bosses and of the clergy who served them'. Building resumed in 1952 but controversy continued. The destruction caused by the civil war meant that successive architects had to fill in the gaps and guess how Gaudi would have wanted the church to look. Indeed, Gaudi continually adapted his plans as the building work progressed; he was spontaneous, open to his architectural muse. It must be said that some of the recent additions to the Sagrada Familia are of an uneven quality, using inferior materials such as reinforced concrete. Some have even argued that work should have stopped with the architect's death.

Sagrada Familia is a building that demands a reaction. George Orwell called it 'one of the most hideous buildings in the world'. Others have been converted after visiting it and it is clear that the basilica leaves a deep impression on many of the camera-clicking tourists. Set for completion in 2026, the centenary of the architect's death, there are hopes that Gaudi himself will be raised to the altars of the Church. While praying for the necessary miracle, many might say that his greatest one was this awe-inspiring, iconic church.

BRAGA (PORTUGAL)

Stairway to Heaven

Travel across Catholic Europe and before long you will stumble across a Calvary. They come in many shapes, sizes and designs, and became popular sites of pilgrimage. Acting as vast open-air catechisms, they were so effective because they involved the whole person: the statues and chapels depicting Christ's Passion and Resurrection formed a vivid 'poor person's Bible'; the bodily ascent up the mountain or mound, often in a place of natural beauty, matched the interior path that was being made; and, especially on a day of pilgrimage, there would be prayers, processions and services to stir the soul.

Calvaries seem to have developed in the fifteenth century, when there was an increase in devotion to the Passion of Christ. The ongoing struggle with the Turks made pilgrimages to the Holy Land increasingly difficult and so pilgrims had to make do with localised versions, a Jerusalem 'down the road' rather than on the other side of Europe. Many of the Calvaries were made as replicas of the holy places, based on measurements and drawings that were popularised by writers such as Androchimius, author of a work on Jerusalem at the time of Christ (1584).

There are notable examples in Italy: Domodossala, Belmonte and Varese, for example. Overlooking the Portuguese city of Braga is another one, which became much-imitated in the Hispanic world: the sanctuary of Bom Jesu do Monte ('Good Jesus of the Mountain'), with its elaborate zigzag sets of stairs (*escadaria*) leading to a neo-classical church. There had been a medieval chapel on the summit dedicated to the Holy Cross and a popular confraternity was founded in the seventeenth century. Then in 1722 the Archbishop of Braga conceived a grand plan for a majestic Calvary; a monumental staircase was constructed, leading pilgrims on a spiritual itinerary up to the shrine. Before the apparitions at Fatima, Bom Jesu was the major pilgrimage site of Portugal. To help the pilgrimage, a hydraulic funicular railway was opened in 1882—the oldest one in the Iberian Peninsula—and this is still in use for those who want to avoid the steep climb up the 573 steps, which was traditionally done on the knees.

Reaching the shrine, the pilgrim zigzags up the mountain, passing five fountains, each representing one of the senses. Most visitors use these as photo opportunities but some continue to use them according to their original purpose. At the 'sight' fountain, for example, water pours out of the eye sockets of a stone face and the pilgrims dip their fingers in the water and touch their eyes. This procedure is repeated for each of the senses, so that the pilgrim follows a ritual of self-purification: 'cleanse my senses, remove all that distracts or tempts me, and lead me closer to God'. As the summit draws nearer, the focus changes and the final section of the staircase is dedicated to the virtues of faith, hope and charity. There are statues of Old Testament figures, too, and chapels portraying episodes of the Passion.

The view from the top is, of course, impressive. On a clear day, you can spot the glittering waters of the Atlantic in the far distance. Before you is the great city of Braga, the 'Portuguese Rome' and the country's third largest city, with its multiple church towers and baroque facades. The suburb of Real boasts what may be the country's oldest-surviving church, built by St Fructuosus on the site of a Roman temple, and the archbishops of Braga claimed (without much effect) to be *Primatus Totius Hispaniae*. The antiquity of the see is reflected in the Rite of Braga, one of the few local liturgical rites to survive the Council of Trent, which made the Roman Missal virtually standard across the West. The most recent edition of the Braga Missal was published in 1924 and its distinctive characteristics included the saying of the Hail Mary at the beginning of Mass and double genuflections, which may have originated as a way of stressing belief in the Real Presence to counter the Priscillian heretics of the fifth century. Though this Rite is now seldom celebrated, the traditional Holy Week customs are still observed, with processions of large statues and barefoot, hooded members of confraternities, similar to those in Seville.

Having admired the panorama, the tired pilgrim enters the church. After the all-encompassing climb, some find the sanctuary disappointing. But there should be other things on the mind of the devotee: the summit represents the summit of Calvary on which Bom Jesu died on Good Friday to bring us new life. This Portuguese shrine represents a true stairway to Heaven.

CIVITAVECCHIA (ITALY)

The Barque of Peter

St Peter was a fisherman and so perhaps it is no surprise that those who succeeded him as Bishop of Rome should have an occasional concern for maritime affairs. This was especially the case as the centre of the Italian peninsula developed into the Papal States, including a long coastline that needed security and surveillance. Concerned largely with the threat of raids and invasions, papal ships also helped transport crusaders to the Holy Land, free Christian slaves in north Africa and patrol the seas for contraband goods. Over time, the Marina Pontificia (Papal Navy) emerged, with Civitavecchia as its headquarters.

Situated 37 miles north-west of Rome, the strategic location of Civitavecchia has been utilised down the centuries by war ships, merchant ships and (now) cruise ships. The Emperor Trajan, who had a villa nearby, rebuilt the harbour, remnants of which can still be seen. Christianity was present from an early date: Pope St Cornelius died in exile here, and the local patron, St Firmina—long regarded as a protector of sailors—shed her blood during the persecution of Diocletian. However, after the collapse of the Roman Empire the port became the regular target of raiders and the citizens moved to the mountains for safety.

By the second millennium the decision was made to return to the 'old city'—for that is what Civitavecchia means. The 1461 discovery in nearby Tolfa of alunite made a tremendous boost to the local economy. This was the source of alum, essential for the dyeing of textiles, and its discovery was interpreted as a triumph over the Turks, since it had previously been imported from Anatolia. Alum quickly became a papal monopoly and a key component of Vatican finances; much of it was stored in and shipped from Civitavecchia.

Such was the port's military and economic importance that famous masters were commissioned to design its defensive structures. The Fortezza Michelangelo bears the name of the great Renaissance artist, who may (possibly) have been responsible for one of its towers. Bramante and Sangallo were also involved in building this large fort, which still dominates the city. Likewise, Bernini designed the Arsenal of the Papal Navy, sadly destroyed by Allied bombers during the Second World War.

Sitting by the harbour and imagining papal ensigns flying from passing ships, I reflected on the little-known connections between the Papal Navy and Great Britain. In April 1755, for example, two thirty-gun frigates, the *San Pietro* and *San Paolo,* arrived in Civitavecchia having been constructed in London. Almost immediately they were used to repel attacks on shipping from corsairs. Occasionally they had other duties, such as transporting two cardinals back to Marseilles after the conclave of 1758.

In 1774 the Duke of Cumberland and Strathearn, younger brother of George III and a vice-admiral, visited Rome and inspected the papal dockyard. The pope then offered him use of the frigate *San Clemente* for part of his return journey, though Horace Mann commented, 'I should doubt whether his prudence in a political light will be approved of, in accepting one of the Pope's frigates to carry him to Toulon'. The ship was 'crammed with all sorts of provisions' and 'new liveries were made for the Bargemen'. On arriving at Toulon, spectators could see the unusual sight of a papal vessel flying the Royal Standard and exchanging salutes with the British ship that waited to take the duke home.

The pope's navy suffered with the French invasion of 1798 and the subsequent Napoleonic occupation of the peninsular. Interestingly, two bronze guns bearing the arms of Pius VI and dated 1787 can be found at Dunster Castle in Somerset; presumably they were used by the French and later captured by the Royal Navy.

After the concordat with Napoleon, two ships were presented by the French to the pope. These included the *San Paolo,* which had started life as *HMS Speedy*. Built in Dover and launched in 1782, this 14-gun brig served the Royal Navy with distinction in the French Revolutionary Wars and was involved in the capture of several French ships and privateers. It was captured by the French temporarily in 1794 and then again in 1801. The following year the ship arrived in Civitavecchia, with the words inscribed in gilt: 'Given by the First Consul Bonaparte to Pope Pius VII'. It was finally decommissioned around 1806 but its former exploits in British service have lived on, inspiring Patrick O'Brien's novel *Master and Commander*.

Three small iron paddle-wheel tugs were ordered from Ditchburn and Mare of Blackwall, on the Thames, for Gregory XVI. They would be used on the Tiber and were named after three pioneers of steam power, *Archimede, Blasco de Garay* and *Papin*. The journey of the small boats from London to Civitavecchia in 1842 was something of a pioneering adventure; after being anchored off Margate, they made the crossing over to Fecamp and then to the Mediterranean through the rivers and canals that cut across France. This caused much interest at the time and the pope himself boarded the *Archimede* once it reached Civitavecchia. This tug was still on the Tiber in 1910.

In 1859 the Thames Ironworks built the final papal ship: the screw corvette *Immacolata Concezione*. Armed with eight 18-pounder guns and a steam engine of 160 horsepower, it was intended to protect papal fisheries and, if necessary, transport the pontiff to safety—this was, after all, an age when the papacy felt threatened by the spectre of revolution and the push for Italian Unification that sought to diminish the pope's temporal power.

The corvette made a speed of 12 knots during her trail on the Thames and was featured in the *Illustrated London News*. While still in London, the ship was visited by Cardinal Wiseman, who expressed 'himself much pleased with the perfect order and arrangement of the whole'.

The period saw several brief campaigns in which the Papal States were forced to defend its territory. In 1860 the London-built *San Paolo* was involved in the blockade of the Piedmontese fleet in the Adriatic and brought safely to Ancona the pay chest of the papal army. In 1867, the *Immacolata Concezione* and the *San Pietro*, another naval vessel built in England, patrolled the coast to prevent the landing of Garibaldi and his Red Shirts.

With the Fall of the Papal States in 1870, the *Immacolata Concezione* was exempted from the general confiscation of all the papal military and naval assets, since as flagship she was regarded the personal property of the pope. She remained untended at Civitavecchia until 1877, when the pope presented the ship to the Ecole St Elme in Arcachon, a French training school for sailors run by Dominican friars. She was briefly in British hands again, as the merchant vessel *Gitana* registered in Glasgow (1885–95), before being destroyed by fire in the Mediterranean in 1905, the last survivor of the Papal Navy.

The Holy See no longer has a navy but the Barque of Peter still continues its journey across the waves, often encountering stormy weather and perilous crossings. But if you find yourself in Civitavecchia—or indeed walking along the Thames—spare a thought for the ships and tugs that once served the pope on the high seas.

DELPHI (GREECE)

The Centre of the World

Where is the centre of the world? For the ancient Greeks, the answer was clear: Delphi, on the mainland of Greece, near the Gulf of Corinth and with fine views of the northern Peloponnese in the distance. According to legend, the site had been selected by Zeus himself after sending out two eagles from the extremities of the earth; the place where they crossed was over Delphi.

Situated at the foot of Mount Parnassus (2,457 m) and near an important crossroads, Delphi had been one of the great Greek sanctuaries since around 1200 BC. At its heart was the Temple of the god Apollo, son of Zeus and Leto, who was normally represented as a young, athletic man, beardless and holding a bow. He was associated with music, healing, light, plague, poetry, truth and prophecy. It seems, though, that Apollo was something of a newcomer to Delphi. Originally a serpent or dragon lived there, eventually slain by Apollo and left to rot in the heat of the sun—the Greek verb 'to rot' is *puthein*, which is perhaps why the place was known as 'Pytho', Apollo given the title of 'Pythios' and the priestess known as the 'Pythia'. The story of the serpent may be a reminder that in the remote past, the first sanctuary on the site was dedicated to the worship of snakes. Other sources claimed that before Apollo, a 'sybil' or prophetess lived there, perhaps a daughter of the sea god Poseidon.

Delphi became a 'pan-Hellenic' sanctuary, recognised by the many different city states, who would present it with riches and gifts. The modern visitor can see the ruins of treasuries built by the Athenians and Siphnians to permanently house the various offerings made. In time, the Pythian Games were held every four years to celebrate the feast of Apollo, At the top of the archaeological site are the remains of an impressive stadium, where athletic contests were once held, while a hippodrome has recently been identified on the plain of Krissa, not far away, where chariot races were organised. Indeed, in the museum, is Delphi's most famous sculpture: that of a victorious charioteer, with eyes made of semi-precious stones which have a magnetic quality. With participants coming to the Games from Greek cities and colonies across the Mediterranean, Delphi had become a centre of the world in fact as well as in mythology.

Most famously, Delphi was the home of an oracle for a thousand years: priestesses who claimed to be mouthpieces of Apollo. The oracle had to be an older woman of blameless life chosen from among the peasants of the area. It was a lifelong commitment, involving chastity (though they could be previously married or widowed). On certain days of the year, alone in an enclosed inner sanctum, the oracle sat on a tripod over an opening in the earth, chewing laurel leaves (one of the symbols of the god) and inhaling the vapours coming from the ground. According to legend, when Apollo slew the serpent its body fell into the fissure and fumes arose from its decomposing body. Intoxicated by the vapours—which some modern scholars have identified as ethylene, formerly used as an anaesthetic—the priestess would fall into a trance, allowing Apollo to possess her spirit.

The majority of visitors, one suspects, asked personal questions about health, love and family. In return for the divine message, they paid a fee, sacrificed an animal and offered a barley cake kneaded with honey. But there were high profile pilgrims too. Croesus, King of Lydia, asked whether he should declare war on the Persians. The mouthpiece of Apollo replied: 'If Croesus crosses the river Halys [on the border with Persia], he will destroy a mighty empire'. Encouraged by this, he took the offensive but, alas, the mighty empire that fell was his own. The Roman Emperor Nero asked about the timing of his death and was told to beware of the seventy-third year. Being still a young man, he went away satisfied, expecting a long life, until he was murdered shortly afterwards by his rival Galba, who was aged 73.

The sanctuary continued into Christian times; even at the end of the fourth century, statues of (Christian) emperors were being placed in the precincts of the pagan sanctuary. But its importance was waning and the much-publicised 'last oracle', during the reign of Julian the Apostate, indicated that 'the fair wrought hall is fallen to the ground' and 'the water of speech is quenched'. Delphi became the home of a growing Christian community, with a bishop's seat and several churches. One was dedicated to dragon-slaying St George, which seemed appropriate the original myths of Apollo killing a serpent. However, the old Temple still stood on the mountain side, an iconic landmark that was never built over. The town was eventually abandoned after an earthquake in the seventh century.

It is significant that intermixed among the Old Testament prophets in Michelangelo's frescoes in the Sistine Chapel are five of the sibyls from Persia, Erythrae, Cumae, Libya and, yes, Delphi. They are all pagan and, indeed, all women and represent the universal importance of Christ's coming. It was not just the people of Israel who yearned for the Saviour. The Delphic Sibyl in Michelangelo's depiction is turning round, her eyes looking at Judith on the other side of the chapel, who is bearing the head of Holofernes. The sibyl's mouth is open in wonder and her hair and clothes blown by the wind of the Holy Spirit. She rolls up her own scroll as she listens to a cherub, reading from a book held by another angelic being. Her work is done; the Lord has come.

FATIMA (PORTUGAL)

One October Day in 1917

The crowds came in their tens of thousands, despite the pouring rain and muddy roads. Our Lady had first appeared to the three shepherd children on 13 May 1917 in the obscure Portuguese backwater of Fatima. She had told them to come back on the thirteenth of each month for six months. Several times she had announced that in October she would perform a miracle 'so that all may believe'. And so, on 13 October, the pious faithful flocked to Fatima to witness the power of God. They stood alongside the gloating secularists, who came hoping the Church would be ridiculed. A devout woman, who had taken the children in to her home, was overwhelmed by the crowds and told them 'if the miracle that you predict does not take place, these people are capable of burning you alive'. But the children responded, 'we are not afraid, because our Lady does not deceive us'.

It was also raining in France, where the Third Battle of Ypres was still being fought, and the soldiers were seeking victory against the swamp that surrounded them just as much as the enemy on the other side of 'no man's land'. The headlines of the *Lancashire Evening Post* that day read 'Rain, The Enemy—Downpour in Flanders Still Continues'. Another correspondent recorded that 'the battlefield was drenched again with rain, and the swollen streams in the furrows below Passchendaele overflowed still further through the wilderness of craters and ruined farms'. An official report from the British Army stated that, despite the rain, 'a large number of defended localities, fortified farms and woods, and concreted strong points were captured by us, together with a number of prisoners'. The Commonwealth War Graves' Commission lists 530 British soldiers who lost their lives on 13 October 1917.

The Germans were one day into 'Operation Albion', a successful amphibious operation aiming to capture the Baltic islands in the Gulf of Riga and thereby threaten nearby Russian naval bases. The Kaiser, meanwhile, was visiting Tsar Ferdinand I of Bulgaria. The previous day he had indulged in some shooting in the Rila Mountains and among the delicacies enjoyed at the royal hunting lodge was an alpine ibex (a wild goat with large, curved horns), brought down by the Kaiser himself.

It was raining too in England and the higher peaks in the Lake District were capped with snow. However, it soon brightened up, allowing Blackpool to beat Stoke City 5–0. In Preston a new record was set for the price of eggs—three for a shilling—revealing the impact the war was having on the home front. In the midst of all this, two new baronets were created by the king, including a Catholic, Sir William Henry Dunn, who had just finished his term as Lord Mayor of London.

British newspapers did not follow events in Fatima. But those who were there would never forget what they saw. Dr Joseph Garrett of the University of Coimbra recalled:

> I remained on the road in the shelter of the hood of my car, looking rather disdainfully toward the place where they said the apparition would be seen, not daring to step on the sodden and muddy earth of the freshly ploughed field. I was a little more than a hundred metres from the high wooden posts mounted by a rough cross, seeing distinctly the wide circle of people who, with their umbrellas open, seemed like a vast arena of mushrooms ... At a certain moment, this immense mass of people, so varied and compact, closed their umbrellas and uncovered their heads in a gesture that could have been one of humility or respect, but which left me surprised and bewildered, because now the rain, with a blind persistency, poured down on their heads and drenched them through.

The Lady had appeared, as she said she would. She identified herself as 'the Lady of the Rosary', asked the children to build a chapel on the spot and pray the rosary. She warned that 'people must amend their lives and ask pardon for their sins'. And she said that 'the war will end soon, and the soldiers will return to their homes'.

The children saw in quick succession visions of St Joseph and the Christ Child, Our Lady of Sorrows and Our Lady of Mount Carmel—reflecting the joyful, sorrowful and glorious mysteries of the Rosary. And then everyone pointed to the sun. It was bright, without harming the human eye, and (wrote Dr Garrett) 'spun round on itself in a mad whirl, when suddenly a clamour was heard from all the people. The sun, whirling, seemed to loosen itself from the firmament and advance threateningly upon the earth as if to crush us with its huge fiery weight. The sensation during these moments was terrible'. Then it stopped. The spectators, who had been sodden moments before, now felt dry. According to Fr Ignacio Lorenco, 'when the people realised the danger was over, there was an explosion of joy, and everyone joined in thanksgiving and praise to Our Lady'.

Though the British press remained silent on what has been called 'one of the greatest manifestations of God's power in the history of the Catholic Church', the *Sunday Mirror* of 14 October 1917 published an article that could be seen as being in the spirit of Fatima. It comes from an unlikely, non-Catholic source: a series of reports from the front written by Horatio Bottomley, editor of the popular periodical *John Bull* and a former Liberal MP, later to be convicted of fraud. However, in his column the day after the 'Miracle of the Sun', he expressed his admiration for the French peasantry,

> humbly believing in the undestroyed Madonna and in the indestructible Child … As they bow their heads in prayerful homage at the ringing of the Angelus bell, I sometimes think that there, in that simple pastoral scene, rather than in learned libraries or in ornate churches, is to be found the true gospel of human destiny … an unquenchable belief that when God has completed His mighty works and fashioned the edifice of His majestic Purpose, all will be well with the storm-stressed souls of honest men.

The war would end in another thirteen months, at the cost of millions of lives and several mighty empires. The message of Fatima took its time to spread beyond Portuguese borders. Approved by the Church in 1930, it was in the aftermath of the Second World War that the devotion became truly popular and Fatima was understood in the context of the Cold War. As one correspondent to *The Tablet* put it, 'at the time when the Red Monster was raising its head in Russia, Mary gave to the world, through the three children at Fatima, her "blueprint" for the peace of the world'.

In 1947 the Jesuit writer, C. C. Martindale, was the one of the first prominent English churchmen to visit, though he went 'not exactly with distrust, but with a certain aesthetic distaste, very puzzled and with as blank a mind as I could'. In 1949 a statue of Our Lady of Fatima was presented by the Portuguese ambassador to Cardinal Griffin, whose own planned pilgrimage to the shrine had been indefinitely postponed through ill health. Before being enthroned at St James's, Spanish Place, it made a tour of churches within the diocese. Books and pamphlets were published telling the story of Fatima, including *A Practical Guide to Fatima* (1950) by the well-known author Susan Lowndes, the niece of Hilaire Belloc. Tour companies began arranging pilgrimages; a trip from Southampton by 'flying boat' in 1950 cost 59 guineas.

A century on we live in similarly confusing and desperate times. Pilgrims still flock to the sanctuary and Francisco and Jacinta were both canonised in 2017. Fatima continues to remind us to trust in God, to 'pray, pray very much' and seek to live a holy life.

GRECCIO (ITALY)

The First Crib

Christmas cribs are a wonderful tradition, showing the stark reality of the Incarnation—that God really did become one of us; that the all-powerful really did become a helpless baby; that the Prince of Peace really did fall asleep in a dirty manger. That was St Francis' intention when he created his famous living nativity just outside the Umbrian town of Greccio at Christmas 1223, three years before his death. He wanted 'to do something that will recall the memory of that child who was born in Bethlehem, to see with bodily eyes the inconveniences of his infancy, how he lay in the manger, and how the ox and ass stood by'.

The story is well known. According to one of his early biographers:

> The manger is ready, hay is brought, the ox and ass are led in. Simplicity is honoured there, poverty is exalted, humility is commended and a new Bethlehem, as it were, is made from Greccio. Night is illuminated like the day, delighting men and beasts. The people come and joyfully celebrate the new mystery. The forest resounds with voices and the rocks respond to their rejoicing. The brothers sing, discharging their debt of praise to the Lord, and the whole night echoes with jubilation ... The solemnities of the Mass are performed over the manger and the priest experiences a new consolation.

Being a deacon, St Francis sang the Gospel of the Nativity at the Mass and preached. Shortly afterwards, a miracle occurred—an infant appeared in the manger and the saint embraced Him.

St Francis had visited the Holy Land and the basilica which St Helena had built over the site of Christ's birth. The cave at Greccio must have reminded him of the one he saw at Bethlehem. Moreover, there were relics of the Holy Crib in Rome, such as at the Basilica of Santa Maria Maggiore (sometimes called Santa Maria del Presepe). He must, also, have been influenced by the tradition of mystery plays and liturgical dramas performed at Christmas, often in churches, which often included the crib scene.

St Francis built upon these, taking them to a new level by using live animals and moving to an outdoor setting. No wonder that, in his telling of the story, St Bonaventure was keen to stress that the saint had 'asked and obtained the permission of the Pope [Honorius III] for the ceremony, so that he could not be accused of being an innovator'.

Of course, it seems quintessentially Franciscan to include real animals in such a crib. The ox and the ass were not mentioned in the Gospels but were referred to elsewhere—Isaiah, for example, writes 'The ox knows its owner and the ass its master's crib'. These animals came to be seen as symbolic of the Jew burdened by the Law (ox) and the Gentile enslaved by paganism (ass). St Francis also admired the ox as an image of humility and obedience and referred to his own body as 'Brother Ass'. These lowly, slightly comic animals were connected to poverty and the livelihoods of the local peasants.

Greccio remains an essential part of any Franciscan itinerary around Central Italy and, as well as seeing the spot where that famous Midnight Mass was held and enjoying spectacular views over the Rieti valley, there is a fascinating exhibition of cribs from around the world.

In the crib at Greccio, we get close to the essence of St Francis and the essence of the Incarnation. The Lord was born in a dark cave, surrounded by brutish animals; He lived as a poor man, with nowhere to lay his head, and lived as a servant king and died on the cross.

St Francis' life was a radical imitation of the Lord. When he left his wealthy family home and wore a ragged tunic, he was not being deliberately eccentric; when he created the crib at Greccio, he was not being overly dramatic. Rather he taught the local people, and us too, a powerful lesson. To find God we have to let go—to let go of worldly attachments and desires, of pride and selfishness, of jealousy and anger. The more we are emptied, the more we are filled by God's grace. In the Christian dispensation, less really is more.

GUADALUPE (SPAIN)

The Spanish Guadalupe

As Christopher Columbus made his famous voyages, he named several of the 'discovered' Caribbean islands after Spanish shrines of Our Lady. Montserrat took its name from the mountaintop sanctuary near Barcelona, while Antigua was a tribute to the Virgen de la Antigua in Seville cathedral. Uninhabited Redonda was round in shape and reminded Columbus of Seville's Santa Maria de la Redonda. Though originally named after St Martin, the island of Nevis honoured another Marian devotion, Nuestra Señora de las Nieves or Our Lady of the Snows.

Then there was Guadeloupe, named not after the popular Mexican pilgrimage site, which was yet to be established, but the great shrine in the Extremadura region, to the west of Madrid, in the province of Cáceres. It is a charming little town, with stalls off the central piazza selling local produce (including copper jugs and a very tasty liqueur made from acorns) and the former hospital of San Juan Bautista, now a parador hotel (think of a National Trust property that you can stay in).

The statue of Our Lady of Guadalupe was one of the many images that were said to have come from the busy artistic workshop of St Luke. It eventually came into the possession of St Gregory the Great when he was working as papal ambassador at Constantinople. He brought it to Rome and may have carried it in procession through Rome during the plague epidemic of 590, when St Michael appeared sheathing his sword over the fortress that is called to this day Castel Sant'Angelo. The statue was then given to St Leander, Bishop of Seville. However, when the region was captured by the Moors in 711, the image, like so many others, was taken away for safety and buried in a remote spot.

The story fast forwards to 1326, when the statue was discovered by a herdsman looking for a lost cow. He found the animal dead and began skinning it for leather when it came back to life. At this moment, the Blessed Virgin appeared and instructed him to dig, recover the hidden image and build a shrine. He went home pondering on what had happened and found one of his sons had died. He prayed to the Mother of God and, once again, there was a resurrection. There was no more doubt in his mind and so he informed the ecclesiastical authorities and together retrieved the ancient statue, which was buried in an iron casket along with documents proving its provenance. A small chapel was built and pilgrims began flocking there. Such was the fame of Our Lady of Guadalupe that she was invoked by Alfonso XI at the battle of Rio Salado in 1340, when a combined Castilian and Portuguese force pushed back the last Muslim invasion of the peninsula. In 1389 the sanctuary was entrusted to the Jeronymite monks.

The monastery gained wealth and prestige and this can still be seen in the splendid buildings—the cloister in the mixed Gothic-Mudéjar style, the sumptuous sacristy with a series of paintings by Zurbaran, and the magnificent antechamber or Camarín built behind the statue, which is normally perched above the high altar. On my visit this formed the climax of the tour, as the kindly (and rather long-winded) Franciscan opened an enamelled door, swung round the statue on its revolving pedestal and allowed members of the group to kiss a medal linked to the Virgin by a ribbon. The image is dark in colour, with a haunting gaze, and forms quite a contrast to the surrounding ornate robes and decoration.

Everything points towards Mary and explains her role in salvation history. Of especial note are the polychrome statues of eight Old Testament women who prefigured the Blessed Virgin: Abigail holding bread and grapes, Deborah leaning on a staff, Esther dressed as a queen, Jael with the hammer and nail used to kill Sisera, Judith with the head of Holofernes, Miriam singing the Lord's praises, Ruth proudly bearing a sheaf of corn in a broad-brimmed hat and Sarah with her hands outstretched in prayer.

At Guadalupe there are many connections between the Old and New Worlds. Ferdinand and Isabella authorised Columbus's first voyage while staying at the monastery and the explorer returned there in 1496, having promised to visit the shrine if he survived a violent storm during his second voyage. Two Native Americans were baptised 'Cristóbal' and 'Pedro' in a stone font which now forms part of the fountain in the village square.

The conqueror of the Aztec Empire, Hernando Cortés, was born in the region and often visited the shrine. It is appropriate, then, that the Spanish Guadalupe should share its name with the more famous Mexican shrine. Opinions vary, however, over how the name was exported to Mexico. Devotion to the Spanish image was widespread in the Americas and it is quite possible that the new shrine was claiming an association with its venerable namesake.

Some suggest that Our Lady revealed herself in a dream in December 1531 to the elderly uncle of St Juan Diego, using the local language of Nahuatl, as *Coatlaxopeuh* ('she who crushes the serpent's head'), *Tequantlaxopeuh* ('she who banishes those who devoured us') or some other title. When this was communicated to the Spanish interpreter, the name was misheard as 'Guadalupe'. Whatever the origins of the name, Our Lady managed to bridge the cultural gap between the two worlds and the Spanish image has been named not only Patroness of Extremadura but Queen of all Hispanic Nations.

GUBBIO (ITALY)

Racing Saints

The Italian hill town of Gubbio, not far from Assisi, is perhaps best known as the second home of St Francis, who tamed a ferocious wolf which was terrorising its inhabitants. 'Brother Wolf', who promised to do no more harm and submitted to the saint by placing a paw into his outstretched hand, has since become one of the great symbols of the town—a statue of the saint and his four-legged friend can be found outside the church of San Francesco, local restaurants are named after the beast and its image clutters the souvenir shops.

I do not mind admitting that, when on holiday, I am always on the look-out for unusual souvenirs that express the vibrant, colourful world of European Catholicism. As I was admiring a St Francis and the Wolf fridge magnet in one of the shops, my eye was drawn to a much more impressive object on the shelves beyond. It is difficult to describe—a model of a decorated octagonal structure in the shape of an hour glass with the image of a saint perched on top and, at its base, large hand-rails. This was a model of one of the famous *ceri* or 'candles' (made of wood and not intended for burning) which form the centre of the celebrations of the local patron, St Ubaldo, a twelfth-century Bishop of Gubbio, on 16 May.

There are three *ceri*, each about four metres high and weighing up to 400kg, with representations of St Ubaldo (patron not only of the town but the builders), St George (patron of the artisans) and St Anthony Abbot (patron of the agriculturalists and students). These bizarre structures are not merely taken through the streets in procession but raced up the steep mountain from the centre of Gubbio to St Ubaldo's basilica. Though much sweat is expended in the endeavour on the part of the *ceraioli* (the teams carrying each particular *cero*, dressed in that saint's colours), there is no real competition because St Ubaldo always wins.

This *Corsa dei Ceri* takes place every year on 15 May, the Vigil of the saint's feast. In the morning there is a Mass and processions of the *ceri* and those who will carry them. A large meal takes place for all those involved; since the vigil of a solemnity traditionally has a penitential nature, no meat is eaten, though the offering of wine adds a festive note to proceedings and perhaps provides strength for what lies ahead. The three statues are fixed to the *ceri* and then raised into a vertical position, following a curious ceremony in which the captain of each team pours water over the 'candle' and throws the earthenware jug to the floor (the shattered pieces are considered to bestow good luck and are eagerly collected).

The *ceri* then pass through Gubbio so that as many can pay their respects as possible. Writing in 1905, Laura McCracken noticed that the *ceri* often paused before 'the house of some favoured person, who has probably earned this distinction by a gift of wine. The spectators at the windows acknowledge the salute by showering down flowers upon the *cero*, which, after a moment, is off again on its mad progress through the town'. Eventually the bishop blesses the *ceraioli* with a relic of St Ubaldo and the signal is given for the 'race' to begin.

I ascended the mountain on which the Basilica of St Ubaldo is located by means of a terrifying funicular, which involved standing in a small hanging cage, totally exposed to the elements, in which there was just about space for two people. As I slowly went up and enjoyed the breathtaking views (if you dare take your hands off the rail and turn round in your cage), I realised what a physical feat it must be to carry one of the *ceri* up the hill.

'The way is long and steep', McCracken wrote, 'and, on a warm May day, would take the ordinary pedestrian fully three-quarters of an hour to make the ascent, if not longer. But it is evening when the *ceri* set out; and, after no more than a quarter of an hour or twenty minutes, these valiant sons of St Ubaldo set down their burdens at the door of the Convent, on the summit of the mountain'.

They run in teams of ten, changing like a relay race every ten minutes but without any halt. There is much excitement and noise and it looks as if the saints themselves are racing through the packed streets and up the mountain, St Ubaldo's golden cope flying in the breeze.

St Ubaldo reaches his shrine first and the doors are closed in the faces of St George and St Anthony. The triumphant saint is taken round the cloister three times and then into the church. Only once this is done are the other saints admitted. In the evening there is a torchlight procession and the saints' images are taken back intro the town. The true winning team, though, is not so much the one that got to the shrine first but the one that showed the most strength and skill in the arduous 'race'.

Watching a video of the ceremony in the little museum beside St Ubaldo's basilica, it would be easy to dismiss the ceremony as picturesque and, yes, insane: the comic-looking 'race' that is always fixed, the mayhem of the crowds and even the danger caused when the *ceri* occasionally topple over. But as I left the mountain-top shrine and steadied my nerves for the descent on the funicular, I was moved by the obvious joy and devotion that the people of Gubbio had for their heavenly patrons. Perhaps we can learn from them in our cooler, greyer climes.

ISTANBUL (TURKEY)

'The New Rome'

As an imperial capital, a self-proclaimed 'second Rome' and a city straddling two continents, it seems fitting to include Istanbul in a European volume such as this. At first glance, the city does not seem particularly Christian: the skyline is dominated by exotic-looking domes and minarets. St Antoine, the largest Catholic church, tucked away beside one of the main shopping streets, is a good twenty minutes' walk out of the historic centre. But look a little closer and things are not what they seem.

Close to our hotel was a rather charming little mosque, surrounded by a peaceful tea garden and saturated with the air of antiquity. This was, in fact, built as a church in 527 by the Emperor Justinian and dedicated to the Roman martyrs Sergius and Bacchus. The kindly gentleman manning the door and policing the observance of mosque etiquette took great delight in showing visitors the Greek inscription honouring the saints in whose honour it was built. This building was a powerful reminder of a largely hidden past. Centre of the Islamic Ottoman Empire from 1453 until the aftermath of the First World War, Constantinople (as Istanbul used to be called) was for well over a thousand years a Christian capital.

English writers often speak of this empire as 'Byzantine'—a term with unfortunately negative connotations (I occasionally find myself ranting about the 'Byzantine' bureaucracy of this or that organisation or diocese). But as far as the inhabitants of Constantinople were concerned, they were Romans and their polity a survival of the great empire that had once reached as far as the Scottish borders. When we talk of the 'fall of Rome' we are looking at history with a typically 'western' perspective and forget that the eastern half of that empire survived almost into 'modern' times.

It was Constantine who transformed the Greek colony of Byzantium into Constantinople in the early fourth century. It was to be a 'new Rome' (*Nova Roma*) and when the city walls were expanded a century later, the city even came to include seven hills, just like its western counterpart. Several impressive buildings were speedily erected, such as the first church of Hagia Sophia (on the site of the structure, built by Justinian, which is perhaps Istanbul's most iconic building). As one writer commented, 'if Rome wasn't built in a day, New Rome very nearly was'.

Over the subsequent millennium, Constantinople flourished as a Christian city despite frequent coups, sieges and earthquakes. It was the location of several important Church Councils—including Constantinople I (381), which finalised the words of the Nicene Creed (Nicaea itself is only fifty miles from the city), and Chalcedon (451, now a suburb of Istanbul on the Asian side of the Bosphoros), which defined the two natures of Christ. The city's Patriarchs, who saw themselves as successors of St Andrew, included St Gregory Nazianzus and St John Chrysostom, both Doctors of the Church. The First Council of Constantinople declared that 'the Bishop of Constantinople shall have the primacy of honour after the Bishop of Rome, because it is New Rome', although this was disputed by some.

Constantinople was alive with theological discussion—not only in clerical circles but, as St Gregory of Nyssa tells us, filling the 'lanes, markets, squares, streets, the clothes merchants, moneychangers and grocers ... When you enquire whether the bath is ready, you are told that the Son was made out of nothing'. In a special way, the citizens of Constantinople believed they were protected by the Blessed Virgin and a much-venerated icon, believed to have 'not been painted by human hands', was often taken in procession.

Constantinople was also a city of relics, many of which were first gathered by Constantine and his mother, St Helena: the True Cross, the Crown of Thorns, the Holy Lance, the *Mandylion* (bearing the image of Christ's face), the body of St Andrew and so on. Many of these were removed to the west, especially as a result of the looting during the Fourth Crusade (1204). Few remain to this day, though the Topkapı (the palace complex of the Ottoman Sultans next to Hagia Sophia) has an extraordinary room of 'Possessions of the Prophets'—the saucepan of Abraham, the staff of Moses, the sword of David and the turban of Joseph. The only New Testament artefacts are some bones of St John the Baptist, including a fragment of his skull. It was interesting to see some Islamic 'relics' on display too, such as the tooth and footprint of their Prophet.

The crusaders ransacked the city in 1204 and two and a half centuries later it was captured by the Turks, who had gradually been closing in on the city. The conquerors of 1453 made their way in triumph to Hagia Sophia. It immediately became a mosque and in time minarets were built on the exterior and huge plaques placed inside, bearing the names of Allah, Mohammed and key Muslim personages. The siege cost the life of the last Byzantine emperor, the eleventh Constantine, and it is said that the Patriarch of Constantinople, who was praying in Hagia Sophia as the city fell, disappeared into the church walls.

Legend has it that he will reappear when the city is once again in Greek (and Christian) hands.

In 1935 Hagia Sophia was opened as a museum rather than a place of worship—a result of Atatürk's secular proclivities—and all that remains of its Christian past are fragments of mosaic and the intriguing 'weeping column'. According to tradition, St Gregory the Miracle Worker once appeared on the spot and the miraculous moisture visible on the column was seen as a powerful sign of his intercession, curing many ailments. On my visit, the queue of tourists waiting to touch the pillar was the one sign of devotion left in this venerable building. Since then, however, in 2020 the great building once again became a mosque.

Constantinople continued to be admired, imitated and (often) misunderstood. Claims were later made that Moscow (a city also with seven hills) was the true successor of Constantinople, a 'Third Rome', and Napoleon once said that if there was one country in the world, Constantinople would be its capital. The dome of Hagia Sophia influenced the design of St Peter's Basilica as well as our own St Paul's and Westminster Cathedral (its architect, John Francis Bentley, visited Constantinople to seek inspiration). Details of Byzantine court ceremonial even came to be found at the Vatican: the sedia gestatoria and the ostrich feather fans, used until recently (commentators speak of papal ceremonies being simplified by Pope Francis but the major changes were made by his predecessors, especially St Paul VI). And, indeed, who can forget that St John XXIII lived here as nuncio between 1934 and 1944 and did much work in this neutral country during the Second World War to save as many Jews as possible. Outside the church of St Antoine is a large statue of him, unveiled by Benedict XVI during his visit of 2006; it describes 'Good Pope John' as 'Friend of the Turkish Peoples'.

Although we might forget it, this great city on the Bosphoros has had a huge influence on Christian theology and culture for the best part of two millennia.

LISBON (PORTUGAL)

An English Exile in Lisbon

They say that Portugal is England's oldest ally. Walking round the streets of Lisbon the observant visitor notices plenty of Anglo-Portuguese connections—for starters the large number of British tourists, and the fact that both countries share a time zone and eat quite early (in marked contrast to Spain).

When Lisbon was captured from the Moors in 1147 it was thanks to a large contingent of English crusaders who were heading for the Holy Land but had been forced to stop due to poor weather. One of their number, Gilbert of Hastings, became the first bishop of the reconquered city and not only began building a new cathedral but, we are told, introduced the Sarum Usage, a local variant of the Roman Rite widely used in England.

The close relationship between England and Portugal grew stronger, especially with the marriage in 1387 of King João (or John) I and Philippa of Lancaster (daughter of John of Gaunt). Her offspring, known as 'the golden generation', included Henry the Navigator.

By the sixteenth century, the English community in Lisbon included not only merchants and diplomats but Catholic exiles. Indeed, by 1624 there was an English seminary in the city, which only closed in 1973. A tomb to one of the most colourful of these exiles can be found at the Jesuit church of São Roque: Francis Tregian (pronounced Trudgeon), who belonged to a wealthy and well-connected Cornish family.

He had spent time abroad studying and had also made sure his face was seen at court. According to family tradition, he had attracted the queen's displeasure when he rejected preferment as well as her flirtatious advances. Whatever the truth of the matter, he returned to his estates and was increasingly watched by the authorities, who were beginning to realise the strategic importance of Cornwall as a Spanish invasion became more imminent.

Tregian was a zealous Catholic and employed St Cuthbert Mayne as chaplain; the priest passing officially as his steward. Little is known of his ministry at Golden, Tregian's house not far from Truro, except it was said that 'not one of those whom he gained to God ever fell away'. On 8 June 1577, the Feast of Corpus Christi, a party of hundred men surrounded the manor, led by Richard Grenville, the strongly Protestant High Sheriff. Mayne was sitting quietly in the garden when the house was raided and, on hearing the clamour, walked in to find himself face-to-face with the Sheriff. 'What art thou?', he was asked, to which he replied 'I am a man'. He was found to have an *Agnus Dei*, suspended from his neck in a case of silver and crystal; to possess such an item was a criminal offence due to an Act of 1571. There were further incriminating items: a chalice and Missal (though there was no proof that they had been used for Mass) and a papal bull (another prohibited item, though this particular bull was of little relevance since it announced a Holy Year two years previously).

Mayne, Tregian and 31 others were taken away for questioning. The priest was hanged, drawn and quartered at Launceston and became the proto-martyr of the seminary priests. Tregian, meanwhile, lost his property and endured many years of imprisonment, spending time at Windsor Castle, and the London prisons of the Marshalsea, Queen's Bench and Fleet. It is interesting that the governor of the Marshalsea had been granted Tregian's confiscated estates.

Through all this, Tregian kept his Faith and managed to write verses with a pin and the snuff of a candle, which were smuggled to his wife (who went on to bear him twelve children). They contained words of consolation:

Let prayer be your practice, wife
Let prayer be your play
Let prayer be your staple of trust
Let prayer be your stay …
Pray therefore still unto that King
Who rules the rolling spheres,
To oppress your grief, to send relief,
He will regard your tears:
Of Him if oft you humbly crave,
As known it is by proof,
You shall obtain what is in truth
Most fit for your behoof.

Afraid that he might die in prison, he movingly wrote to her:

Farewell, the anchor of my hope,
Farewell, my stay of life,
Farewell, my poor Penelope,
Farewell, my faithful wife:
Bless, in my name, my little babes,

God send them all good hap,
And bless withal that little babe
That lieth in your lap.

Fortunately, conditions eventually improved. His wife and children were able to visit, he was given a more comfortable room with a servant, and eventually granted parole. With the accession of James I and after 26 years of captivity, he was freed on the condition that he left the country. In Catholic Europe, Tregian was treated as a celebrity. He visited the English College at Douai, where Mayne had studied, and, on arriving in Spain, was given the privilege of entering Madrid in one of Philip III's royal coaches. Tregian was seen as a living martyr, a confessor of the Faith, and the king granted him a generous pension so that he could end his days in peace and comfort. He moved to Lisbon, which was then part of Spanish territory, and became closely associated with the Jesuits at São Roque.

Francis Tregian died in 1608; 17 years later his body was exhumed and found to be intact, causing a sensation. According to Fr Ignatius Stafford, 'his hair is upon his head and beard, his nails upon his hands and feet, and all whole and entire; his flesh soft, and being pressed down, riseth up again; his arms, fingers, and legs flexible'. A body buried more recently nearby had almost entirely decomposed.

An unexpected cultural fruit was produced by the long years of imprisonment faced by the Tregian family. Francis' eldest son, who shared the same name, worked for Cardinal Allen in Rome and Archduke Albert in what was then the Spanish Netherlands. Given this background, it is little surprise that he was placed in the Fleet Prison on his return to England. But if his father wrote verses in captivity, the younger Francis had an even more ambitious goal. For two years he copied and arranged music for the virginal (an early keyboard instrument) from both English and continental sources. The collection is now known as the 'Fitzwilliam Virginal Book' (named after the Cambridge museum where it is kept) and is one of the most important sources for Elizabethan and early Stuart music in existence. Even from the silence of the prison cell, the heart of Francis Tregian sang.

LORETO (ITALY)

The Holy House

Walk inside the Shrine of the Holy House at Loreto (Italy) and there is much to attract the eye: the constant stream of pilgrims, works of art by the likes of Signorelli and Domenichino, and numerous chapels—one of which (the American Chapel) features astronauts and UFOs. A fascinating and unexpected detail, often passed over by guides, can be found on the walls of the nave: large plaques recording the miraculous story of the Holy House in English, Welsh, Gaelic and Lowland Scots. These were produced by the Jesuit Robert Corby (or Corbington) in 1634 and also printed as broadsheets, with titles such as *The Wondrous flittinge of the kirk of our B. Ledy of Loreto* (to take the Lowland Scots version). Even during the period of persecution, British pilgrims made their way to Loreto, including the martyrs St Edmund Campion, St Ralph Sherwin, St Henry Walpole and St Robert Southwell. Corby's inscriptions made an important point. British Catholics may have been persecuted but they were just as much part of the Universal Church as the Italians or Spanish.

Corby belonged to an extraordinary family. His parents, Gerard and Isabella, moved to Kildare (Ireland) from northern England to escape persecution. Of their sons, three became Jesuits (including Blessed Ralph Corby, martyred at Tyburn in 1644) and one died as a student at St Omers. The two surviving daughters became nuns at the English Benedictine Convent in Brussels. The parents meanwhile had moved to the Spanish Netherlands and both decided to separate and follow in their children's footsteps: Isabella became a Benedictine at Ghent at the tender age of eighty while Gerard became a Jesuit lay brother, living (it is said) to see his own father reconciled to the Church at the age of a hundred!

Corby told the story of the 'miraculous origin and translation' of the Holy House, which had once stood in Nazareth and was the 'chamber' where Our Lady 'was born and bred, and saluted by the Angel, and therein conceived and brought up her son Jesus to the age of twelve years'. It was frequented by many pilgrims until angels took it to Trsat, now part of Rijeka (Croatia), and then finally to Loreto, where it arrived on 10 December 1294. It was apparently seen by shepherds being borne across the sky and this rather startling image can be seen in many old pictures. Little wonder that Our Lady of Loreto is regarded as the patron of pilots and all those involved in aviation, and that even UFOs can be seen in the paintings of the shrine!

Others explain the tradition by referring to the Angeli family, descended from the Byzantine Emperors, who arranged for the Holy House to be brought to the west. This was at a time when the Holy Places were being threatened and many precious relics were moved to Christendom for safety. The year 1291, let us not forget, was the year that the Christian stronghold of Acre fell after a long siege and the crusader kingdoms destroyed.

At the end of the day, the means of the Holy House's translation does not really matter. Certainly, there are strong arguments for its authenticity: the house is of early origin, there are details that confirm that it came from Palestine (such as the stones and methods used in its construction and the discovery of remains of an ostrich egg) and evidence that it has long been regarded as holy (there is graffiti made by pilgrims from the first centuries of Christianity).

Another inscription in the basilica affirms that 'the whole world has no place more sacred. This building is more holy even than the Basilica of St Peter, Prince of the Apostles. For here was the Word made Flesh, and here was born the Virgin Mother. From the west, where the sun goes down, to the east, where it rises from the waters, no place is more holy'. There are little reminders of its sacred origins—not only the antiquity of the structure but the dramatic inscription, which can also be seen in the basilica at Nazareth: *Hic Verbum caro factum est*, Here the Word was made flesh. Just behind the altar is a little cooking pot or bowl which is said to have been used by Our Lady, reminding us of the domestic reality of the Holy Family.

Corby's multi-lingual inscriptions are not the only British link to Loreto. The seventeenth-century poet Richard Crashaw is buried in the basilica. He was an Anglican cleric and a Fellow of Peterhouse, Cambridge, who was closely associated with the Metaphysical Poets. A Royalist and a supporter of Archbishop Laud, he fled overseas in 1643 and soon afterwards converted to Catholicism. He sought support from Henrietta Maria, the wife of Charles I who was herself in exile, and ended up in Rome with several other exiled Cambridge fellows. He found a post in the retinue of Cardinal Palotto and was given a canonry at Loreto, even though he was not ordained. He died there in the summer of 1648 after contracted an illness on his journey from Rome—some say he was poisoned.

The most obvious link between England and Loreto is the shrine of Our Lady of Walsingham, centred round a replica of the Holy House built by Richeldis de Favarches, with the help of angels, in 1061. In a vision she was shown the dimensions of the house and it is interesting to note that these roughly match the house in Loreto. Of course, it is quite possible that Richeldis or one of her associates had visited Nazareth and seen the Holy House, returning home to build a copy in the same way that many medieval pilgrims returning from Jerusalem built structures based on the Holy Sepulchre. The original replica was situated just outside the priory church, in a separate building, and it was Our Lady's desire that 'all that seek me there shall find succour'. Though the original Holy House was destroyed at the Reformation, modern replicas were built at King's Lynn (where the Catholic shrine was originally located) and the present Anglican shrine. Walsingham is indeed England's Loreto, England's Nazareth.

LUCCA (ITALY)

A Royal Pilgrim in Tuscany

The walled Tuscan town of Lucca has many beautiful churches and sanctuaries. Perhaps the most famous is the shrine of the *Volto Santo* in the cathedral—a miraculous crucifix, solemnly processed through the streets every September and thought to have been carved by Nicodemus himself. In another part of the town is the shrine of St Gemma Galgani, the 'Holy Maid of Lucca', a Passionist tertiary, stigmatic and mystic, who died aged 25 in 1903.

For English visitors, there is a little-known but fascinating shrine that should be discovered just to the north of the city centre in the church of San Frediano. Named after a sixth-century Irish missionary who became Bishop of Lucca, it contains the shrine of St Zita, a servant who worked for one of the great Lucchesi families in the thirteenth century. In a nearby chapel, the 'Cappella Trenta', there rests the body of an English saint, still remembered in Lucca but almost forgotten in his homeland—St Richard 'of Wessex'. He is depicted here in a fine fifteenth-century altarpiece, created by the Sienese Jacopo della Quercia, standing beside the Virgin and Child, together with St Ursula, St Lawrence and St Jerome.

The basic story of St Richard is neatly summed up in his epitaph:

> Here King Richard lies, gentle and regal,
> An English King, he is now of the Kingdom of Heaven.
> He left his kingdom, he abandoned all for Christ.
> So from England he comes to us as St Richard.
> He was the father of St Walburga the virgin,
> And father of SS Willibald and Winebald:
> May their prayers earn for us the Kingdom of Heaven.

We know very little about his early life. We are even unsure of his name, since the first mention of 'Richard' is from a much later date. Tradition names him as 'King of the English', although all we can say for certain is that he was of noble, possibly royal, blood. He may have been the grandson of St Sexburga, brother-in-law of St Boniface and a kinsman of many other royal saints, including St Etheldreda, St Ethelburga, St Withburga, St Ermengilda and St Ercongota.

Helped by his wife, Wunna, St Richard passed this family tradition of sanctity to his children, three of whom became saints and missionaries: SS Willibald, Winebald and Walburga. If we know scant details of St Richard's life, we can learn much about him from the circumstances of his death and from the lives of his children.

In 720 St Richard, together with his two sons, set out from the south coast on a pilgrimage to Rome and the Holy Land. Eighth-century travel was full of risks, not the least of which was sickness. By the time the band of pilgrims had reached Lucca, early in 722, St Richard had to take to his bed with a violent fever. He died a few days later. Having buried their beloved father in Lucca, the two brothers continued their pilgrimage. According to the earliest account of the legend—the *Hodoeporicon* by Hygeburg, an English nun of Heidenheim—they made their way 'through the vast land of Italy, through the deep valleys, over the craggy mountains, across the level plains' to the Eternal City, where they offered prayers of thankfulness and praise at the tomb of St Peter.

According to Thomas Meyrick, who wrote *The Family of St Richard* in 1844 as part of Newman's series on the English saints, it is from the sanctity of his children that we can argue the piety of the father, 'under whose fostering care such stately plants grew up to adorn Christ's earthly paradise'.

St Willibald followed in the footsteps of his father as a pilgrim *par excellence*—he reached both Rome and the Holy Land, and spent two years in Constantinople. On his return to the West, he settled at the great Benedictine abbey of Montecassino, before being sent by the pope to Germany. Here he assisted his uncle, St Boniface, in his great work of evangelisation. St Willibald founded a double monastery at Heidenheim and became first Bishop of Eichstätt. Here his brother, St Winebald, who was appointed first Abbot of Heidenheim, joined him.

St Walburga, started off as a nun at Wimborne, Dorset, before joining the double monastery at Heidenheim, where she became abbess. She remains the most popular of the three siblings—giving her name to the great spring festival of *Walpurgisnacht* (1 May) and still attracting pilgrims to her tomb at Eichstätt through the mysterious flow of an aromatic fluid, called 'St Walburga's Oil'. Small bottles of this liquid, mixed with water, are freely available to devout visitors.

Given his children's astonishing contribution to the religious life of Germany, it is little surprise that two clerics from Eichstätt arrived in Lucca in 1150, seeking the body of St Richard. The body was promptly discovered and miracles claimed. However, the canons of San Frediano were reluctant to give up the relics, which seemed to provide ample ammunition in their long-standing rivalry with the cathedral.

Nevertheless, the Germans tried to claim St Richard's remains, even calling him 'Duke of Swabia', but it was in Lucca that the bones remained. His cult continues there to this day, although that of St Zita eclipsed it in the late thirteenth century and soon reached England—altars to 'St Sitha' existed at several churches and a shrine with the relic of the saint's toe and hair could be found at Eagle, Lincolnshire. Her image (unlike that of St Richard) can even be found in Henry VII's chapel at Westminster Abbey.

The prayer cards available in the church's repository refer to our saint as 'St Richard the Pilgrim' rather than 'St Richard the King'. His feast is celebrated on 7 February.

METEORA (GREECE)

Monks Suspended in the Air

The rocks of Meteora rise up like a family of giants, transforming central Greece into a landscape truly beyond this world. Patrick Leigh-Fermor, in his unsurpassed prose, speaks of 'the tremendous spikes and cylinders of rock that soared perpendicular for hundreds of feet into the sky' making an 'improbable geology'. It is sometimes called a *lithopolis*, city of rocks, while the name 'Meteora' itself means 'suspended in the air', deriving from the same root as the meteors we sometimes spot in the night sky.

Hermits first scaled the heights, possibly as early as the ninth century; they 'braved the storms and the fierce weather', says a modern guidebook, 'and, armed with their indomitable will, they climbed up on the rocks like the wild birds of the sky nested in the hollows of these wind-beaten crags in quest of fulfilment of soul and redemption'.

The caves in which they lived still pocket the face of some of the rocks. Once a week they would descend to worship together in a simple, white-washed chapel at the base of one of the rocks. In time monasteries were founded, originally over twenty foundations on the various summits, though some are now desolate, 'mute and sad without the sweet sounds of psalmody and the sweet smell of incense'. Thus, the monastery of Hagia Mone is now just a collection of inaccessible ruins, while a painted image on the rock-face and the remains of a wooden ladder hanging just below the summit is all that remains of the monastery of Hypsilotera (The Higher One).

St Athanasios, who glories in the title 'the Meteorite', did much to organise these monastic communities. Educated in Constantinople, where 'like a bee he gathered what was ripe' and the island of Crete, he entered the monastic life Mount Athos around 1332. However, due to the attacks of the Turks he was forced to leave the 'Holy Mountain', along with his spiritual master, Gregory, and finally settled at Meteora. Such was the holiness of his life that he attracted many disciples, forming the nucleus of the largest of the monasteries, the Great Meteoron.

St Athanasios is considered the chief saint of Meteora, along with John Uroš, the last Serbian ruler of Thessaly and titular Emperor of the Serbians and the Greeks. He abdicated his throne to embrace the monastic life at some point in the 1360s and his presence at Meteora brought much prestige and patronage.

I was able to visit two monasteries: those of Varlaam (named after the hermit who once lived on the spot) and the convent of Hagios Stephanos. The views are magnificent and the churches full of fine frescoes. In the words of Leigh-Fermor, 'the walls were devoted to wild scenes of martyrdoms—inverted crucifixions, flayings, impalements, draggings by wild horses, tearings apart by bent saplings, brandings, mutiliations, and, above all, beheadings. Phalanxes of splendidly clad figures knelt or lay prostrate with blood gushing from their headless trunks while their heads, still haloed, rolled away over the sad plain'. Their ultimate witness was to the Lord, who sits enthroned at the highest point of the church ceiling.

Outside the church of St Stephen, it was interesting to see the 'semantron', a long plank of wood used to summon the monks to prayer. Tradition holds that it originated with Noah, who was told by God: 'Make for yourself a bell of box-wood, which is not liable to corruption, three cubits long and one and a half wide, and also a mallet from the same wood. Strike this instrument three separate times every day: once in the morning to summon the hands to the ark, once at midday to call them to dinner, and once in the evening to invite them to rest'. The sound echoes around the rocks and monasteries of Meteora, calling the faithful to gather in the ark of the church.

Access to many of these monasteries was traditionally rather perilous. When a nineteenth-century English visitor, Robert Curzon, arrived at Varlaam a gun had first to be sounded 'to answer the same purpose as knocking at the door in more civilised places'. After seeing his servants being hauled up some 22 feet in a net, Curzon decided to climb up the 'series of ladders which were suspended by large wooden pegs on the face of the precipice'. Half-way through the ascent, he panicked as he glanced down and saw 'that the precipice went sheer down to so tremendous a depth, that my head turned when I surveyed the distant valley over which I was hanging in air like a fly on the wall'. The monks shouted out words of encouragement and he eventually reached the monastery safely, through a door in the rock.

After staying at the monastery, Curzon decided to leave by means of the net. He described how 'the net was spread upon the floor and having sat down upon it cross-legged, the four corners were gathered over my head, and attached to a hook at the end of the rope. All being ready, the monks at the capstan took a few steps round, the effect of which was to lift me off the floor and launch me out of the door right into the sky, with an impetus which kept me swinging backwards and forwards at a fearful rate; when the oscillations had in some measure ceased, the abbot and another monk, leaning out of the door, steadied me with their hands, and I was let down slowly and gently to the ground'.

The souvenir shop sells several depictions of a happy-looking monk being hoisted in such a device. 'The net says to the monks', one hymn states, 'be careful, not only do I lift you up from the ground to the top, but also the heaven'. When one visitor asked how often the ropes were renewed, the abbot answered: 'only when it breaks'. Fortunately, access these days is easier—stone steps have replaced the flimsy ladders and nets, and groups of tourists are safely deposited in the coach parks of the more accessible monasteries—access to St Stephen is via a small bridge.

The solitude of the Meteora has been affected over the years by war, earthquakes, declining vocations and loss of property. In *For Your Eyes Only* (1981), James Bond (Roger Moore) ascended the rock and broke into the enclosure to retrieve an ATAC decoder from bad guy Aristotle Kristatos (Julian Glover). The monks and nuns put up with the groups of tourists and no doubt make much-needed profits from the admission charges and shops.

Yet, despite all this, Meteora remains a wondrous oasis of peace, where the cobwebs of this world are quickly blown away and one feels closer to God. I would agree with Curzon, that 'nothing can be more strange and wonderful than this romantic region which is unlike anything I have ever seen either before or since'.

MONTE GORDO & THE ALGARVE (PORTUGAL)

A Place Apart

From the balcony of our hotel at Monte Gordo I admire the golden sands of Portugal's last beach before the Spanish border and the deep blue of the Atlantic—a very different guise from the greyish waters surrounding the British Isles. Once, well within living memory, this was a largely unknown fishing village. The Vasco Da Gama was opened in 1960, one of the first grand hotels on the Algarve, and the tourist industry began to take hold. It took time for the area to adapt—Ingrid Bergman stayed a night in 1963 and was fined for appearing on the beach in a bikini. One could say that, in the interests of making money, much of the local character of the Algarve was quickly lost. The traditional white-washed houses of Monte Gordo are now dwarfed by higher-rise buildings, and previous generations would surely be bemused by twenty-first-century golfers, surfers and sun worshippers.

Despite its new-found popularity, the Algarve remains a land apart. Before the opening of railways, motorways and an international airport at Faro, the area was isolated from the rest of the country. It was easier to get to Cadiz or Seville than to Lisbon. Indeed, the road leading northwards out of nearby Tavira was once known as the road 'to' Portugal.

Many peoples have passed through these parts and sailed within sight of Monte Gordo. In the mists of time came the Phoenicians from the Levant. These adventurous traders did much to lay the foundations of the Mediterranean world that we know today by the eighth century BC, founding outposts at Seville, Cadiz, Lisbon and (in this part of the Algarve) Cacela Velha and Tavira. At the entrance to Tavira's municipal museum are the remains of ritual pits where they may have sacrificed to the god Baal. Then came, among others, Celts, Romans, Greeks, Visigoths and, of course, Arabs, who controlled the area between the eighth and thirteenth centuries. Indeed, the name 'Algarve' comes from the Arabic 'al-gharb', meaning 'the west': the western part of al-Andalus.

It was largely through the military orders that successive Christian kings of Portugal pushed southwards and drove out the Arabs in an ambitious reconquest. The Algarve was gradually captured, town by town, stronghold by stronghold, between 1238 and 1249. The magnificent church of Santa Maria do Castelo, built on the site of a former mosque beside the old Moorish fortress at Tavira, claims the tomb of the great hero of these campaigns: Paio Peres Correia, Grand Master of the Order of Santiago. Also in the church chancel are the tombs of the 'seven martyred knights'—six knights and a merchant who were murdered nearby by the Arabs in 1242. This so enraged Correia that he breached the walls, captured the town and used it as a base for subsequent campaigns in the region. Soon, the new kingdom of the Algarve was part of the greater kingdom of Portugal, though its late addition and geographical isolation, separated from the north by ranges of mountains, always made it a distinct entity.

As with the rest of Portugal, there were close relations with England, especially in terms of trading. In the museum of Santa Maria do Castelo can be seen an alabaster Calvary dating from the fifteenth century and made in the workshops of Nottingham; it once stood in an archway leading to a hermitage on the outskirts of the town. Such work was widely in circulation around southern Europe before the Reformation. The great Portuguese prince, Henry the Navigator, was himself half-English—the son of Philippa of Lancaster—and acted as governor of Algarve. He sponsored many voyages from Lagos in search of new trade routes and colonies, including Ceuta and Madeira. Indeed, thanks in part to his vision, the monarch became known from 1471 as 'King of Portugal and the Algarves of either side of the sea' (that is, what we call the Algarve as well as several north African territories).

The 'old ally' did not always behave peacefully. In 1587, at a time when the Spanish and Portuguese crowns were united in the person of Philip II, Sir Francis Drake mounted raids on the area around Lagos and Sagres as he made his way back from Cadiz, where he had successfully 'singed' the King of Spain's beard. Nine years later the Earl of Essex led a raid on Faro and brought back with him the bishop's precious collection of books. Many of these volumes were donated to Thomas Bodley's library at Oxford, where they remain to this day. Despite such destruction, there was an English consul at Faro from the seventeenth century and Protestant merchants from those northern climes quietly got on with their business, though carefully watched by officials of the Portuguese Inquisition.

The waters brought in other threats, too. Just as the Portuguese were pioneers of the slave trade, the Algarve itself was frequently attacked by corsairs from north Africa and locals were taken into slavery, right up until the early nineteenth century. Algarvians, often living in remote, poorly defended areas, were permitted to keep a gun at home so that they could defend themselves, and many decided to move further inland. Between 1607 and 1778 over 4,500 Portuguese slaves were successfully ransomed and returned to their homes.

Then there was the great earthquake and tsunami of All Saints Day 1755 which not only destroyed Lisbon—the resulting fires quickly spread by the many candles that had been lit in the churches—but devastated the Algarve coast. The disaster traumatised Europe and led many to ask questions about how a loving God could let such a tragedy happen. The earthquake also led to what has been called a 'Humanitarian Big Bang'—Portugal received unprecedented aid from other countries, including a British man-of-war loaded with gold, silver, clothes, tools and food.

Many villages and towns had to be rebuilt, along with their churches. A prime example of this lies a few miles east of Monte Gordo in the town of Villa Real de Santo Antonio, perched on the Guadiana river and staring across at the Spanish town of Ayamonte, where the inhabitants follow a clock that is an hour later. Villa Real replaced an earlier fishing village that been destroyed in the tsunami (Santo Antonio de Areniha) and its grid pattern of streets resembles those of the newly rebuilt Lisbon. This was the brainchild of the Marquis de Pombal, the autocratic chief minister to the king, who is also known for his opposition to the Jesuits and their expulsion from the kingdom in 1759. His methods could be harsh; to encourage the development of his new town at Villa Real it is said he burnt the fishermen's huts at Monte Gordo.

On the second weekend of September Monte Gordo celebrates its great feast in honour of Our Lady of Sorrows (Nossa Senhora das Dores). Alongside the stalls and live music is a religious procession along the beach, accompanied by devotees on foot, fishing boats on the waters and the town band. Then, after the fireworks have dimmed and the crowds dispersed, the town returns to its usual rhythms. The waves continue to crash into the golden sands. Each night, as the holiday-makers sleep, the lamps of the fishermen can be spotted on the waters, in search of sole, tuna or bream, just as their ancestors did.

MONTE SANT'ANGELO (ITALY)

Holy Michael the Archangel

The remote Gargano promontory juts out from the eastern coast of Italy into the Adriatic and is home to one of the oldest as well as one of the newest shrines in the Catholic world. Both celebrate their feasts in September: the shrine of Padre Pio in San Giovanni Rotondo, with its modern pilgrimage church, and the ancient sanctuary of St Michael at Monte Sant'Angelo.

Though Padre Pio has now displaced the Archangel in popularity, many saints, princes and popes have made the arduous journey to Monte Sant'Angelo over the centuries. There were ordinary men and women too, many of whom were on the way to Rome or the Holy Land. Some left their names on the grotto's walls, including the runic inscriptions of 'Hereberehct', 'Herraed', 'Wigfus' and 'Leofwini', Anglo-Saxon pilgrims. One wonders what stories they might have told.

I was fortunate to be at Monte Sant'Angelo one Michaelmas. The little town was heaving with people and the many shops showing off their wares: finely decorated walking sticks, local produce, and statues of St Michael, with his raised sword over a chained devil. Such were the crowds that it took a full half hour to descend the steps to the sacred cave of St Michael for Mass. In the afternoon there was a grand procession through the narrow streets, with confraternities and clergy accompanying a statue of St Michael and the 'Archangel's Sword'—not to be understood in a literal sense but as the sword from the famous sixteenth-century marble statue in the sanctuary. One small child with a solemn expression and wavy hair caught my eye: he was dressed up as the Archangel, complete with a golden crown and a plastic sword.

The shrine's origins can be traced back to three visions, normally dated to the 490s. These were commemorated in the old calendar on the feasts of the Apparition of St Michael (8 May) and the Dedication of St Michael (29 September). According to the legend, a wealthy man called Garganus was reviewing his herd one evening when he realised his prize bull was missing. The next day it was located in an inaccessible cave high up in the mountain. In order to force the animal out, he shot a poisoned arrow at it, which inexplicably rebounded out of the cave and wounded the bewildered man. This caused much amazement, and three days of fasting and prayer were ordered by the local bishop so that God's will could be discerned. At the end of this period, St Michael appeared saying, 'I am the Archangel Michael, and I have chosen to dwell in that place on earth and to keep it safe. I wished by that sign to indicate that I watch over the place and guard it'.

Shortly afterwards, the Archangel appeared to the bishop, once again after a three day fast, foretelling victory in a battle, during which the soldiers were assisted by mysterious earthquakes, clouds and lightning. Historians believe the battle actually took place a century or so after the first apparition and probably involved a Lombard victory over the Greeks.

At long last, arrangements were made for the grotto to be formally consecrated to the Archangel. However, St Michael appeared a third time (after the usual period of prayer and fasting) and announced that he had already performed the consecration himself: 'I myself founded it, built it and dedicated it'. When the bishop went to the solitary spot in procession on 29 September, he discovered that an altar had been erected and dressed, with a miraculous spring nearby. Moreover, the Archangel left his footprint in the rock as a sign of his presence. From that day forth, the sanctuary at Gargano was called the 'Celestial Basilica'.

Many years later, in 1656, a fierce plague raged over the area and the archbishop prayed for protection. St Michael appeared to him and told him to put the cross and the letters 'M.A.' (Michael Archangel) on stones from the sacred cave. Whoever kept these stones devoutly in their homes would not be visited by the pestilence. A statue of St Michael was subsequently placed in the main square, allowing the grateful locals to pay tribute to their 'Conqueror of the Plague, Patron and Guardian'.

The Feast of the Dedication of St Michael on 29 September—'Michaelmas'—became an important feast throughout the Christian world and gave its name to university and legal terms. Situated near the equinox, it marked the end of the harvest and the beginning of autumn.

British folklore suggests that Michaelmas is the last day for picking blackberries, since when St Michael expelled Lucifer from heaven, he fell to the earth and landed on a blackberry bush. The devil scorched the berries with his fiery breath and spat on them, giving them a bitter taste if picked after the feast. Another popular archangelic delicacy was Michaelmas Goose, well fed on the fruits of the harvest and often paid in lieu of rent for the next quarter of the year; 'Eat a goose on Michaelmas Day', it was said, 'Want not for money all the year'.

Sanctuaries such as Monte Sant'Angelo inspires to us ask for St Michael's protection in our day of battle and become more aware of the ministrations of blessed spirits around us.

MONTSERRAT (SPAIN)

The Black Madonna

When I was studying at the Venerable English College in Rome, my address was the 'Via di Monserrato' and for several years I lived on the 'Monserra' corridor—named after the neighbouring church of Santa Maria in Monserrato. Though often closed (at least in my time), this unassuming church is the city's Spanish Church and once had a hospice for Spanish pilgrims attached. The church houses the tombs of the (Spanish) Borgia popes, Callistus III and Alexander VI, and on occasion there would be a flurry of excitement on the narrow street below my room when a member of the Spanish Royal Family paid a visit.

The church is, of course, named after the famous shrine of Our Lady of Montserrat. This is the perfect pilgrimage site—situated near a major city and port and in an area of outstanding natural beauty. The mountain itself stands out in the Catalan landscape, just over 4,000 feet high, with its serrated edges which resemble the edge of a saw (hence the name). On a clear day it can be seen from as far as Mallorca. The poet Verdaguer suggested that 'with a saw of gold the angels cut down these hills' to make a sanctuary for Our Lady. As well as attracting pilgrims the area is a popular haunt of climbers and walkers and over the years the unusual rock shapes have gained nicknames: 'Spellbound Giant', 'Death's Head', 'Elephant's Trunk', 'Friar'.

It is little surprise that hermits had settled in this beautiful spot by the eighth century. A monastery was eventually founded and pilgrims visited the image of Our Lady, known as *La Moreneta* (the little dark one) owing to the black colour of the face. Some say the statue was miraculously found by shepherds amidst the rocks, others that it was brought here for safety at the time of the Arab invasions.

The cult spread, in part, thanks to the expanding Spanish Empire. Over 150 churches dedicated to Our Lady of Monserrat were established in parts of Italy under Spanish rule, the Habsburgs promoted the devotion in central Europe, and the first churches in Mexico, Chile and Peru bore her name—as does a Caribbean island (now a British Overseas Territory).

The Emperor Charles V and his son, Philip II of Spain, both died holding candles from Montserrat. Many saints have visited Montserrat, including St Peter Nolasco, St Raymond of Penyafort, St Vincent

Ferrer, St Francis Borgia, St Aloysius Gonzaga and, most famously, St Ignatius Loyola. He came here for the Feast of the Annunciation 1522, shortly after recovering from a serious battle injury and experiencing a great conversion of heart. He passed several days in prayer and made a general confession of his life, asking permission of his confessor to hang up his sword and dagger as an offering at the shrine and a sign of his new way of life. 'This confessor', we read, 'was the first to whom he unfolded his interior, and disclosed his resolution of devoting himself to a spiritual life. Never before had he manifested his purpose to anybody'. Before leaving, he met a poor man and gave them his expensive clothes, putting on instead the garb of a pilgrim, complete with a hat and a staff. He spent the night in prayer and then left after receiving Communion first thing in the morning. However, 'at about a league's distance from Montserrat, he was overtaken by a man who had ridden after him at a rapid pace. This man accosted him and inquired if he had given certain garments to a poor man, as the latter had declared. Ignatius answered that it was true that he had given them to a beggar. On learning that the latter had been ill-treated because he was suspected of having stolen the clothes, the eyes of Ignatius filled with tears, in pity for the poor man'.

A particularly appealing aspect of the life of Montserrat is the *Escolania*, the famous choir school that dates back to at least the thirteenth century—a useful corrective to any snobbery on our parts that few worthwhile choral traditions exist beyond British shores! Visitors flock to hear them sing the *Salve* at the shrine on most days and they have recorded over a hundred discs.

Despite the peace that is so apparent today, Montserrat has had its moments of tension and violence. The Napoleonic Wars left the abbey in ruins. The Spanish Civil War led to the deaths of 23 monks, at various places, and these are included among the beatified martyrs of the period. It is said that Himmler visited the monastery in 1940 while negotiating with Franco in Barcelona. Wagner's opera *Parsifal* had spoken of the Holy Grail being kept in 'the marvellous castle of Montsalvat in the Pyrenees' and the Nazis hoped to find it at Montserrat and use its mysterious power in their armoury of weapons!

Life under Franco did not necessarily make things easier for the monks, especially since the monastery gained a reputation as a safe refuge for scholars, artists and others who were critical of the regime. It was also a centre of Catalan culture and language, which the government was trying to suppress. This was especially apparent in 1947 when the image was solemnly placed on a new throne before crowds of a hundred throusand. Catalan was spoken in public for the first time in years and the Catalan flag flown. Unsurprisingly, the organisers were punished. In 1963 the abbot had to go into exile after criticising the General. In 1970 300 Catalan intellectuals organised a sit-in at the abbey in protest to the death sentences given to sixteen Basque ETA activists. Although the police sealed off the monastery and the protestors were eventually removed, the government commuted the death sentences.

Montserrat, then, is not only a monastery and a shrine with a long and distinguished history but the beating heart of a nation's culture and identity.

PADUA (ITALY)

A Pilgrimage to St Anthony

Like so many Italian cities, Padua is full of interest, boasting the peerless frescoes created by Giotto for Enrico degli Scrovegni, one of the oldest universities in the world and what claims to be the largest European square—the Prato della Valle. Moreover, at the famous Pedrocchi Café, I had one of the finest coffees I have ever tasted, an espresso with a creamy mint top.

Everyone knows that nearby Venice is the city of St Mark, but few realise that Padua claims the body of St Luke. Recent investigations have confirmed that the bones at S Giustina are indeed of a man of Syrian descent, dating from the first few centuries of the Christian era. However, Padua is not the city of St Luke. There is another patron who has so captured the popular imagination that he is known locally as 'Il Santo', *the* saint: Anthony of Padua.

Born in Lisbon, he initially joined the Augustinians and later transferred to the Franciscans, only becoming associated with Italy accidentally. He was on his way to Morocco to preach the Gospel and (if God willed it) receive the martyr's palm, when ill health necessitated his return home. Then his ship ran into storms and he ended up in Sicily—and so he stayed on the Italian peninsula. God so often acts through the unexpected ups and downs of life, writing straight with crooked lines!

It is appropriate that his most famous relics in Padua—the jaw, the tongue, the vocal chords, which can still be venerated today—are connected to his voice since it was principally as a preacher that St Anthony was remembered by contemporaries. This was a perhaps unexpected development for in his early years as a friar, St Anthony kept a low profile. Then in 1222 St Anthony attended an ordination and, at the meal afterwards, the provincial asked one of the friars to preach a short sermon. You can imagine the scene—the assembled company trying to avoid catching the provincial's eye, hoping they would not be picked. St Anthony offered to say a few simple words—and everyone was deeply impressed not only by the content of his preaching but by his obvious holiness and sincerity. Soon he was much in demand, travelling round Italy and France bringing people to Christ and doing much to counter the Cathar heresy, then much prevalent—indeed, he is known as the 'Hammer of Heretics'. By the end of his life, tens of thousands gathered to listen to his sermons and confess their sins to him; people waited all night to listen to him and he needed bodyguards for protection. We are told that 'women, carried away by enthusiasm, brought scissors to cut pieces off his tunic as a kind of relic' and that 'you could see knights and noble ladies hurrying through the dark; and people who were more used to spending no small part of the day lazing about on soft couches, keeping awake without any discomfort (they say) and gazing on the preacher's face'.

St Anthony is a very popular saint—in fact, there are 68 cities and towns named after him (more than other saint) and many of our churches have a statue of him. Those of us who frequently lose or misplace things have frequent recourse to his intercession. This custom arose from an incident in the saint's life: a novice who left the friary took with him a book of psalms that was very dear to St Anthony and in which he had made many notes. He prayed for the book's return and also that of the novice—and his prayers were answered!

Images of St Anthony often show him holding the Christ Child, thus ranking him alongside Our Lady and St Joseph. This refers to a vision that the saint had just before his death, when light was seen streaming from his cell and St Anthony was observed cradling the Christ Child. Franciscans have a great devotion to the Incarnation—as seen in St Francis constructing a crib at Greccio—and perhaps there is a deeper meaning since, just as Our Lady led us to Christ through her maternity, so St Anthony led us to the Word Incarnate through his preaching. At the site of this vision in Camposampiero, 30 miles north of Padua, there is a charming statue of the saint crouched on the floor, playing with the divine Infant.

He had retreated to Camposampiero to spend more time in contemplation amid the toils of preaching; moreover, he was physically exhausted and suffering from dropsy. Near to the Franciscan hermitage was a large walnut tree, 'from the trunk of which six limbs reached towards the sky to form a kind of crown with its branches'. The saint had a tree house built and spent his days 'like a busy bee' in meditation and writing sermons. However, his first biographer noted, by climbing into the tree, the 36-year-old saint 'showed that he was drawing near to heaven'. On 13 June 1231 he died at the friary of Arcella, 'absorbed into the abyss of light'; he had been taken ill earlier that day and was on his way back to his beloved Padua.

The deathbed was a scene of peace, accompanied by the singing of psalms and hymns. Things changed soon afterwards. Although the friars tried to hide news of St Anthony's death, the local children ran about the streets shouting 'The holy father is dead'. Soon a vast crowd had gathered at Arcella and miracles were already being claimed. There was an unedifying tussle for his body between the inhabitants of nearby Capo de Ponte, the Poor Clares of Arcella and the friars of Padua. Tensions mounted so quickly that armed guards were called and the intervention of the bishop was needed before the holy relics could be taken back safely to Padua. The construction of the present basilica was begun almost immediately and completed by the end of the century.

It was moving to visit the basilica early on the last morning of our pilgrimage and stand near St Anthony's tomb. People restrf their heads on the shrine, others were looking at the prayer requests and photos pinned up nearby, one lady walked away in tears—all with the backdrop of a continuous stream of Masses. In death as in life, St Anthony remains the most popular of saints.

PHILIPPI (GREECE)

The First European Christian

We know very little about how Christianity reached Britain—legends and speculation have long tried to fill the gap—but we do know something about how the Faith reached Europe. Around AD 49, while ministering at Troas (now in Turkey), St Paul had a dream: 'a Macedonian appeared and appealed to him in these words, "Come across to Macedonia and help us"' (Acts 16: 9). He may have had other plans but instead decided to follow the promptings of the Spirit, arrange a passage across the Aegean and travel into the unknown. Such flexibility, it seems, is a necessary characteristic of missionary discipleship.

The journey to the northern Greek port of Neapolis, east of Thessaloniki, took two days. Modern day Kavalla, as it is now called, remains a bustling town, with a picturesque old centre, lines of seafood restaurants along the front and stray dogs lurking round cafes and tourist coaches hoping for scraps of food.

A church dedicated to St Nicholas marks the spot where St Paul landed and Christianity came to Europe. The apostle's arrival was probably largely unnoticed, except perhaps by the odd port official, shop owner or dog. As far as the apostle was concerned, he was simply travelling to another part of the Roman Empire. Yet, with hindsight, it was a truly momentous event; one small step for the man from Tarsus, one giant leap for humanity. Perhaps it was no coincidence that in Byzantine times the town was known as Christoupolis ('city of Christ').

St Paul's first stop was Philippi, an important city on the Via Egnatia, the great road that connected the East with Rome. Named after the father of Alexander the Great and famed for its gold mines, Philippi was the chief city of the Roman province of Macedonia. Two great battles had been fought there in 42 BC between Julius Caesar's assassins (Brutus and Cassius), who had taken over the eastern part of the Empire, and his avengers (Mark Antony and Octavian). The latter were victorious and the path was cleared for Octavian to eventually become Caesar Augustus, the emperor in power at the time of Christ's birth. After the battle, Philippi became heavily Romanised, a useful means of awarding land to military veterans.

Philippi is now a ghost town in ruins, a huge archaeological site of columns, walls and rubble, situated (like most ancient Greek cities) at the foot of an acropolis, a fortified hill often with an important religious sanctuary. Here and there are signs of its lost magnificence—an impressive amphitheatre, mosaicked floors, remains of several churches (dating, of course, from a later period) and a section of the mighty Via Egnatia.

Standing in the midst of the huge *agora*, once a bustling meeting place and commercial centre, it was astonishing to think that this was the first place in Europe to hear the Gospel. On arriving, St Paul immediately sought out his own people. At the time, there were not enough Jews to support a synagogue so they met in the open air, 'a place of prayer' outside the city walls and near the river, where the necessary ablutions could take place.

The first European convert was Lydia, given the title 'equal to the Apostles' by Eastern Christians; 'a devout woman from the town of Thyatira who was in the purple-dye trade' (Acts 16: 14). Purple dye was greatly prized in antiquity, a sign of high status. This explains the phrase 'born in the purple' or the fact that new cardinals are said to have been 'raised to the sacred purple'. Lydia was obviously a well-to-do businesswoman, possibly widowed: she 'and her household' were baptised.

St Paul and his companions stayed at Philippi for a while, initially using Lydia's house as a base. One day, however, a slave girl possessed with an evil spirit met them and shouting continually 'Here are the servants of the Most High God; they have come to tell you how to be saved!' (Acts 16: 16–17). She is described as a soothsayer, in the Greek oracular tradition, who made money by telling fortunes. St Paul eventually exorcised the girl; however, the steady income she had earned for her masters was lost and they sought revenge. Paul and Silas were arrested for causing a disturbance, flogged and then thrown into prison. A Roman cistern is traditionally identified as Paul's prison and a church ('Basilica A') later built on the site.

The *Acts of the Apostles* goes on to speak of the miraculous deliverance of Paul and Silas when an earthquake shook the prison and the doors flew open. The apostle reassured the distraught, suicidal gaoler that the prisoners had not escaped. He and his family were converted and (like Lydia) invited the apostles to their house for a meal. The authorities seemed nervous they had ill-treated a Roman citizen and advised Paul and Silas to discreetly leave the city.

St Paul remained close to the Philippians and a decade after his first visit wrote a letter to them that forms part of the New Testament. He records some of the names of the congregation—Epaphroditus,

Evodia, Syntyche, Clement, Syzygus—and wrote 'I miss you very much, dear friends; you are my joy and my crown'.

It was moving to celebrate Mass near the spot where Lydia was baptised. The altar, together with a shrine to St Lydia, was located on a tiny 'island' on the river. Two tiny bridges connected this sanctuary to the banks, where the congregation were seated in a sort of small amphitheatre. It was obvious from the steps going down into the river that baptisms sometimes took place there.

The waters in front and behind me gushed past like a torrent and I had to strain my voice to be heard. It seemed an appropriate symbol not only of the dynamic power of baptism but the unstoppable evangelisation that started with Lydia and stretched the length and the breadth of the continent—in God's time, from Philippi all the way to Preston, Paisley and Port Laoise. And if the first European converts to Christianity were a businesswoman, a slave girl and a gaoler, it was clear that everyone was invited to embrace this new Faith.

RABAT, MALTA

St Paul's Shipwreck

Oh, hear us when we cry to Thee,
For those in peril on the sea!

Our group of pilgrims sang these words at the beginning of Mass, their voices ascending from the dark little chapel at the Assumption church in Mosta (Malta) up into its vast dome, one of the largest in the world. In April 1942 a bomb crashed through the dome and rolled across the church floor, watched nervously by the 300 people who were attending Mass. To everyone's amazement it did not detonate and, as a thanksgiving, a replica of the bomb was placed in a sort of 'shrine' in the sacristy.

The words of the hymn were appropriate because we were following in the footsteps of St Paul, who was shipwrecked on the island in AD 60. The account can be found at the end of the *Acts of the Apostles* and I must confess I had never paid much attention to it. So much of our working knowledge of the Bible comes from the readings at Mass and this dramatic passage is not included in our lectionary.

St Paul was on his last journey to Rome. There were 276 people on board, many of them Roman soldiers and their prisoners. St Luke was there too, as was St Aristarchus, a 'fellow labourer' from Thessalonica. It was a troublesome journey, with heavy winds, and the ship was blown off course. St Paul tried to keep morale up and encouraged the sailors to throw sacks of wheat into the sea to lighten the load, but they were forced to run the ship aground on the island of 'Melite'. This is normally identified as Malta, though there are rival claimants in Cephalonia (one of the Ionian islands off the western coast of Greece) and Mljet (near the Croatian coast). In Malta the 'bay with a beach' was later called 'St Paul's Bay' and a nearby uninhabited island, with a large statue of the apostle, 'St Paul's Island'.

What is striking is the welcome the shipwrecked men were given. The locals emerged out of their humble dwellings and must have groaned when they realised that prisoners were stranded on their beach. However, they helped the drenched and exhausted survivors, some of whom had clung onto planks and other parts of the broken ship. They built a fire to warm them up and provided them with food.

The church of St Paul's Bonfire now marks the spot—one of the oldest on the island, though rebuilt after wartime bombing.

When St Paul threw some brushwood upon the fire a viper attached itself to his hand but he remained unharmed, much to everyone's astonishment. Scholars quickly point out that Malta has no poisonous snakes. Of course, that may have been different 2,000 years ago and some commentators, such as Mgr Ronald Knox, suggested that the snake in question came over to the island in an African grain ship. Perhaps the reptile that so alarmingly attached itself to the apostle's hand was the harmless leopard snake, still to be found there.

Popular tradition honours St Paul for ridding Malta of venomous reptiles—St Patrick would work a similar miracle for Ireland 400 years later. The fossilised shark's teeth found all over Malta were once believed to be the tongues of the snakes driven out by the Apostle and were kept as talismans—*Ilsien San Pawl* (St Paul's Tongue). Moreover, ground limestone from St Paul's cave at Rabat was for centuries diluted and used for treating snakebites. Despite the large quantities of scrapings, the size of the grotto never seemed to decrease.

Of course, the whole point of the story is that the coming of St Paul resulted in the triumph of good over evil, of truth over error. The miracles wrought by the Apostle opened the minds and hearts of the Maltese to the Gospel. A particularly important moment was his cure of the Roman governor, St Publius, who became a Christian and the first Bishop of Malta.

St Paul left many traces in Malta. His relics are kept in the church of the Shipwreck in Valletta, including his right wrist-bone and part of the pillar on which he was beheaded (given by Pius VII in 1817). At Rabat many visit his grotto, where he lived during his three-month sojourn in Malta. Nearby, at St Paul's Cathedral in Mdina, built on the site of St Publius's residence, there is a much-venerated image of the Madonna and Child, popularly believed to have been painted by St Luke who was shipwrecked with the apostle. When the Saracens laid siege to the city in 1429, shortly before the island was given to the Knights of Malta, it is said that St Paul appeared in a vision riding a white horse and brandishing a flaming sword. There is a vivid depiction of this in one of the cathedral's transepts.

At the village of Naxxar the chapel of 'St Paul of the Step' commemorates one of the places where he preached, his words (it is said) being heard in Gozo, which can be seen from there on a clear day. The shipwreck even has its own feast, on 10 February, and it is always supposed to rain that day, calling to mind the stormy weather St Paul encountered.

When Pope Benedict visited Malta in 2010, he said that 'it was from the shipwreck that Malta's good fortune to acquire the faith was born so we may likewise believe that the shipwrecks of life can fulfil God's plan for us and can also be useful for new beginnings in our own lives'. St Paul's arrival in Malta was not planned. 'Sailors can map a journey, but God, in his wisdom and providence, charts a course of his own'. St Paul knew this only too well. His life was completely turned upside down after he dramatically encountered the Risen Lord on the road to Damascus. The course of his life was suddenly changed; henceforth, his every thought and action was directed to proclaiming the mystery of the Cross and of God's reconciling love.

SAN GIOVANNI ROTONDO (ITALY)

A Visit to Padre Pio

Padre Pio—St Pio of Pietrelcina—can be felt around every corner of San Giovanni Rotondo. When the famous friar arrived at the small friary nearly a hundred years ago, it looked radically different to what pilgrims see today: there were no hotels or souvenir shops but rocks and rough paths. The nearby village, like many in Puglia, was desperately poor. That all changed as the fame of St Pio spread far and wide; this once obscure area now boasts the largest church to have been built in Europe during the last century, designed by Renzo Piano, the architect of London's Shard.

Despite his popularity, we often miss the point about Padre Pio. Perhaps understandably, we are fascinated by the extraordinary phenomena reported during his lifetime: how he is said to have emitted a 'pleasing fragrance, almost a mixture of violets and roses'; how there were well-attested accounts of bilocation; how he read hearts and foretold future events; how he cured the sick and, most famously, bore the wounds of Christ in the stigmata, which remained with him for fifty years and bled constantly until they disappeared shortly before his death in 1968.

Padre Pio should not be treated merely as a religious celebrity or curiosity but remembered primarily as a friar, a priest, a fellow Christian who followed his calling in an extraordinary way. His name is, in itself, telling—we prefer to call him 'Padre' rather than 'Saint' because the Priesthood was absolutely central to who he was. In the midst of his community he was a kindly, jovial, though sometimes challenging brother. He spent much of the day in the confessional—such were the number of penitents that the church opened at 4 AM. He could treat penitents with apparent severity, especially if they were not sincerely repentant and did not intend to change their life, but they almost always came back for 'the peaceful embrace of sacramental forgiveness'.

When one English woman arrived in the confessional, for example, Padre Pio closed the window saying: 'I am not available to you'. The lady repeated her efforts during the following days but was met with the same reaction. Finally, he consented to hear her confession. When she asked why he had kept her waiting, he answered: 'And you? How long have you made Our Lord wait? You should wonder how Jesus could welcome you after you committed so many sacrileges. You have delayed your judgment for years; besides sinning against your husband and your mother, you have received Holy Communion in mortal sin'. The woman received absolution and returned to England with great joy.

The Mass was at the centre of his life. He rose early to prepare for it—often at 1am—and sometimes the celebration lasted as long as three hours, though this reduced in his later years. He regularly celebrated it at 5am before a crowded congregation—over his lifetime around twenty million attended his Masses. According to one witness,

> The Capuchin's face which a few moments before had seemed to me jovial and affable was literally transfigured ... Suddenly great tears welled from his eyes, and his shoulders, shaken with sobs, seemed bowed beneath a crushing weight ... Between himself and Christ there was no distance ... I defy those who have been at San Giovanni Rotondo to attend Mass as mere spectators.

All priests, of course, act in the person of Christ at Mass but Padre Pio made the link between Christ and the Priesthood especially clear, as the stigmatised friar acted in the person of the crucified Lord and, if you like, lived the Passion. This characteristic extended into his whole life. St Pio may seem to be an impossible example to follow but one of the most essential aspects of his life was his patience in suffering. As a young man he suffered loss of appetite, insomnia, exhaustion, fainting spells, and terrible headaches. For long periods he had permission to live at home as a friar, to gather up his strength, and when he was called up for military service during the First World War, he spent much of it on sick leave. He suffered rejection and jealousy from those that might have naturally been his greatest supporters. The Church was at first nervous about the crowds who flocked to San Giovanni Rotondo and were unsure about the genuineness of his mystical phenomena; for many years he was banned from celebrating Mass in public and hearing confessions, though there was nearly a riot when reports reached this place that Padre Pio might be transferred to another friary. Several books about him were placed on the Index. There were claims of immorality and fraud; even his fellow saint, Pope John XXIII, referred to him on one occasion as a 'straw idol'. When he founded a hospital, the House to Relieve Suffering, he was accused of misappropriating the funds.

This foundation still stands at San Giovanni and would put many of our hospitals to shame. It was established thanks (in part) to the help of an English woman, Barbara Ward, who was a noted economist and later became Lady Jackson of Lodsworth. It is interesting to note St Pio's other British connections. Graham Greene attended one of his Masses in 1949, while travelling with his lover, Catherine Walston. Though he declined an invitation to meet him personally, he was much impressed and for many years carried the friar's image in his wallet. Many British servicemen visited him while stationed in the area during the Second World War. Padre Pio is said to have protected the friary from British shells, just as a flying friar was supposedly spotted in front of American bombers as they flew over San Giovanni in 1944. Then there is the story about Padre Pio talking to a friend on the evening of 20 January 1936, when he suddenly knelt and prayed 'for a soul that is soon to appear before the tribunal of God'. Shortly afterwards he revealed that he had prayed 'for the king of England'. The following day the king's death at Sandringham was formally announced.

Perhaps the thing I was most impressed by while at San Giovanni was the modernity of his holiness. Some of the saint's belongings carefully displayed in the museum are things you might find in my room, such as a wing corkscrew or a Vicks Inhaler. Padre Pio belongs to the modern age. Although his sanctity is unique in so many ways, he shows that holiness is possible for all.

SAN MARINO

The Little Republic

The Republic of San Marino is perhaps best known for its Grand Prix and international football team. Despite being ranked joint last by FIFA and never having won a competitive match (until September 2024 against Liechtenstein), in 1993 the Sanmarinesi famously scored a goal against England within 8.3 seconds of kick-off: a record in the annals of World Cup qualifiers. Perhaps we tend to be rather dismissive of these European microstates, especially if sport is involved. My day trip to San Marino, while on holiday in Italy, acted as a timely corrective.

The first thing that strikes the visitor is the republic's remoteness. There are no railways, no fast motorways. Our drive was only about twenty miles and yet it took an hour and a half due to the winding mountain roads. From afar you see the vast, jagged shape of Monte Titano and assume that only the most intrepid mountaineer could reach its peak. Then, as you get closer, you realise that a city is perched precariously on the mountain's south-western side, with the three towers that can be seen on the national flag.

The 'historic centre' of San Marino is interesting enough, though you can see the main sights in an hour or two and most tourists (many of them Italian) seem more interested in the shops selling firearms, perfume and alcohol. As with so many tourist destinations, there are several attractions of the 'lowest common denominator' variety, such as the Museum of Curiosities or the Museum of Torture (which, I was saddened to see from the publicity, contained replicas of such devices as the Iron Virgin, that infamous fabrication of anti-Catholic writers).

I was particularly struck by the neo-classical Basilica del Santo, which contains the relics of St Marino or Marinus. His story takes us back to the very origins of the republic. Very little is known for certain of his life and he is first mentioned in the eighth-century *Liber Pontificalis*. Originally from Rab (in what is now Croatia), he was a stone-cutter by trade and travelled to Rimini at the beginning of the fourth century to escape the anti-Christian persecution of Diocletian (which was more ferocious in the eastern part of the Empire). St Marinus continued in his professional work and is thought to have first encountered Monte Titano since it provided a useful quarry for stone.

St Marinus was also fervent in preaching the Christian Faith in his new home and formed a community around him. He was ordained a deacon by the Bishop of Rimini and retired to Monte Titano to live the life of a hermit. Many miracles are associated with his time there—the taming of a bear, the healing of the sick, the driving out of evil spirits. A dispute arose with the family that owned the territory in the area but he managed to convert them and was eventually granted possession of Monte Titano.

Interestingly, his companion, St Leo, who had fled from Croatia with him, also left adopted the eremitical life. He was ordained a priest and settled on nearby Monte Feltro, where there is a town called San Leo. As Pope Benedict put it during his pastoral visit to San Marino, they 'brought new perspectives and values to the local context, resulting in the birth of a culture and a civilisation centred on the human person, the image of God and therefore with intrinsic rights that precede all human jurisdiction'.

St Marinus's death is normally dated as 3 September 366 and his last words were given much import in later years: *Relinquo vos liberos ab utroque homine,* 'I leave you free of the one and the other man', normally interpreted as bestowing independence on his followers from the temporal power of both emperor and pope. This was certainly believed down the ages: a document from 1296 relating to a tax dispute reports that 'they do not pay because they have never paid. It was their saint who left them free'. Some suggest that St Marinus actually lived at a slightly later date—perhaps around the seventh century—and founded the monastery that existed on Monte Titano, his chronology being pushed back a century or two in order to stress the independence of San Marino.

The republic's subsequent history has been as precarious as the city's position on the edge of Monte Titano. The English guidebook that I purchased was patriotic in its tone, describing the republic's struggle for liberty against the 'tyranny' of its opponents, whether it be the neighbouring city-state of Rimini, the dukes of Urbino or the Holy See.

The Sanmarinesi were, of course, loyal children of Holy Mother Church but resented the various attempts to make San Marino part of papal territory. In 1739 the pope's governor in Ravenna, Cardinal Giulio Alberoni, invaded the republic on the pretext of capturing some outlaws, apparently without the support of his master, Clement XII. The cardinal briefly managed to impose the temporal authority of the pope until the experiment was ended by an appeal to the pontiff himself. The day of 'liberation', the Feast of St Agatha, is still a national holiday, while Cardinal Alberoni is regarded as the 'baddie' of San Marino history. One of the national heroes from these days was

Antonio Belzoppi, who secretly travelled to Venice to obtain help. He was followed on his gondola by three men in Alberoni's pay and the fog that descended, allowing Belzoppi to escape, was attributed to the intercession of St Marinus.

Thanks to good luck, political cunning and (the Sanmarinesi would add) help from above, San Marino remains the oldest and smallest republic in the world. Good relations with Napoleon and Garibaldi meant that the city state survived during periods where many larger entities fell. San Marino remained neutral during the world wars of the last century, though an Allied bombing on 26 June 1944 resulted in about 60 fatalities; it was wrongly believed that the Germans had occupied the republic.

Whatever the truth behind the legend of St Marinus, he has become a symbol of the republic's long Christian history and concern for liberty for well over a millennium—worth remembering next time San Marino features in a World Cup qualifier.

SAN PELLEGRINO IN ALPE (ITALY)

The Hospice on the Mountain

The remote hilltop shrine of San Pellegrino in Alpe (Tuscany) stands some 5,000 feet above sea level—higher than Ben Nevis—and it made for a rather frightening drive. On the way back, just as we reached the foot of the mountain, we discovered that the breaks of the car had failed. If this had happened a few minutes earlier or we had been caught in heavy traffic, we could have been in serious trouble.

San Pellegrino was for centuries an important stopping point on the road from Modena to Lucca and the site of a hospice for pilgrims and travellers. The poet Shelley came here in August 1820 and was inspired by the experience to write *The Witch of Atlas*. However, the mountaintop village is best known for the shrine of St Pellegrino.

According to tradition, Pellegrino (or Peregine) was the son of King Romanus and Queen Plantula of Scotia. This is often translated as 'Scotland'—indeed, as late as 1782 the Bologna Calendar called St Pellegrino 'King of Scotland'—but it is worth remembering that *Scotti* confusingly referred to the Irish. At his baptism, the saint amazed the witnesses by answering 'Amen' to the prayers and the priest predicted a great future for the child. He grew up at the Court but, as a young man, renounced his birthright and left his homeland for a great pilgrimage.

His first stop was the Holy Land, where he prayed at the places sanctified by the Lord, visited the Monastery of St Catherine on Mount Sinai and spent (we are told) forty years in the desert. He preached at the Sultan's court but was led in chains to the mosque to offer worship. When he refused to do this, the pilgrim was flung into prison until, after five days, he was miraculously freed by Christ Himself. Returning to the Sultan, he proposed an ordeal by fire to establish the truth of the Faith. After thirteen hours in the flames, he remained unharmed and Pellegrino was set free, though he was disappointed that his efforts had won no converts.

Boarding a ship bound for Italy, he experienced a terrible storm, during which he was thrown into the sea by the sailors, who had been convinced that Pellegrino was the cause. However, thanks to the grace of God, all was not lost. His pilgrim's garb miraculously turned into a ship—his cloak became a raft, his stick a mast and his purse a sail. Having reached Italy, a star then led the holy pilgrim into the wilderness of the Appenines, where he lived for twelve years in a wood afterwards called 'Romanesca'. Here he worked many miracles and fought the devil, who tested him through the extremes of snow and rain. In the end, Pellegrino won and drove the evil spirits out of the dark woods and hills. He then went to live in a cave, where he was looked after by the leopards that lived nearby, and finally reached a place called Thermae Salonis. He wrote a brief spiritual testament on the bark of a tree and rested inside the trunk, which was hollow. It was here that Pellegrino died at the age of 97 years, 9 months and 23 days.

The body remained inside the tree, untouched and indeed protected by the animals of the forest, until the saint's resting place was revealed in a dream to a noble woman. She and her husband gave Pellegrino a fitting burial. Devotion to the holy man soon spread and the Tuscans and Lombards both tried to gain possession of the relics. The local bishops suggested that the body be placed on a cart and the oxen be allowed to go wherever they wanted. They stopped near the place the saint had died and a basilica was built and dedicated on 1 August 643 (which became the saint's feast day). The bones of a companion, St Bianco, also rested nearby.

The legend, of course, contains numerous inaccuracies and many of the motifs that can be found in the lives of other saints: childhood prodigies, extreme penances, miraculous escapes and the discovery of the body through a vision. The legend itself is only first mentioned in a fifteenth-century manuscript and provided a powerful spiritual message to pilgrims making an arduous and dangerous journey—the saint persevered despite the obstacles of demons, severe weather, savage beasts, hunger, thirst and other humans.

Having said that, there is no reason to doubt the existence of an Irish (or Scottish) pilgrim who ended his days in the wilderness of the Appenines. From the sixth century, numerous Irishmen trusted in Providence and became 'voluntary exiles' by leaving their homelands and going on a 'wandering for the love of God', many of whom are still venerated across Europe. The fame of these holy men was such that the term 'pilgrims' (*peregrini*) came to denote the Irish and it is little surprise that a generic name like 'San Pellegrino' was used for our saint, in the absence of his baptismal name.

It is also interesting to note that there are two saints with royal Irish connections venerated in nearby Lucca: St Frediano (son of the King of Ulster and Bishop of Lucca in the late sixth century) and St Silaus (an Irish bishop who died at Lucca on his way back from Rome in 1100). The church of San Frediano also boasts the tomb of St Richard the Pilgrim, who we deal with elsewhere.

Historians have come up with many clever arguments to explain this cult: that, through a complex of factors, the memory of a holy Irish pilgrim became mixed with the medieval hospice's dedication to another St Pellegrino, Bishop of Auxerre (popular among French pilgrims), and that when the mountaintop church gained relics of the Roman martyrs, they quickly became the bones of the Irish saint. Whatever the truth, there is much to admire in the life of the saint, who continues to attract visitors and—judging from my experience driving back from his shrine—protects them!

SANTAREM (PORTUGAL)

The Holy Miracle of Santarem

The Eucharist is the 'source and summit' of the Christian life. Yet, despite this treasure in our midst, there are many who approach the sacrament mechanically, indifferently and unworthily. For this reason, on certain extraordinary occasions, the Lord's presence in the Eucharist has been made visibly manifest, so that the change wrought at the consecration affects not only the substance but the accidents of the bread and wine.

One of the most famous of these eucharistic miracles can be found in the Portuguese city of Santarem, south of Fatima. In 1247 (or some say 1266), a century after the city was recaptured from the Arabs, a poor woman was fretting over her husband's unfaithfulness. Such was her desperation that she visited a sorceress (some sources say a Jew), who promised a speedy resolution provided she was brought a consecrated Host. The next time the woman received Holy Communion at the nearby church of St Stephen, she did not swallow the Host but removed it and wrapped it up in her veil. She then hurried home.

Much to her horror, she immediately noticed bloodstains on her veil. Soon it was dripping blood and bystanders offered their help, thinking the woman was injured. Once she was home, she quickly hid the veil, and the Host that was wrapped inside, in a wooden chest and hoped the problem would go away.

As the unhappy couple lay in bed that night, the chest emitted a strange, unearthly light, which illuminated the whole house and attracted the attention of neighbours. This led the husband to ask questions and the woman confessed what she had done. The couple experienced a conversion of heart and spent the rest of the night kneeling in wonder beside the chest.

In the morning they fetched the parish priest, who took the Host back to the church in a more solemn and dignified procession than the one the day before. The Host, which continued to bleed for several days, was encased in wax, in order to preserve it. A further miracle occurred some years later when it was discovered that the wax had broken into numerous pieces and the Host had unaccountably been placed within a crystal pyx. The house where the miracle took place was eventually converted into a chapel; St Stephen's, meanwhile, became known as the 'Church of the Holy Miracle' (Santo Milagre).

The relic was processed through Santarem not only on solemn feasts, but at the time of some calamity, such as floods, droughts and war. The shrine received visits not only from ordinary pilgrims but members of the Portuguese royal family. In 1322 St Elizabeth of Portugal ordered a penitential procession, in which she wore a noose around her neck and covered herself in ashes, praying that her husband (King Dinis) and son (Prince Alphonsus) would be reconciled. Another famous pilgrim was St Francis Xavier, who came before setting off on the missions.

In 1810, as Napoleon's troops approached Santarem, the rector of the shrine buried the monstrance in a local vineyard and placed the miraculous Host in a purse around his neck. This was soon entrusted to the safekeeping of the Patriarch of Lisbon.

The people of Lisbon became very proud that this famous eucharistic miracle was in their city and showed no intention of returning it to Santarem once peace was restored. Then someone came up with a cunning plan. A claim was made that a man would cross the River Tagus while standing on the water wearing boots made of cork. On 2 December 1811, we are told, much of the city gathered to watch this marvel. Meanwhile, the precious relic was hurried through the deserted streets back to Santarem.

Today thousands of pilgrims continue to venerate the Host, passing through a room behind the high altar, where there is a display of paintings and artefacts linked to the devotion, and then climbing a rickety set of stairs so that they are at eye level with the monstrance. The Host appears to be flesh, with delicate 'veins' running through it. On occasion images of the Lord have been perceived on the surface. At the bottom of the phial is a pool of coagulated blood, which (according to a recent investigation) appears fresh and recently clotted.

O memorial wondrous of the Lord's own death;
Living Bread, that giveth all Thy creatures breath,
Grant my spirit ever by Thy life may live,
To my taste Thy sweetness never failing give.

SANTIAGO DE COMPOSTELA (SPAIN)

Onwards and Upwards!

The scallop shell can be found on signs and pavements all over Europe—in Paris and Vienna, Vezelay and Lisbon, even Valka on the Estonian-Latvian border. Guidebooks and websites describe the different paths, including the Camino Inglés, which either starts at Ferrol or A Coruña on Spain's northern coast. Like a complex religious nervous system, the various routes eventually reach Santiago de Compostela—the city built around St James's tomb, situated at what the medievals considered the end of the world (Finisterre).

Modern pilgrims might say the journey is the destination. Afterall, many are the stories told, the friendships made, and the hospitality received, not to mention the daily triumphs over exhaustion, blisters and the temptation to give up. Indeed, pilgrims typically greet each other not only with a polite *Buen Camino* but an encouraging exchange of *Ultreia—et suseia* (loosely translated as 'Onwards—and upwards').

Motivations are, of course, mixed and highly individualist: religious devotion, a quest for redemption and healing, an escape from the busyness of modern life, a physical challenge, a personal reboot, recreational tourism, and/or a tick off the bucket list. There are many enriching stops as the holy city is approached: the walled town of Astorga, with its episcopal palace designed by Gaudi; the mountain village of O Cebreiro, which celebrates the Celtic heritage of the region; the Benedictine monastery of San Xulian de Samos.

Yet one cannot diminish the power of the final goal—the tomb of St James. The first glimpse of the city's towers is an emotional, tear-jerking moment for many. Once through the cathedral's magnificent Pórtico da Gloria, pilgrims embrace the statue of the apostle above the main altar, attend Mass and obtain the much-coveted Compostela certificate. There are well-deserved celebrations in local restaurants and taverns, and a much-needed rest in a hotel—for the lucky ones, a stay in the Hostal de los Reyes Católicos opposite the cathedral. Then, perhaps, there is an onward journey to Finisterre for a dip in the ocean and the (now much-discouraged) ceremonial burning of clothes.

It is curious that this remote corner of Galicia should rank alongside Jerusalem and Rome as a premier pilgrimage site. The history of the *Camino* is centred around two burials and rediscoveries, separated by many centuries. Tradition records, firstly, how, after the Ascension,

St James preached in northern Spain, though with little apparent success. On returning to Palestine he became the first of the Twelve to shed his blood for the Gospel. His followers placed his body on a rudderless boat and set sail across the Mediterranean; landing at the scene of his labours in Galicia, the apostle was buried and the location of his tomb eventually forgotten.

Fast forward to the ninth century and a hermit named Pelayo, who saw stars shining over a field (Compostela means 'field of the star'). The relics were rediscovered, a chapel built and St James became a powerful patron for the Christian kings of the Asturias as they reconquered their lands from the Arabs. The twin imagery of the saint developed over the centuries—the humble pilgrim, complete with broad hat, staff and cockle shell, and the fearsome Matamoras ('Moor-slayer'), on horseback, with raised sword.

Pilgrims flocked to the shrine, including, in the fifteenth century, Margery Kempe of King's Lynn and William Wey of Eton, both of whom left accounts of their journey. The twelfth-century Codex Calixtinus collected together accounts of St James's life and miracles, and, in describing some of the main routes, constituted Europe's first 'guidebook'. An infrastructure developed around the pilgrimage—hostels, monasteries, secondary shrines, and military orders. St Dominic de la Calzada is venerated in the region around Burgos for the care he gave to pilgrims and the building of a bridge and causeway. Indulgences were granted and in 1122 Pope Calixtus II declared a 'Holy Year' whenever the Feast of St James falls on a Sunday—a tradition that not only continues to this day but was a useful precedent for popes calling their own Roman jubilees from 1350.

International pilgrimages began to decline in the sixteenth century and it is often forgotten that one of the causes of this was Sir Francis Drake, the Elizabethan hero who terrorised the Iberian coast. In 1589, when the English were mounting counter-offensives following the Armada, the relics of St James were hidden for safety. They seem to have been forgotten, which seems surprising given the Catholic character of the region and the fact that devotion to the apostle continued locally. Indeed, Santiago remained an important ecclesiastical centre. British Catholic exiles occasionally found themselves there—St John Roberts, the Welsh Benedictine martyr, completed his novitiate at the abbey of San Martiño Pinario and an Irish college was founded in the city in 1605, one of five such institutions to exist in Spain. It only closed in 1769 after the suppression of the Jesuits.

Ongoing wars, political instability and, from the eighteenth century, a growing criticism of seemingly superstitious practices also had their impact. Writing in the 1840s, Richard Ford reported in his handbook for travellers that Santiago was 'much shorn of its former religious and civil dignities' and that pilgrims, though few in number, were generally unwelcome 'since they bring no grist to the mill, but take everything, and contribute nothing'.

Nevertheless, archaeological excavations led to the 'rediscovery' of St James's body in 1879 and their authentication by Leo XIII in the 1884 Bull *Deus Omnipotens*. Here, once again, there is a British dimension. Non-Catholic antiquarians, architects and photographers were impressed by their visits to the city and raised the profile of its treasures. John Charles Robinson, a curator at what later became the Victoria & Albert Museum in London, judged the twelfth-century Pórtico da Gloria to be 'incomparably the most important monument of sculpture and ornamental detail of its epoch'. A cast was duly taken in 1866 and carefully taken back to South Kensington, where it stands to this day. Such initiatives led to a renewal of Spanish interest in the shrine. Once the shrine was restored to its former glory, pilgrimages were once again arranged—including the first English one in the 'Holy Year' of 1909, led by the Archbishop of Westminster. That same year a total of 140,000 pilgrims were registered—compared to several hundred in the typical jubilee of the nineteenth century.

St James was rediscovered as a symbol of Spanish identity, rooted in Catholicism, and devotees hoped that Santiago Matamoros would join the fight against liberalism and anti-clericalism. Pilgrimages were promoted in 1896 to pray for Spain's war effort in Cuba. In his turn, General Franco used the shrine to bolster his regime and encourage visitors to the country.

The modern *Camino* is very much a result of the late twentieth century, flourishing especially from the 1980s and benefitting from the popularity of hiking and cycling. Yet, despite being a restored tradition, pilgrims are very much motivated by following in the footsteps of previous generations and discovering their cultural and religious roots.

A highlight for many at the Pilgrim Mass is the astonishing sight of the *botafumeiro*—the giant thurible that requires eight men (*tiraboleiros*) to operate. Seen at ground level, it appears huge, but once lifted up and swinging from transept to transept, it resembles the small models on sale in the souvenir shops. Guides delight in explaining how the sweet fragrance of incense cleverly disguised the smells of sweaty, dusty pilgrims. Yet the primary purpose of burning incense is to honour the sacred—Almighty God and His faithful apostle, yes, but also the pilgrims assembled together, tired but exuberant, as they have overcome their personal demons and attained their goal. May the fruits of their *Camino* be echoed through the greater pilgrimage through life.

SEGNI (ITALY)

An English Bishop in the Volscians

Segni is a sleepy hill town in the Volscians, south-east of Rome. It was occasionally used as a residence by the popes and it was here that Alexander III canonised St Thomas of Canterbury in 1173. The Victorian travel author, Augustus Hare, noted that 'nothing can be more kind than the reception which the inhabitants of Segni give to strangers' and that when the people returned from the fields with their animals at sunset, the steep streets were 'blocked up for a time, and the cries, the shouts, the braying, the barking, and, above all, the squeaking and grunting, baffle description'.

It perhaps comes as a surprise that one of the town's most distinguished bishops was an Englishman, who had been previously been Vicar Apostolic of the Western District (covering Wales and the west country): Philip Ellis (1652–1726).

Born on 8 September 1652, the future bishop belonged to a distinguished family that bore the scars of the religious and political divisions of the time. His eldest brother, John, became Under Secretary of State to William III and Queen Anne, while another brother, William, acted as Secretary of State to the exiled James II at St Germain-en-Laye. If Philip became a Catholic bishop, his brother Welbore was Church of Ireland Bishop of Kildare.

Philip was sent to Westminster School in 1667 and converted to Catholicism the following year; he then went overseas. A nineteenth-century edition of *The List of the Queen's Scholars of St Peter's College* claimed that Ellis had been 'kidnapped by the Jesuits from Westminster School, and brought up by them in the principles of the Romish faith, at St Omer. He was not heard of by his family for many years; and might never have been discovered, but for his having at St Omer the nickname of "Jolly Phil", by which he had also been known at Westminster.'

He was professed at the English Benedictine priory of St Gregory at Douai in November 1670, taking the name Michael. With the accession of James II, Ellis found himself back in England as a member of the newly established Benedictine community at St James's Palace. The young monk became one of the king's chaplains-in-ordinary and was noticed as an effective preacher.

In 1688 Blessed Pope Innocent XI divided England into four ecclesiastical districts and Ellis was among the new bishops, taking charge of the Western District. He was consecrated at the Chapel Royal in St James's on 6 May by the papal nuncio. At first all went well: the new bishop confirmed at the new Jesuit school in the Savoy and, it is said, reconciled the earls of Sunderland and Melfort to the Faith. However, it seems that the bishop never actually reached his district for the 'Glorious Revolution' broke out in November 1688 and with it died Catholic hopes. Ellis was arrested, having been betrayed by a serving girl, and incarcerated in Newgate prison. Early the following year he was released and took a ship overseas, never to return to England again.

In France, Ellis became chaplain to the exiled queen, Mary of Modena and, due to a misunderstanding concerning his surname, became known as the 'Bishop of Ely'. In early 1693 he travelled to Rome and acted for a time as secretary to the English Dominican cardinal, Philip Howard. Not surprisingly, as time went on, he was accused of abdicating his responsibilities to the Western District and preferring a privileged life in Baroque Italy. Ellis was aware of these accusations and complained of 'misrepresentations and ill offices from abroad and at home'.

Eventually, in September 1705, Ellis officially resigned from the Western Vicariate and was appointed the following year to the Legation of Bologna, an important office in the Papal States. In October 1708 he was translated to Segni. Ellis had been a bishop for twenty years and yet for most of that time had virtually been without a flock. Now, at Segni, he exercised his office with a new-found energy. During his first two years, he only left the diocese three times—an impressive record for an early modern prelate. Within three months he had founded a seminary and secondary school in a disused Poor Clare convent at the top of the town, although the use of this property led to a lengthy legal dispute.

'Mylord Ellis of Wales', as he was known, carried out regular parish visitations, widened roads and organised missions, with the help of the Jesuit Blessed Anthony Baldinucci. He repaired the episcopal palace and cathedral, which was in a poor state; indeed, the bishop's chief means of entering his cathedral was at first through a wine cellar. He added a new roof and choir-stalls, promoted devotion to 'Our Lady of the Mountains' and erected statues to two local saints: Pope St Vitalian and St Bruno, a twelfth-century bishop. In November 1710 Ellis oversaw the first diocesan synod, which was held in the choir of the duomo. About seventy of the clergy attended and Ellis had to provide them with hospitality in his palace, seminary and elsewhere. It became something of a model for other dioceses in the Papal States and Clement XI ordered the decrees to be published.

Ellis was still interested in English affairs and remained close to the Jacobite court, which had settled in Rome. He was present at the birth of 'Bonnie Prince Charlie' in 1720 and gained chapter rights with the English Benedictines in 1725. In Rome he was also involved in the process that led to the canonisations of Pius V, Andrew Avellino, Felix of Cantalice and Catherine of Bologna in 1712.

Ellis had, at first, been shocked by the condition of his flock. 'The people of Segni', he wrote, 'are only a little more civilised than the ancient Volscii, their ancestors. They appear to take no interest in education and culture and, what is far worse, seem to be quite averse from religion. For the most part they do not even know the basic truths of the faith'. The people, on their part, had been suspicious of Ellis's reforming zeal. However, by the time of his death from dropsy of the chest on 16 November 1726, aged 74, Ellis was much-loved by the Segnini and he is still regarded as one of their most important bishops. He was buried in the chapel of his seminary, to which he left most of his belongings.

Ellis's episcopal ring, along with his library, was eventually given to Bishop Baines by Leo XII for the use of his successors in the Western District and then the diocese of Clifton. In 1981 Segni was united to Velletri to make a new Suburbican Diocese, a see administered by a bishop but also given as a title to one of the senior curial cardinals at the Vatican. At the time of his election as Benedict XVI in 2005, Joseph Ratzinger was Bishop of Velletri-Segni, thus claiming (in one sense) to be a successor of 'Jolly Phil'.

SEVILLE (SPAIN)

Seville and its English Cardinal

Seville is surely one of the great cities of Europe. Famed for its oranges and Holy Week celebrations, its magnificent cathedral was, until the completion of the new St Peter's, the largest church in the world. When the Chapter decided to build the cathedral at the beginning of the fifteenth century on the site of an old mosque, they declared: 'let us build a church so beautiful and so grand that those who see it finished will think we are mad'. There is much to interest the visitor: the belfry (or Giralda) which originally served as a minaret, the image of Our Lady 'Antigua' (after which a Caribbean island is named) and shrines both secular (the resting place of Christopher Columbus) and sacred (the tomb of St Ferdinand, a hero of the *Reconquista*).

Walking around Seville you feel as if you could be in South America. This 'New World feel' is perhaps unsurprising since the city effectively acted as the capital of the Spanish Empire, at least in its early years. Some of the buildings point to this imperial legacy: the General Archive of the Indies, the Torre del Oro (a safe place for many of the treasures brought back to Spain) and the House of Trade (which levied a 20 per cent tax on all goods that passed through between New and Old Worlds). Little wonder that Seville became so prosperous.

Seville was also a major Catholic city and unsurprisingly had links with the beleaguered British Catholics, who (unlike many of their countrymen) were happy to look beyond the Channel. It was at Seville, for example, that William Weston underwent his Jesuit novitiate. Then, in 1592, Robert Persons founded an English College, with the support of Philip II and the Duke of Medina Sidonia. It was never very large—supporting the studies of nearly 450 students between 1592 and 1767—and relied on the generosity of benefactors, including some of the *nouveaux riches* of the Spanish Empire. The widow of the Captain-General of the Indies Fleet sponsored its chapel in 1595 and a quarter of a century later permission was granted to raise funds for the seminary in the New World. The priests based at the college were also able to serve the English community in that part of Spain—including exiles, merchants, labourers and soldiers—as well as the foreigners in the city's prisons, galleys and hospital. Seville was very much an international city.

The college closed in 1767, when the Jesuits were suppressed in Spain, and the buildings passed into the hands of a local medical society. This caused much controversy in later years, for the property was owned by English Catholics rather than the Society of Jesus. Attempts to claim compensation continued into the twentieth century. Although the college buildings have sadly been destroyed, the church still stands and is now in the hands of the Mercedarian Fathers.

Seville not only boasted an English College but produced the father (one might say) of modern English Catholicism—Nicholas Wiseman. This may come as a surprise, for he is normally associated with Rome (where he was a student and seminary rector) and Westminster (where he became the first Cardinal Archbishop in 1850).

Wiseman's paternal grandfather was a merchant from Waterford who settled in Seville during the second half of the eighteenth century. The house of the future cardinal's birth can be found in the city centre; the street is now named after his popular novel set in the early centuries of the Church, *Fabiola*. If in Britain we remember him as the first Metropolitan Archbishop of the restored hierarchy, overseas he was chiefly known as a scholar and writer. *Fabiola* was translated into many languages and the pope even commented that this work had done more good than many a papal encyclical.

It is curious to think of this quintessentially English cardinal playing as a child in the narrow streets or spacious plazas of Seville. Spanish would, indeed, have been his first language, perhaps accounting for his shyness when he moved to colder British climes after the premature death of his father in 1805. A childhood friend later remembered 'little Nicholas' generously distributing his treasured sweetmeats among his playfellows in Seville. Wiseman had a prodigious memory and, despite only being a toddler, recalled seeing the British ships at Cadiz after the battle of Trafalgar.

It was at the Cathedral of Seville—the *Magna Hispalensis*—that his mother laid him on an altar and consecrated him to God. His protégé, Cardinal Manning, thought that 'the first *stratum* of his mind was deeply tinged by the soil in which he was born' and especially his view of the Church: 'he had been born in an atmosphere of Catholic splendour, and all his conceptions and visions of the sanctuary were as he had seen them in childhood, and as it ought to be, rather than as it is in the chill and utilitarianism of Modern England'. He tried, in other words, to import the Catholic values and splendours of Seville (and, of course, Rome) to Victorian London.

It is interesting that a friend of the family in Seville was Blanco White, then a gifted priest who, like Wiseman, had Irish ancestry.

In 1810 White left for England and studied at Oxford, befriending (and influencing) the likes of St John Henry Newman. By this stage he had become an Anglican and later a Unitarian. 'An old friend of mine', Wiseman later wrote, 'never mentions him without tears in his eyes. He was, he says, the most pious, the most amiable, and the most clever young man he ever knew'.

It is reassuring that Wiseman's place of birth at no. 5 Calle Fabiola has a plaque in his honour, erected by the city authorities shortly after his death in 1865. Not only is he described as a 'luminary of the Catholic clergy' and 'an honour to his country', but it is made clear that the monument was erected in memory not so much of a foreigner but 'of so illustrious a Sevillian'.

So, one could say, that the English Catholic hierarchy, which died out after the death of the half-Spanish Mary I and which might have been re-established had the Spanish Armada been successful, was only fully restored in 1850 under the leadership of a Spanish-born cardinal. History is full of recurring themes.

URBINO (ITALY)

Jacobites at Urbino

Urbino is one of the most spectacular cities of central Italy. Once an independent duchy, it reached the peak of its glory in the fifteenth century under Federico da Montefeltro, a true Renaissance prince who was immortalised in his portrait by Piero della Francesca.

For the historically observant, however, there is an unexpected undercurrent to Urbino's rich history. Visit the Oratory of St Joseph, one of a number of beautiful confraternity chapels in the city, and you will find on the walls a list of its prominent members, including 'Jacobus III, Rex Brittanie'. Walk around the impressive art collection on the first floor of the Palazzo Ducale and you will pass the 'King of England Room', which (the guide book explains) 'takes it name from the fact that James III once resided in this room as a guest of Clement XI'.

Urbino, then part of the Papal States, was the headquarters of the exiled Stuart Court between July 1717 and October 1718. When the Catholic James II and his family fled to France in 1688, they settled at the palace of Saint-Germain-en-Laye, just outside Paris, thanks to the support of Louis XIV. However, after the death of the 'Sun King' it was agreed that James II's son, James Francis Edward Stuart (known by his supporters as 'James III'), should be expelled from French territory to 'the other side of the Alps'. The Stuart Court spent a short time at Bar-le-Duc (then in the independent Duchy of Lorraine) and Avignon (still a papal city), before moving briefly to Pesaro and then Urbino, where it was given not just a room but the whole of the Palazzo Ducale (with the exception of the apartments used by the papal governor). The rooms were set up as you might have found them at St James's or Kensington Palace. Thus, in Urbino you could find a guard chamber, a presence chamber, a privy chamber with canopied throne and so on. Among those given the task of defending 'the king over water' was a small detachment of Swiss Guards, sent from Rome.

The king and his immediate circle would have been much concerned with promoting their cause and spent a great deal of time writing and receiving letters. There were occasional moments of drama, such as the intelligence that Charles Mordaunt, Earl of Peterborough and Knight of the Garter, was on his way to Urbino to assassinate James. The authorities were persuaded to arrest him at Bologna in September

1717. When the British government heard of this, they threatened to send the Navy to deal with the papal forces. The earl, who was merely making a private visit to Italy as many well-to-do gentlemen did at the time, was quickly released. The episode only goes to show the insecurity felt at the Jacobite Court.

On the whole, it has to be said, life in Urbino must have been rather dull for the Stuart court. Many of the courtiers spoke little or no Italian and complained of Urbino's isolation and the weather (too hot in the summer, too cold in the winter). The food was good, although the exiles obviously had no taste for the local wine and insisted on shipping their own provisions from France. Courtiers whiled away the time playing billiards and shuttlecock. Music was also an important feature of life at the Palazzolo Ducale and regular concerts were arranged, with visiting musicians and *castrato* singers.

James would often attend Mass at the cathedral, situated next to the palace and linked to it by a private entrance. When news of the death of his mother, Mary of Modena, reached Urbino in May 1718, a Solemn Requiem was celebrated by the archbishop 'with sumptuous music'. As already mentioned, James joined the Confraternity of St Joseph, founded to help the families of those condemned to death. As the historian of the Urbino Jacobites, Edward Corp, has noted, this was 'something which no doubt had a particular appeal to James III after the failure of the rising of 1715–16, when so many Jacobites, notably the third Earl of Derwentwater, had been executed'.

The exiled court was somewhat unusual for eighteenth-century Italy. Despite James's staunch Catholic Faith, many of his entourage were Anglican. James believed that, as rightful King of Great Britain, he had to be a father to both Catholics and Protestants. Anglican services were therefore conducted in the Palazzo Ducale by a resident chaplain—a unique arrangement in the Papal States.

There were inevitable tensions at Urbino, between Scots and English, Catholic and Protestant, but the Jacobites were ultimately united around the person of their monarch and his claims to the Throne. One key concern was that, at the age of 30, he was unmarried—which not only put the future of his cause in doubt but meant that his Court was almost exclusively male. At last a suitable bride was found—a Polish princess, Maria Clementina Sobieska, whose grandfather had turned the Turks back from the gates of Vienna in 1683. Maria Clementina was beautiful, devout, well connected and wealthy.

News of the forthcoming marriage filled the Jacobites with great hope. However, as she made her way through Habsburg territory to reach James, she was placed under house arrest by the emperor—pressure had been placed on him by his ally, George I, to put a stop to the wedding. Diplomacy seemed unable to gain her release and the solution was only found in a daring escape that would not be out of place in a swashbuckling movie. An Irish Jacobite, Charles Wogan, who had originally selected the princess as a suitable bride for James, managed to smuggle her out of an Innsbruck castle disguised as a maid in April 1719.

Maria Clementina eventually reached Bologna and found that her bridegroom was away in Spain preparing for his latest ill-fated invasion attempt (sometimes referred to as 'the Nineteen'). A marriage by proxy was quickly arranged and the couple later exchanged vows in person at Montefiascone, where the bishop was a friend of James. Shortly afterwards the Royal Family moved to Rome, a more convenient location for the Court, and the succession was secured by the happy birth of two princes.

James's marriage later broke down, Maria Clementina retiring to a convent, and the Stuarts never succeeded in overthrowing the Hanoverians. 'James III' and his sons were destined to be buried not in St Peter's Abbey, Westminster but in St Peter's Basilica, far away in Rome. A walk through the streets of Urbino called to mind a time of hopeful expectation, when the old cause had not yet died and there was reason to think that a Catholic Stuart would once again sit on the British throne.

VALENCIA (SPAIN)

Finding the Holy Grail

Not far from the Spanish city of Burgos, a stop for many a pilgrim to Santiago, lie the Atapuerca mountains. Here astonishing discoveries were made in the twentieth century, thanks in part to the efforts made by an Englishman, Richard Preece Williams, in building a railway. Large amounts of early human burials dating back tens and hundreds of thousands of years were unearthed. In 1997 excavators found skeletal remains of a group of *Homo heidelbergensis* (a precursor of *Homo sapiens*) dating back at least 350,000 years and crucially including a hand axe that was dubbed 'Excalibur'.

Why such excitement about an axe head? Its presence in a burial suggests, many scholars think, a funeral ritual and belief in the afterlife, no matter how primitive. Humanity is characterised by a search for the truth and a belief in God. No atheist civilisations have been found (at least until now) and the caves of Atapuerca show that this spiritual quest goes back hundreds of thousands of years. An astonishing thought indeed.

This search for the truth has left its mark on literature. In the west, one thinks of the legends surrounding the quest for the Holy Grail—knights in shining armour travelling through vast wildernesses and dense forests looking for this great treasure which promised eternal life. This was the stuff that the Arthurian legends were made from: heroic tales of Perceval and Galahad.

On a visit to another part of Spain—to Valencia, about 360 miles from Atapuerca—I discovered the Holy Grail. It lay not in a mysterious castle, cave or lake but in a slightly understated side chapel in the cathedral. In order to find it I had to pay the entrance fee (a rather sad commonplace, it seems, in Spanish cathedrals) and follow signs to the 'Capilla del Santo Caliz'.

Valencia is Spain's third largest city, with a bustling port and its own language, Valencian. Founded as a Roman colony more than a century before the birth of Christ, the name derives from the Latin 'Valentia', alluding to the strength or valour of the soldiers who went there. It was the location of one of the first psychiatric hospitals and the much-venerated statue of Our Lady of the Forsaken (La Mare de Déu dels Desemparats), originally kept in its chapel, is the centre of a colourful celebration each May. As far as most tourists are concerned, the city is the home of paella and its traditional ingredients include chicken, rabbit, saffron and even snails. The presence of the Holy Grail, however, is beginning to be included in tourist itineraries.

The Holy Grail normally refers to the cup that the Lord used at the Last Supper, although the word comes from the old French *graal*, describing a deep dish rather than a cup. Several places claim to have the original vessel, but Valencia has one of the more convincing claims. The cup in question is made of dark red agate and mounted on a much later stem and base, with two curved handles. It was probably produced in Palestine or Egypt between the fourth century BC and the first century AD, and intended for ceremonial usage, such as the Passover.

Tradition records how the cup was kept safe by the Lord's disciples and eventually brought to Rome, where the first popes used it for the celebration of Mass. It has even been suggested that the Roman Canon (the First Eucharistic Prayer}, used in the papal liturgies from time immemorial, alludes to this treasured vessel in the words of consecration: 'he took this precious chalice' (*hunc praeclarum calicem*). This would have had particular meaning when Mass was offered with the precious chalice once used by the Lord.

In the Valerian persecutions of the third century the treasures of the Church were smuggled away into hiding; thanks to the ministrations of the Spanish-born deacon St Lawrence, the Holy Grail was taken to his homeland. Hidden not only from the Romans but the Moors, who invaded Spain in the eighth century, it was kept at the monastery of San Juan de la Peña by the twelfth century. At the turn of the fourteenth century it was in the possession of the kings of Aragon and eventually deposited in Valencia Cathedral. It was hidden with great courage during the Spanish Civil War and both St John Paul II and Benedict XVI used the chalice at Masses celebrated during visits to the city.

As I sat in the chapel, looking at the sacred chalice, I wondered whether this was the actual cup used by the Lord in the Upper Room—a tantalising if unprovable possibility. I thought of the legends of the Grail, which fascinate us not so much because of the finding but because of the searching. I reflected on the search for truth that we each make throughout life, with all its twists and turns. As Christians, how fortunate we are compared to those early humans in the caves in northern Spain. We have received the gift of faith and the definite revelation of Christ Jesus.

In the midst of this journey of faith is what we do each Sunday: we encounter the Lord at Mass, hearing His Word and partaking of the one bread and one cup (*hunc praeclarum calicem*). This nourishes us and gives us the graces we need as we live out our faith. We need to make it part of us, as natural as the air we breathe, and continue delving into its depths—squeezing out its meaning, just like squeezing those delicious oranges of Valencia.

YUSTE (SPAIN)

The Cloister Life of an Emperor

I can still remember where I was when Pope Benedict XVI announced his resignation: visiting my late mother at her nursing home. Some of the sisters joked that there was now a vacancy in Rome. I was stunned and lost for words.

Abdications always have the power to shock and unsettle, and history gives us several notable examples: Edward VIII, Christina of Sweden, Napoleon, and Charles V, who stepped down as Holy Roman Emperor and King of Spain in 1556. That abdication was so shocking because his territories were vast—not only Germany, Austria, Italy, Spain and the Netherlands but the Spanish Empire on the other side of the Atlantic and beyond. Little wonder that it was described as 'the empire on which the sun never sets' and that his personal device were the twin pillars of Hercules with the words *Plus Ultra*, 'Further Beyond'.

Despite his immense territories, Charles was no dictator. He respected the authority of local elites, preferring to rule through them, and attempted to keep a precarious balance between them, despite their various needs and circumstances. Above all, he dreamed of making Europe a Christian commonwealth and of liberating the holy city of Jerusalem. However, in middle age he became tired and disillusioned after decades of costly warfare with France, internal strife caused by the Lutheran Reformation, and declining health. Ever since his youth he had made known his desire to retire one day to the peace of a monastery.

The monastery he eventually chose for his retirement was suitably remote: Yuste in Spain's Extremadura. The house had its origins in a shrine of 'St Saviour of the Mountains', dating back to the time of the Muslim invasion. A hermitage was erected there in the early fifteenth century. The numbers drawn to the secluded spot grew and the community joined the Hieronymite Order, which was particularly popular with the Spanish Crown. A century after its foundation, the community could claim some outstanding members, famed for their holiness. Fray Juan de Xeres, for example, had a great devotion to the semi-legendary martyr St Ursula and was nursed, it was said, upon his deathbed by her eleven thousand virgins (or at least some of them). Likewise, Fray Rodrigo de Caceres had a vision of Our Lady shortly before his death. Given its reputation for sanctity and its attractive location, surrounded by woods and mountains, it is little wonder that Charles chose Yuste for his final retreat.

A moving ceremony was held in Brussels in which he handed over Spain, the Netherlands and the New World to his son Philip. For the time being he retained the imperial title until the College of Electors met to choose a successor. In September 1556 the emperor left his native Flanders for the last time. A fleet was assembled to take him to Spain and he enjoyed the comfort of a suite of rooms on board, including a bed suspended from the ceiling by ropes in view of his gout and seasickness. As he sailed through the Channel he was greeted by the Lord High Admiral of England (where his daughter-in-law, Mary Tudor, was still queen) and had to take shelter for a day and a night on the Isle of Portland. He eventually landed on Spanish soil on 28 September and set out on a grand progress, via Valladolid, to Yuste. As he drew near he reached the mountain pass at Tornavacas and remarked 'I will never walk on another pass except when I would pass on'.

The imperial apartments at Yuste were not yet ready and so he stayed for three months at the castle at Jarandilla de la Vera, now a parador hotel. Members of his household, many of whom were Flemish, were less than impressed with their damp temporary home; as one historian put it, 'the chosen paradise of the master was regarded as a sort of hell on earth'. However, Charles seemed at peace. A notorious *gourmand*, he enjoyed not only the local mutton, pork and game but delicacies sent regularly from Valladolid, which only aggravated his gout. More edifyingly he enjoyed conversations with St Francis Borgia, who had given up the dukedom of Gandia to join the Jesuits. 'Both the prince and the Jesuit', we are told, 'had withdrawn themselves from the pomps and vanities of life; but custom being stronger than reason or faith, their greeting was as ceremonious as if it had been exchanged beneath the canopy of estate at Augsburg or Valladolid. Not only did the Jesuit, lapsing into the ways of the grandee, kneel to kiss the hand of the prince, but he even insisted on remaining on his knees. Charles, who addressed him as duke, finally compelled him to assume a less humble attitude, only by refusing to converse with him until he should have taken a chair and put on his hat'

On 3 February 1557 Charles finally arrived at Yuste as the monastery bells rang and the monks chanted the *Te Deum*. His 'palace' was modest enough for an emperor, comprising of eight rooms with pleasant views of the gardens and pond. From his bedroom he could look through a special window into the sanctuary of the church. When his health allowed him, though, he attended the services with the monks and even joined them on Fridays in Lent to scourge himself.

Charles lived a life of solitude and piety but, of course, he required a sizeable household, including twenty kitchen staff and even the presence of his clockmaker, Gianello Torriano, to look after his collection of timepieces. Torriano was also skilled as a maker of automatons and, perhaps inspired by his stay at Yuste, made the 'Clockwork Prayer' in the 1560s—a mechanical monk who repeatedly beat his breast, raised and kissed his cross, turned and nodded his head, rolled his eyes and mouthed silent prayers. The emperor also received visitors, including his sisters Eleanor, formerly Queen of Portugal and of France, and Mary, Queen of Hungary, and kept up to date with imperial business.

Outside on the covered terrace a plaque can still be seen that reads: 'His Majesty Charles V our Lord was seated in this place when he fell ill on 31 day of August [1558] at four o'clock in the afternoon'. He had come down with the dreaded marsh fever or malaria. His thoughts were increasingly drawn to the subject of death and, shortly before being taken ill, had ordered the funeral liturgy to be celebrated for members of his family and even (the day before becoming sick) for himself—'the pious monarch himself was there attired in sable weeds, and bearing a taper, to see himself interred and to celebrate his own obsequies'. When death finally came, on 21 September 1558, it was Charles's wish to be buried under the high altar at Yuste: 'one half of my body to the breast', he instructed, 'shall lie beneath said altar, and the other half, from the breast to the head, shall project from it, so any priest who shall say Mass shall have his feet over my breast and head'. This proved to be impractical and his body was placed behind the altarpiece, until it was moved to El Escorial by Philip II in 1574.

Yuste was granted many privileges, including the title of 'royal' monastery, but it eventually declined and had to face the destruction of much of its contents by Napoleon's troops in 1809 and then secularisation in 1833. When William Stirling visited in 1849, it was inhabited only by a lay proprietor 'who eked out his wages by showing the historical site to the passing stranger'; the imperial rooms were used as a store for maize and olives, 'and the silk worm wound its cocoon in dust and darkness'.

Yuste was restored in the twentieth century, forming part of the *patrimonio nacional* under the Spanish Crown. Walking around today the peaceful cloisters, the austere church and the modest imperial apartments, there were more security guards than tourists, and the silence was interrupted by requests for photos not to be taken. Nevertheless, the place was haunting and, in the words of Stirling, 'there was enough to show how well the imperial eagle had chosen the nest wherein to fold his wearied wings'.

ZARAGOZA (SPAIN)

Our Lady of the Pillar

The Marian Basilica of Zaragoza (Spain) sits magnificently on the river Ebro. At first sight it resembles a mosque, with its multiple domes and four minaret-like towers. But a quick consult of the guidebook reveals that this is not only a church but the second largest in Spain and possibly the earliest sanctuary dedicated to the Mother of God.

The best place to view the basilica is from the stone bridge. Here you can find several monuments relating to the bloody sieges that took place there during the Peninsular War. One marks the spot where three resistance leaders were bayonetted and thrown into the river by the French on 22 February 1809, including the priests Basilio Boggiero Spotorno and Santiago Sas. An engraving exists of Sas dressed in cassock and skullcap and brandishing a sword. Such was the stubbornness of the citizens in resisting the forces of Napoleon that the city was given the titles of 'noble', 'heroic' and 'immortal' that can be seen on the coat of arms.

On crossing the bridge, another magnificent church comes into view on the left. Zaragoza actually has two cathedrals. One is the Basilica of Our Lady of the Pilar, with its multiple domes and towers, and the other is La Seo, dedicated to the Saviour. Also built on the site of a mosque, it was the place where St Pedro de Arbués was murdered in 1485 as he knelt in prayer. The Augustinian had recently been appointed as a senior official of the Inquisition but had to wear armour for his own protection. It was not so much because of his cruelty that he was so despised but because many saw the Inquisition as a threat to Aragonese privileges. Unsurprisingly his canonisation in 1867 was regarded as highly controversial.

Another dramatic moment in the cathedral's history came when a hearing was held there to gather evidence regarding the proposed annulment of the marriage of Henry VIII and Catherine of Aragon. The hearing supplemented the more famous one at Blackfriars in London.

Zaragoza is best known for Our Lady of the Pilar. Tradition dates the origin of the shrine to AD 40, when the greater St James visited the Roman city of Caesaraugusta. He won seven converts but became disheartened as to the slowness of his progress and the apparent hopelessness of his cause. As he rested by the banks of the river, wondering what he should do, the Virgin Mary appeared to him. This was no ordinary Marian apparition for Mary was still living out her days in Ephesus. Legend tells how the angels brought her to distant Spain and how she exhorted the apostle to continue. She also asked him to build a church in her honour and left behind a pillar of jasper to mark the spot of this happy encounter—hence the title 'Our Lady of the Pillar'.

As Mary promised, Spain was indeed evangelised and Zaragoza became a place closely associated to the Mother of God. Down the centuries, pilgrims have thronged there, including many kings, queens and saints. The wooden statue of Our Lady itself stands only 15 inches (39 cm) tall and is placed on the pillar of jasper, normally covered in elaborate clothes. At the back of the chapel an opening has been made so that pilgrims can touch part of the stone. A small shop within the porch sells ribbons in different colours that measure the same height as the statue. These are often worn about the person, taken into exams or tied to car mirrors.

The most prominent miracle of Zaragoza occurred on 29 March 1640. Miguel Juan Pellicer Blasco from the town of Calanda had lost a leg in an accident and, unable to work, often sat at the entrance of the shrine praying and begging for money. That night he dreamt he was at the sanctuary and his leg miraculously restored. On waking he found, to his astonishment, that his leg had indeed returned. As word spread of the miracle, the number of pilgrims to Zaragoza greatly increased and the basilica was soon rebuilt and enlarged in the baroque style. Like so many Spanish churches, the basilica faced destruction during the Spanish Civil War. If you look closely at the walls around the shrine you will notice two holes made by bombs dropped here in 1936. Miraculously, perhaps, they did not detonate.

Another reason for the shrine's popularity is the fact that Columbus set foot in the Americas on the feast of Our Lady of the Pilar, 12 October 1492. Little wonder that she is considered Patroness of the New World and, in the words of St John Paul II, Mother of the Hispanic Peoples. For this reason, the flags of the Hispanic Nations hang near the statue, from Argentina to Venezuela.

The tradition of Our Lady of the Pilar is unique and extraordinary. What are we to make of it? As I venerated the tiny statue, I thought of one clear lesson that she teaches modern pilgrims. How easy it is, like St James, to be discouraged in doing the Lord's work. In the labour of evangelisation we worry about how others perceive us, we ask whether it is worth all the effort, we become disheartened by our failings. Our Lady of the Pilar's message is to embolden us with holy daring and to restore our hope and purpose. This is as necessary today as it was in AD 40.

WESTERN EUROPE

Andorra, Belgium, France, Ireland, Luxemburg, The Netherlands

ALBERT (FRANCE)

The Leaning Virgin

Despite the violence and devastation of the First World War, the countryside of the Somme has largely reverted to its original appearance, marked by rolling fields, modest ridges and small hamlets. Nevertheless, the landscape still bears the marks of conflict and every year produces a potentially deadly 'iron harvest' of unexploded shells, shrapnel and even the remains of the dead. In places you can still see the lines of trenches and collections of craters.

One of the few towns in the region is Albert, situated on the river Ancre. At its centre is the impressive Basilica of Notre Dame de Brebières, which during the war was famous for its leaning statue of the Virgin and Child.

This Marian shrine had been popular among locals for centuries. According to tradition, a medieval shepherd noticed a sheep pawing at the ground one day. He sent a dog over but the ewe remained stationary and so he went over and struck the ground. He heard a mysterious voice: 'Stop shepherd, you hurt me', and discovered that his crook was covered with blood. The shepherd nervously bent down and uncovered a stone statue of the Virgin and Child, with a sheep grazing at their feet. Our Lady's head was marked by the shepherd's blow.

A chapel was built at the spot and the statue was given the title 'Our Lady of Brebières'—deriving from *brebis* ('sheep') and *berger* ('shepherd'). Devotion quickly spread, especially among shepherds. St Colette turned to her at the age of fourteen with her typically teenage concerns over delicate health and lack of height. The Virgin heard her prayers, we are told, and not only did her constitution improve but she miraculously gained several inches. The saint went on to reform the Poor Clares.

In 1637 the sanctuary was partially burned by Spanish troops and eventually in 1727 the image was moved for safety to the nearby church at Albert. During the French Revolution the image survived after being hidden in a coffin—a lucky escape for the church was briefly turned into a temple to the 'Goddess of Reason'.

Whether known as 'Notre Dame de Brebières', 'the Virgin of Albert', 'Our Lady of the Ewes' or 'the Divine Shepherdess', devotion revived in the second half of the nineteenth century. A new basilica, with the famous gilded Virgin and Child on the tower, was completed and Leo

XIII even called it the 'Lourdes of the North'—though the numbers of pilgrim never began to compete with that Pyrenean shrine.

During the First World War, the medieval statue was moved to Amiens Cathedral for safety. On 15 January 1915 a German shell caused the gilded statue on the tower at Albert to lean forward, almost at a right angle. 'It is really wonderful', wrote one British officer, 'and personally I think it is a miracle. The statue is huge (with an immense base), and of metal; all the girders which used to support it are smashed, and the statue appears to be suspended in mid-air'.

It soon became the focus of much legend—that whoever caused her to fall would (depending on the version you heard) win or lose the war, or simply 'when the Virgin fell, the war would end'. It became an iconic image, appearing on numerous postcards, and was known as the 'Golden' or 'Leaning' Virgin. The Australians were less reverent—they christened it 'Fanny Durack', the Olympic swimmer, because the statue looked as if it was about to dive into a pool. In March 1918, the Germans occupied Albert and the British artillery deliberately targeted the church tower, to prevent it from being used as an observation post. The Virgin finally fell that April, six months before the Armistice.

Allied troops recaptured the town in August 1918. A soldier of the 8th East Surreys wrote: 'Streets, once picturesque and lively with the business of British military life, had become mere paths littered with rubbish, lined with stumps of walls and wrecks of buildings, and undermined in every direction with land-mines and charges. The basilica from which the golden image of the Virgin and Child had hung for so long was there yet, and its vast nave still dominated the town, but it had become a mere huge forbidding shell of red brick'.

The church was subsequently restored and re-opened amid much jubilation in 1931, thanks to a large grant from the French Government and the gifts of many donors. A special relationship existed with the people of Birmingham, who raised a considerable sum of money towards the town's reconstruction and opened an almshouse for the aged poor. To this day, the street on which the basilica is located is called 'Rue de Birmingham'.

Thus, the ancient image returned to its rightful place and a copy of the original gilded Virgin once again looks over Albert and the surrounding war-scarred countryside. In the words of poem by M. E. Francis,

> Mother, this place was peaceful once, and blest,
> That golden statue on its tower poised high

Held the Child Jesus—not upon its breast,
But raised aloft, with little arms outspread
As once upon the rood's unyielding bed
— And all who passed might hear thy voiceless cry,
From break of dawn until the day was done:
'Look up, my children, look upon my Son'.

ANDORRA

'The Only Remaining Daughter of the Carolingian Empire'

When is an elected republican president also a reigning prince? And which Catholic bishop, other than the Bishop of Rome, is an *ex officio* head of state? The answers both relate to the tiny principality of Andorra, sandwiched in the Pyrenees between France and Spain. Much of its history has consisted of territorial struggles and compromises made to ensure its independence. As a result, Andorra has two heads of state—the Bishop of Urgell (just over the border in Spain) and the president of France.

Small microstates often accumulate an impressive list of quirky trivia. Andorra, for example, was not included in the Treaty of Versailles and so technically its First World War only ended in 1958. It also claims the highest European capital, the longest life expectancy in the world and the only country to have Catalan as its official language. Today, of course, it is a tax-free haven and a shopper's paradise, as well as being a centre of tobacco production.

A look at its national anthem reveals two essential aspects of its identity. Firstly, we hear: 'The Great Charlemagne, my Father / From the Saracens freed me'. The origins of the principality are usually traced back to Charlemagne, who is said to have granted sovereignty to the 'Valleys of Andorra' in recognition for their brave fight against the Moors, who had taken control the Iberian Peninsula. Modern Andorra, it could be said, is the sole survivor of the network of buffer states set up under the emperor's protection between the Christian West and al-Andalus. Charlemagne is still very much remembered as Andorra's founding father. Only in 2007 it instituted a civil decoration, the 'Order of Charlemagne', while houses where he is said to have stayed, even his footprint, are sometimes pointed out to visitors. With some justification, Andorra can claim to be the 'only remaining daughter of the Carolingian Empire'.

After the break-up of the Empire, power over the area passed to the Count of Urgell and (from 1133) the bishop of that place. Prolonged claims by the neighbouring Count of Foix led to the 1278 treaty which established the concept of co-sovereignty between the bishop and the count. When Henry of Navarre, who included Count of Foix among his titles, became King of France in 1589, that part of Andorra's sovereignty passed to the French Crown and (eventually) Republic.

The national anthem continues, 'And from Heaven he gave me life / Of Meritxell the great mother'. The spiritual heart of the country is the shrine of Our Lady of Meritxell. It is said that the principality cannot be explained without her and vice versa; 'Meritxell' remains a popular girl's name. A fire in 1972 sadly destroyed much of the sanctuary and the original twelfth-century statue, though replicas were quickly created. The statue shows a seated Mary, holding the Child Jesus and wearing the flat wooden shoes typically worn by mountain farmers in those parts. She stretches out her right hand, drawing the faithful into the mystery of her Son—this hand is exaggerated in its size, giving her the name of the 'Virgin of the Long Hand'.

According to legend, the statue was discovered one Epiphany by some inhabitants of Meritxell as they made their way to Mass. By the roadside they noticed a rose in flower—an unusual sight in the middle of winter—and in its branches the statue of Our Lady. With the encouragement of the parish priest, they took the statue to the local church at Canillo. However, next morning the statue had made its way back to the original spot by the roadside and, though it was snowing, none had fallen on the statue or the rose. And so, the shrine of Meritxell was built on that spot and continues to this day. Pilgrims flock to her shrine on 8 September and dance the traditional Catalan circle dance, the *sardana,* out of pure joy at Mary's maternal protection.

ANTWERP (BELGIUM)

An English Carmel in Antwerp

The Carmelites have long had a presence in England, as can be seen in the tradition that St Simon Stock received the Brown Scapular from Our Lady either at Aylesford or Cambridge. Carmelite houses were among those dissolved at the Reformation; by this time there were about 280 friars. Although the Order produced no recognised martyrs during this period, the Prior of Doncaster (Laurence Cooke) seems to have been put to death in the aftermath of the Pilgrimage of Grace (1536).

In the midst of all this, unknown to any of the subjects of Henry VIII, Teresa de Ahumada entered the Carmel at Avila in 1535. For many years she was a somewhat lukewarm nun, as she herself later confessed, but, after experiencing a radical conversion, went about reforming her Order and founding houses for her 'Discalced' sisters.

Among St Teresa's closest companions were Blessed Anne of St Bartholomew, a humble shepherd who had felt the call of the cloister, and Venerable Anne of Jesus, who was much esteemed by St John of the Cross. In the early years of the seventeenth century these two nuns founded a series of reformed Carmels, first in France and then in what is now Belgium, including one at Antwerp (1612). The legacy of St Teresa was thus brought to the doorstep of England. Anne of Jesus even wrote that 'if the doors were open to us to go to England, I would go even if I had to crawl there'.

Instead, the Teresian nuns had to make do with their first English recruit: Anne Worsley, known in religion as 'Anne of the Ascension'. In 1619 she became the lynchpin of a new specifically English Carmel that was founded at Antwerp. This was made possible through the financial support of Lady Mary Lovel, one of the great Catholic women of the period. A widow and mother, she first joined the English Benedictines at Brussels, where her daughter was a nun, but left after a year. Shortly afterwards she received a message from Our Lady to found a Carmel and gained permission from the authorities, both civil and religious. We read that when her Jesuit confessor showed reluctance in supporting the idea, 'he was severely reprehended by our Blessed Lady in his morning prayer for opposing the designs of heaven, so much conducing to the glory of God'. Lady Mary was not the sort of lady who took 'no' as an answer.

Several signs showed further divine approval: Mother Anne of the Ascension had herself seen the location of the new convent in a vision and, as the building was erected, an image of Our Lady was discovered which was treasured by the community in subsequent years. But there were tensions. Having contributed so much to the foundation, it was natural that Lady Lovel should assume a certain authority over the nuns, much to the prioress's discomfort. There were disputes over who should act as confessor to the community—St Teresa favoured liberty of choice in this matter—and whether local Flemish women were allowed to join. The Foundress even threatened to withdraw her support, although in time her enthusiasm for a new initiative (the establishment of another community, this time Bernardine, in Bruges) took the pressure off the Antwerp house.

As the historian, Peter Guilday, writes, 'the 175 years of the English Carmel's residence at Antwerp were spent in what would seem to the outside world a continual monotonous round of religious duties and exercises, but in the divine economy which regulated the scattered English flock of the Church, their life merits as high a place as the activity of the missionaries or the preparation of boys and girls of the time for the struggle which inevitably awaited them on their return home'. By the time of Mother Anne's death in 1644, over 50 English ladies had received the habit, including Teresa Ward, whose sister, Mary, founded the Institute of the Blessed Virgin Mary. Further foundations were made at Lierre and Hoogstraete and the English Carmelites gained a strong reputation.

Several nuns became famous for their sanctity. After the death of Mother Margaret Wake (of the Angels) in 1678, shortly after her election as superior, her body was found to be incorrupt. This caused great excitement; guards were stationed around the convent to prevent any disorder and it was taken to a place of honour in the convent, beside the choir, where it was visited by many devotees. Another Antwerp prioress, Mother Mary Xaveria of the Angels (Catherine Burton), and a prioress at Lierre, Mother Margaret Mostyn, also died in the odour of sanctity; the latter being known for her many visions and prophecies.

As with most of the English religious houses overseas, the three Carmels were closed during the aftermath of the French Revolution, and continued in the safer environment of Protestant England. The Antwerp nuns set up a house at Lanherne (Cornwall), those of Lierre at Darlington (County Durham) and Hoogstraet at Chichester (East Sussex).

An interesting footnote is provided by the fact that, just before the house at Hoogstraet closed, one of the community, Mother Bernardine of St Joseph, founded the first Carmel—indeed, the first contemplative house—in America, at Port Tobacco in her native Maryland. The life of the cloister, so violently attacked by the proponents of the Protestant Reformation, refused to die and burst into new life, even in distant and new worlds.

ARS (FRANCE)

The Curé's Village

Every village has its *curé* or priest—no matter how many churches he may have to run—but there is only one place known as the '*curé*'s village'. If Ars is synonymous with its nineteenth-century parish priest, so his identity has become subsumed into the place that he served. Few people refer to him by his baptismal name, Jean-Marie Vianney; he is known across the world as the '*curé* of Ars'. His priestly life was no 9 to 5 job, compartmentalised alongside other interests and pursuits. It was as if he was ontologically linked to his parish and his pastoral role. This was who he was.

The *curé* was born in Dardilly, near Lyon, in 1786, a few years before France broke out into Revolution. As a result of anti-Christian legislation, the young saint had to attend catechism classes at the dead of night, make his First Confession beside the grandfather clock in his family home and receive his First Communion at a secret Mass in a local barn. He later recalled the wagons of hay placed against the door to ensure that the revolutionaries did not disturb proceedings.

By the age of seventeen he announced his desire to become a priest but was delayed by his father's wish that he should help on the farm. Formation was interrupted, too, when he was called up by the French army in 1809. This he managed to avoid—on one occasion he hid in a hayloft and suffered so much under the weight of the hay that he vowed never to complain about anything again. We seldom think of the *curé* as a deserter from Napoleon's Grande Armée, whose lot might have been fighting the British in Spain (campaigns made familiar to many through Bernard Cornwell's *Sharpe* novels).

Vianney found his studies challenging. A contemporary admitted that 'he knew little of Latin, having begun his studies late, and gone through them very rapidly' and that 'he was not strong in philosophy; there were many others, however, no further advanced in it than himself'. This is, perhaps, a consolation to many seminarians!

He was eventually ordained in 1815, the year of Waterloo, and three years later was sent to the village of Ars in the Dombes region. Famously, in approaching his new home by foot he asked for directions from a local shepherd, Antoine Givre. The priest knelt down and prayed, exclaiming how small the village was, and then said to the boy: 'You have shown me the way to Ars, I will show you the way to Heaven'. A statue marks the spot of this memorable pastoral encounter, the first of so many over the subsequent forty-one years, until his death in 1859.

It is two centuries since Abbé Vianney arrived in Ars, on 13 February 1818. Walking around the little village, memorials of the saint can be found everywhere and there is much for a priest pilgrim to think about. I found that the life of the saint, despite living in a very different time, shone a light on my own ministry and especially on the many areas where there was room for improvement!

Despite his many duties, the *curé*'s life was solidly rooted in prayer. As he knelt before the tabernacle, 'bathing in the flames of love which issued from the divine presence on the altar', his face was visibly transformed. This is shown in the famous sculpture by Emilien Cabuchet, based on a wax bust made while watching the saint pray and catechise, before which pilgrims are encouraged to light a candle. 'I have seen it many a time myself', wrote one of his spiritual children, 'it seemed as if he saw our Lord'.

At the heart of everything was the Eucharist. He made sure his church was worthy of the divine mysteries—indeed, like so many priests, the *curé* found himself forced into the role of builder and made many improvements to the little medieval church of St Sixtus. He rebuilt the tower, enlarged the façade and chancel, added side chapels, and embellished the interior with statues and other decorations.

The saint did this with one aim in mind: the salvation of souls. He gave regular catecheses and these, along with his sermons, used vivid images and examples drawn from everyday life which could be understood by all. Rather like Padre Pio, the *curé* spent long hours with penitents. By the 1850s, by which time crowds were flocking to the little village, he would spend up to seventeen hours in the confessional. 'The mercy of God', he used to say, 'is like an overflowing torrent'.

Although the church was the centre of his ministry, he was much concerned with social outreach and charity. In 1824, for example, he founded La Providence, an orphanage and school for girls, now a pilgrim hostel and a place for perpetual adoration. He also worked closely with the laity. A particularly important associate was Catherine Lassagne, who directed La Providence until it was handed over to a community of sisters in 1847 and henceforth became the *curé*'s housekeeper, dealing with his many visitors and the torrent of letters he received. Her evidence proved essential to the cause for his beatification.

The saint actively engaged the devil in combat, especially at night, when he would be woken by taps, blows and strange noises; on one occasion his bed was even set on fire. He referred to this infernal foe as the 'grappin', named after a pitchfork commonly used to dig up potatoes. Such attacks highlight not only his sanctity but the struggle that everyone faces—priests included—with sin and human weakness.

He carried the crosses, too, of poor health, of suspicion from his brother priests, who thought him ignorant, imprudent and even fraudulent, and of self-doubt. On several occasions he tried to leave Ars, feeling overburdened by his pastoral duties and attracted to the solitude of the Carthusian life. One night, this internal crisis reached fever pitch and he left Ars for the nearest Charterhouse, but as he stumbled through the darkness he reasoned: 'Am I really doing the will of God now? Is not the conversion of one single soul worth more than all the prayers I can offer up in solitude?' He returned to his parish; despite the relentless toil; that was where the Lord had planted him.

In May 1854 William Bernard Ullathorne, Bishop of Birmingham, visited Ars during his pilgrimage to La Salette. 'To understand him', he wrote, 'one should see his face, always glowing when he speaks of God, always bathed in tears when he thinks of evil'. Such was his popularity that he could not leave the presbytery or church 'without being thus surrounded and pressed upon by the people'; indeed, 'penitents will lie all night on the grass, fifty at once, either in order to gain the earliest admission to the church and the confessional'.

AUXERRE (FRANCE)

'Then Came the Bishop of Old Auxerre'

The Burgundian city of Auxerre straddles the river Yonne, with the towers of its magnificent cathedral and abbey rising above the historic centre. The abbey, which is now a museum, is dedicated to St Germanus, the fifth-century bishop who is the city's patron. His bones rested there, until desecrated by Huguenots in 1567. Yet his image is still everywhere to be seen, along with vestments purporting to have belonged to him. He is particularly interesting because of his close connections with Christians on the other side of the Channel: his pupils included St Patrick and he visited Britain on two occasions, giving valuable insights into this rather obscure period of history.

Born around 380, St Germanus received a good education and trained as a lawyer. He was appointed as a 'dux' or governor of one of the provinces, possibly Brittany, married a lady whose name is sometimes given as Eustachia, and enjoyed the pleasures that his position gave him. One tradition has him falling out with the then Bishop of Auxerre, St Amator, because of his habit of hanging hunting trophies on a tree that had been considered sacred by the pagans. The prelate had the tree cut down, which turned out to be a moment of conversion for the governor. When the old bishop died in 418 St Germanus was elected by the people as his successor; rather like St Ambrose of Milan, he was a layman at the time of his appointment. Given his legal and political background, he was perhaps an obvious choice in a society that relied on episcopal authority for stability.

According to his biographer, Constantius of Lyon, 'he deserted the earthly militia to be enrolled in the heavenly; the pomps of the world were trodden underfoot; a lowly way of life was adopted, his wife was turned into a sister, his riches were distributed among the poor, and poverty became his ambition'. St Germanus is remembered as a model bishop, devoted to his people, pious in his duties, fervent in eradicating the vestiges of paganism and keen to promote monasticism. Among the bishop's disciples were two of the great Celtic saints, St Patrick and St Illtud, who are believed to have spent time at Auxerre under his guidance.

Constantius tells us that in 429 'a deputation from Britain came to tell the bishops of Gaul that the heresy of Pelagius had taken hold of the people over a great part of the country and help ought to be brought to the Catholic faith as soon as possible'. Pelagianism was one of the most widespread heresies of the period. Originating in Britain, it denied original sin and downplayed the necessity of grace. Human beings could work for salvation through their own effort. St Germanus was chosen to undertake a mission to Britain, together with St Loup (or Lupus), Bishop of Troyes. On his way to the coast he passed through Nanterre and met the young St Genevieve, the patron of Paris, predicting her future sanctity.

Constantius depicts evil spirits brewing up a storm to obstruct the voyage of the two bishops across the English Channel: 'the ocean was assaulted by the violence of demons, haters of religion ... They heaped up dangers, roused the gales, hid the heavens and the day under a night of clouds, and filled the thick darkness with the terrors of the sea and air ... The sailors were powerless and abandoned their efforts; the vessel was navigated by prayer and not by muscles'. St Germanus eventually managed to calm the sea by sprinkling the waves with holy oil 'in the name of the Trinity'. Those who have had rough crossings across the Channel may feel a certain sympathy with this experience.

Arriving on British soil, Constantius refers to the bishops' ceaseless round of preaching and miracle-working: 'since it was a daily occurrence for them to be hemmed in by crowds, the word of God was preached, not only in the churches, but at the crossroads, in the fields, and in the lanes'. Eventually the heretics challenged the bishops to a contest, before a vast crowd, somewhere near Verulamium (modern-day St Albans, Hertfordshire). 'Empty arguments were refuted', we read, 'the dishonest pleas were exposed, and their authors, as each point was made against them, confessed themselves in the wrong by their inability to reply'. The turning point came when a well-born couple brought their blind ten-year-old daughter into the assembly. St Germanus prayed over her, along with St Loup, and then placed a reliquary on her eyes: 'immediately it expelled their darkness and filled them with light and truth ... From that day onward the false doctrine was so completely uprooted from men's minds that they looked to the bishops for teaching, with thirsty souls'.

While in Hertfordshire, St Germanus visited the place of St Alban's martyrdom to give thanks for the successful outcome of this conference. It is not clear whether the shrine was already known; the *Passio Albani*, which may even have been commissioned by St Germanus, says that the martyr appeared to the French bishop in a dream, allowing his tomb to be discovered and the details of his passion to be written down. St Germanus left relics of the apostles and martyrs in the tomb and took some bloodstained earth away with him. It is often claimed that he dedicated a church in Auxerre to the martyr. The evidence for this is weak, though it is highly likely that the text of the *Passio Albani*, the earliest account of the martyr's life and death, was written on the walls of a church in that city. Moreover, the emphasis on visions and miracles in the story (like the miracles in the life of St Germanus) was a useful way of attacking the Pelagian stress on human effort as opposed to divine grace.

St Germanus also became involved in the struggle between the Britons and an invading force of Picts and Saxons; the last Roman legion had departed twenty years previously and Britain was in turmoil. The bishop was asked to visit a military camp to give spiritual comfort and protection to the British troops; indeed, he seems to have spent much of Lent 430 with them. Constantius records that many 'sought the waters of salvation' and 'a church was built of leafy branches'; 'the soldiers paraded still wet from baptism'. A great battle was fought and the outnumbered Britons charged at the enemy, shouting out 'Alleluia!' The Saxons and Picts promptly fled, resulting in a much-celebrated 'Alleluia Victory'.

St Germanus was a devoted pastor and, like many other bishops of his time, had his warrior side. As Hilaire Belloc wrote rather mischievously:

> Then came the bishop of old Auxerre
> Germanus was his name
> He tore great handfuls out of his hair
> And he called Pelagius shame.
> And with his stout Episcopal staff
> So thoroughly whacked and banged
> The heretics all, both short and tall—
> They rather had been hanged.

St Germanus was back in Britain around 447 to deal with the ongoing Pelagian threat, this time accompanied by the Bishop of Trier, St Severus. He died while on a diplomatic mission to Ravenna three years later and his body returned to Auxerre.

St Germanus has been surprisingly neglected by the British. Very few church dedications exist, the two most celebrated examples being St Germans in Cornwall (though there is some doubt over which saint this was named after) and Selby Abbey in Yorkshire, founded by a monk from Auxerre in 1069. The story of this foundation is intriguing. The saint appeared in a vision to Benedict of Auxerre, asking him to establish a monastery at a place that he would identify outside York and to take with him a relic of his finger. On approaching his community, permission was denied and, spurred on by further visions, the monk took the relic and left Auxerre on his own accord. Not knowing England very well, he accidentally went to Salisbury and the saint appeared to him, laughing at his mistake. He finally reached Selby and set up a hermitage that would later become the great abbey.

Along with St Loup of Troyes and St Severus of Trier, St Germanus was one of the earliest saints that we know for sure ministered on English soil. His life by Constantius is one of the most important sources for fifth-century Britain. Moreover, the bishop popularised the story of St Alban, our first martyr, using it in his attack on the Pelegian heresy. St Germanus should indeed be better known.

BANNEUX & BEAURAING (BELGIUM)

Two Belgian Apparitions

Sorting out the papers of my late father, I read a series of autobiographical notebooks that he had kept over the years. Of course, for me these were fascinating, although (thankfully) there was nothing sensational in them!

His memories went back to the late 1920s and one particular highlight were the regular trips made to Belgium to see his mother's family—for my grandfather had fallen in love with a Belgian girl while billeted in her village at the end of the First World War. Catholicism therefore entered our staunchly Methodist family.

These family holidays took place in the area around Tournai, one of the oldest Belgian cities and the only one to have been ruled directly by England for a brief time (1515–19) after Henry VIII conquered it during a war with France. 'The garden of my mother's house', my father wrote, 'had tall cherry trees on to which the bedroom windows looked. The bird-song on summer mornings was delightful. To a child from industrial Lancashire it was like waking up in paradise! Often I would dream that I was in bed in that house, only to find that I was back in England. The sense of disappointment and deprivation was terrible'. There were many unusual sights, sounds and smells—'there were priests in their black cassocks and hats; men and women religious in their habits, often riding bicycles; more horse-drawn vehicles than at home and mules, some of them, I believe, Army mules still employed from the 1914–18 War.'

I found it interesting to ponder that while my father was being intoxicated by this colourful world, Our Lady was appearing to some children not that far away. In 1932–3 two apparitions in Belgium, both later approved by the Church, rocked the Catholic world. The first of these took place at Beauraing, a poor farming village about 60 miles south-east of Brussels. On 29 November 1932 a group of five children saw Our Lady near a railway viaduct, just outside the convent school. All in all, there were 33 apparitions. The children described the Lady as being dressed in white, with a crown of golden rays and (on one occasion) showing her golden heart. Just as at Lourdes (where Our Lady was associated with a rosebush) and at Fatima (where she appeared near an azinheiras), so at Beauraing she stood under a hawthorn tree—appropriate not only because it is a member of the rose family but because the thorns point towards her Son's Passion. She told the visionaries to 'always be good', to pray and 'if you love my Son and love me, then sacrifice yourself for me'.

Almost at the same time, Mariette Beco noticed a mysterious lady standing in her back garden at Banneux, near Liege. As the apparitions continued, she encountered much hostility—perhaps not surprisingly, many thought Mariette was simply copying the recent events at Beauraing. But Mary came with a distinct message: she was the Virgin of the poor, who had come for all nations and to relieve the sick and the suffering. Mariette was shown a spring of water (rather like Lourdes) and this still remains a focus for many pilgrims, who take bottles of the water to give to the needy. Mariette died in 2011 and, despite encountering many trials, remained until the end a humble witness to these extraordinary events.

When I visited these two Belgian shrines, I was struck by their ordinariness. Banneux is now a very attractive complex, with pleasant walks, numerous chapels and a whole parade of pilgrim shops. But at its heart is the chapel of the apparitions, still in the little garden of the Beco house. The family was very poor and Our Lady's coming coincided with a time of economic hardship.

Beauraing seemed a little neglected on the day of my visit; there were only a handful of pilgrims but the statue of Our Lady, under the hawthorn, still stands in the shadow of the railway bridge and beside a busy road. Our Lady does not simply choose picturesque spots for her sanctuaries but the real world, which is so often gritty and noisy. It reminded me somewhat of London's Marian shrine, Our Lady of Willesden, in Harlesden—once a quiet Middlesex village but now a hectic, multi-cultural suburb which tends not to feature in the tourist guides.

As I sat before Our Lady of Beauraing, a car zoomed past with a megaphone advertising some sort of 'reptile world'. There was a telling contrast between the two: the traffic on the road and the peaceful oasis of prayer and pilgrimage; the local tourist attraction with its snakes and lizards and the Lady who came to crush the ancient serpent.

BOULOGNE-SUR-MER

& SAINT-JOSSE-SUR-MER (FRANCE)

Two Shrines in Picardy

The English Channel has long been a source of fascination. Just 21 miles separates Dover from Calais and yet, it could be said, that stretch of water defines much of English history and identity. Day-trippers cannot fail to notice the many differences found over the Channel, within sight of the white cliffs—not only the price of a bottle of wine, the fine cuisine and the peculiar custom of driving on the right but even the trees lining the roads, the architecture of the buildings and, of course, the religious culture.

This is made immediately apparent in two ancient shrines that await the visitor just over the Straits of Dover. Firstly, in the charming port of Boulogne-sur-Mer, there is a famous shrine to Our Lady particularly beloved by seafarers. Tradition records how the statue arrived at the town in the seventh century, drifting into harbour in an empty boat which glowed with an unearthly light. The image was soon enshrined and busy working miracles; pilgrims came to include St Bernard, the Black Prince and five English kings.

The last King of England to visit Boulogne as a pilgrim was Henry VIII (1532). He attended Mass and gave a generous offering to the shrine. No one could have guessed that twelve years later the king, having broken with Rome and fighting a war against France, besieged the town, looted the church and carried off the wonder-working statue. This was returned during the reign of Edward VI as part of a peace treaty. At least on this occasion the image was not destroyed. It is fitting that an image of Our Lady of Walsingham stands in the present church in Boulogne.

Our Lady of Boulogne's vicissitudes had not ended. The statue was stolen by the Huguenots later in the sixteenth century and thrown down a well; then during the French Revolution the church was destroyed and the statue publicly burned. The shrine experienced a revival in the nineteenth century; a new statue was produced and a splendid basilica built, although the Victorian travel writer Augustus Hare complained of 'the absurd dome which outrages the older buildings beneath it'. The town was damaged during the Second World War but Our Lady of Boulogne became a symbol of French resurgence in its aftermath. Four replica statues made a tour of France, visiting 16,000 parishes and acting as a focus of prayers for the deliverance of France and the restoration of peace.

Another Catholic shrine near the Channel is that of Saint-Josse-sur-Mer, close to the charming town of Montreuil and a few miles inland, although (as the name suggests) it once sat directly on the coast. In the days when France was a patchwork of independent and semi-independent territories, this area belonged to the Count of Ponthieu. One day in the seventh century a strange-looking pilgrim appeared at his castle: St Judoc (or Josse). He belonged to the royal family of Brittany and had been offered the crown around 636 after his older brother, St Judicäel, abdicated and retired to a monastery.

St Judoc is often shown with a crown or orb at his feet for he too turned his back on worldly riches and power and became a pilgrim, visiting the shrines of Europe. With eleven companions he went to Chartres, Amiens, Paris and eventually Rome, where he may have been ordained.

Eventually he settled in what is now northern France and lived as a hermit at Saint-Josse-sur-Mer, under the protection of the Count of Ponthieu. Together with his disciple Wulmar, St Judoc faithfully celebrated the Sacred Liturgy, spent hours in silent prayer and cared for the poor and the sick. Various miracles were attributed to him, including the appearance of a holy spring, which is still visited by devotees, and the cure of blindness. On one occasion four poor men arrived at his hermitage one after another. The saint divided the scrap of bread that he had but this had become very small by the time the last poor man arrived. At that moment, Wulmar spotted four ships, which brought sufficient supplies—a gift from the Lord Himself who had appeared to the saint under the guise of the beggars.

Like many of the Celtic saints, Judoc had a close relationship with nature. The weather on the Atlantic coast must have been harsh at times but, we are told, he 'fed birds of every kind, and little fishes from his hand as if they were tame creatures'. He was less charitable towards an eagle that carried off some of his hens; he made the sign of the cross, uttered a prayer and the eagle dropped dead (after returning his prized cock).

St Judoc died on 13 December 668. It is said that (like St Cuthbert) his hair, beard, and nails continued to grow after his death and that his disciples had to trim them. His hermitage was still used as a place of prayer and charity and pilgrims began visiting the saint's tomb. Charlemagne eventually entrusted the hermitage to Blessed Alcuin, the well-known English scholar who worked at the imperial court, and it was turned into a hospice for travellers. Many English men and women who crossed the Channel sought shelter there; perhaps they were on their way to one of the great shrines and so it was appropriate that they asked for the protection of this pilgrim saint.

St Judoc's cult soon spread to England and many other countries. These were turbulent times, with Viking raids on both sides of the Channel. In 902 some of the saint's relics were taken to Winchester for safety, where they were enshrined at the new cathedral. 'Judoc' was anglicised to 'Joyce' and this became a popular name for both boys and girls. He was invoked against fever, harvest fire, storms and snakebite and medieval pilgrim badges depicting the saint have been found in London and elsewhere.

Chaucer's Wife of Bath exclaimed on one occasion 'by God and Seint Joce'. Indeed, she also made a pilgrimage to Boulogne, reminding us of the close connections between English Catholics in the age of faith and these French shrines just a few miles away from the Kentish coast.

BRUGES (BELGIUM)

Relics of the Precious Blood and an English Convent

As a child, an occasional treat was provided by my father when he set up his projector in the living room and entertained us with his slides. The technology may seem charmingly old-fashioned in this digital age but there was something rather exciting about the whole ritual—the darkening of the room, the erection of the screen and the sound of the machine as each slide was slotted into place. Many of my father's slides were of my early years or our first family holidays together, but some dated from my parents' first years as a couple, before I was born. One set of pictures sticks in my memory. It was of a holiday they had spent in Bruges in the early 1970s and featured the famous procession of the Precious Blood, which takes place every year around the Feast of the Ascension—a very colourful affair with an impressive array of floats and costumes.

The little basilica of the Precious Blood (Heilig Bloedbasiliek) is unusually located on the first floor of an ornate building, squeezed into one side of the Burg, next to the town hall. When I eventually visited as an adult, my timing was fortunate because public veneration of the famous relic was about to begin. Being used to scenes of devout chaos at some of the continental shrines—noisy pilgrims, some of whom (religious sisters included) push to the front with their elbows—I was very impressed by the simplicity and dignity of the short service. After a brief exhortation in several languages, we formed an orderly queue and each person mounted a platform to venerate the relic. This was in a rock crystal tube, attached to a chain which went round the neck of a member of the confraternity, who kept his eyes downcast in prayer. In that time-honoured Catholic way, pilgrims were invited to put a donation in the box as they paid their respects and, in return, were handed a prayer card.

The relic of the Precious Blood consists of a piece of cloth used to wash the body of Christ before his burial and contains, it is believed, His saturated blood. The relic seems to have been given by the Patriarch of Jerusalem to Thierry of Alsace, Count of Flanders (rather quaintly translated in some guidebooks as 'Count Derrick') in 1150 on account of his bravery during the Second Crusade. More recent research suggests that the Precious Blood arrived slightly later, following the Sack of Constantinople in 1204 and the coronation of Count Baldwin IX of Flanders as the first Latin emperor.

Whatever its provenance, the relic soon became an important focus for the citizens of Bruges and a symbol of their identity. It was soon being taken around the city once a year in a procession that included clergy, soldiers, politicians, guildsmen and other dignitaries. In time there was a pageant too, at one time involving mythical characters and giants.

Belgian history is rather complicated; the country, which was created in 1830, was previously in the hands of Burgundian, Spanish, Austrian and Dutch rulers and several times the procession was stopped and the relic had to be hidden—during the French Revolution and the two world wars, for example, and, going further back in time, the period when Bruges was dominated by Calvinists (1578–84). However, the procession remains to this day, attracting thousands of visitors. The pageants no longer includes rollicking giants but there are scenes from the Old and New Testaments, historical characters from the city's history (including the story of the relic's arrival) and, finally, the reliquary itself, surrounded by the 'Noble Brotherhood of the Holy Blood'. In 1972 the future John Paul II participated in the procession and there is a striking photo of the Polish cardinal escorting the relic along the street.

The relic of the 'Holy Blood' at Bruges is not the only one in Christendom. The Basilica of Sant' Andrea at Mantua claims to have a similar relic, brought there by St Longinus, the Roman soldier who pierced the Lord's side with his spear. Portions of the Precious Blood were sent to Rome and to Weingarten Abbey in Germany, where it is taken in procession each year on Ascension Friday, carried on horseback by *der heilige Blutritter* (as the rider is called). In medieval England, relics of the Holy Blood were deposited at Hailes in Gloucestershire and Ashridge, near Berkhampstead in Hertfordshire.

Generations of the faithful have been understandably desirous of accessing physical relics of their Lord and Master. It is little wonder, then, that pilgrims flocked to shrines like that at Bruges. This is not the place to question their authenticity; for whatever their provenance, they have been the cause of prayer and conversion.

*

On my visit to Bruges I had the privilege of visiting the English Convent and celebrating Mass in its eighteenth-century chapel. I used a chalice that had belonged to the first chaplain, with the year 1629 very clearly inscribed on the base, and felt as if I was in a long line of priests who had stood on that spot, celebrating the sacred mysteries. And that sense of continuity and timelessness was present at every corner of the house: the long white corridors with the portraits of prioresses, their often very English faces starring out from very Flemish-looking wimples; the picture and relic of St Thomas More, donated by the martyr's family; the names of several hundred sisters inscribed on plaques near the site of the conventual cemetery.

The convent, dedicated to Our Lady of Nazareth, was founded on 14 September 1629, as a daughter house of another English house, St Monica's at Louvain (1609). The new community claimed a twin ancestry. Firstly, the mother house, St Monica's, had itself been founded from St Ursula's, also in Louvain, which a number of English Catholics had entered in the sixteenth century. This house belonged to the Windesheim Congregation and stood in the tradition of the Flemish mystics and spiritual writers such as Thomas à Kempis.

Added to this was a strong link with pre-Reformation England. The foundress of St Monica's was Mother Margaret Clement, whose mother, Margaret Giggs, had been the adopted daughter of St Thomas More. She had entered St Ursula's and became its prioress in 1557; another early English member was Elizabeth Woodford, who had been an Augustinian Canoness at Burnham in Buckinghamshire before the Reformation. Many of the sisters at Bruges had blood ties with the martyrs: Mother Augustina Bedingfield, for example, was directly descended from both Blessed Margaret Pole and Blessed Adrian Fortescue, while Mother Mary Augustina More was an eighth generation descendent of St Thomas More and donated the fragment of the saint's vertebrae that I had the opportunity of venerating in the chapel.

The young community faced many trials, including the effects of war and plague, financial hardship and the pressure of persecution in England. The poverty of the house did not deter the occasional arrival of royal visitors. On the eve of St George's Day 1656, for example, the exiled Charles II was entertained in the refectory with 'a little collation' and then 'walked in our garden'. He undoubtedly felt at home for almost all the sisters had relatives and friends who had fought for the king in the recent Civil War.

The convent grew and flourished, its main activity being the running of a school for 'ye young gentlewoman pensioners'. However, in 1794 the community was forced to flee due to the French Revolution. For eight years the sisters lived out their vocation at Hengrave Hall in Suffolk, thanks to the generosity of the Gage family. Meanwhile, three nuns remained in Bruges and were able to protect the property. When it was expropriated and put up for sale, Sr Olivia Darrell discreetly bought it at auction. Thus in 1802, after France and England had signed the Treaty of Amiens, the community were able to return to Bruges. Given the delicate political situation, they had to keep a low profile. The entrance to the church on Carmersstraat was walled up, making the sanctuary only accessible internally, although the community managed to successfully fight an imperial decree declaring that they 'may no longer admit new members'.

The community returned to living the religious life and educating young ladies. In 1843 the young Queen Victoria visited the school with Leopold I, King of the Belgians, and 'seemed altogether pleased and expressed her admiration of the richness and precision of the children's singing'. At the end of the century the Flemish poet, Fr Guido Gezelle, briefly acted as chaplain. Although the nuns were happily settled back in Bruges, an English foundation was made at Haywards Heath in 1886 (it later moved to Sayers Common) and between 1959 and 1983 the sisters also looked after a daughter convent in Kaduha, Rwanda.

The house at Bruges, though English in its origins, became increasingly international and in 1901 the first Belgian prioress was elected. The two world wars caused much anxiety: during the first the school building was used as a field hospital for both sides and in the early 1940s it was opened up to incurables threatened by hostilities in Antwerp. In more recent years the community reconsidered its activities and closed the school so that the nuns could focus on the contemplative and liturgical life. Though much has changed over the centuries, the convent remains an oasis of peace just outside the bustling tourist centre of Bruges and the sisters that I met remain inspired by the heroic English ladies who first came to this venerable spot.

BEAUVAIS (FRANCE)

The Wonders of Beauvais

As you approach the town of Beauvais, north of Paris, you immediately notice a large object towering over the other buildings. According to the nineteenth-century writer Benjamin Winkles, it is 'lofty enough to be the tower of a church, yet the form of it forbids the supposition, and judging from all previous experience, it is far too lofty to be the main body of one'. Some might mistake it for a rock or castle, but it is Beauvais Cathedral, magnificent as it soars into the grey skies of Picardy. And also regarded as a glorious failure.

We tend to take the skills of medieval cathedral builders for granted, their creations looking so sturdy and permanent all these centuries later. Yet they were at the cutting edge of technology and sometimes the dreams of their builders proved to be too ambitious. Work began on the cathedral in 1225, replacing a much older structure. It would be the highest-vaulted cathedral in Europe, reaching 159 feet and far surpassing the cathedrals at nearby Amiens and Paris. The choir was completed in 1272 but twelve years later part of it collapsed—due, it seems, to an imbalance in the forces that hold up such a building, combined perhaps with moving foundations or the effects of strong winds.

It was repaired in 1337 but work only began on the transept in the sixteenth century. Disaster struck again in 1573 when the 502-foot tower fell down. The result is an unfinished cathedral, without a nave, full of props and brackets that reveal the fragility of the structure, but still considered one of the highlights of French gothic. Indeed, it is said that the perfect cathedral would consist of the choir of Beauvais, the nave of Amiens, the façade of Rheims and the spire of Chartres. Perhaps Beauvais would have won all the prizes had it been completed.

There are several interesting characters celebrated by the town, many of whom are strong-willed women. One of its patrons is St Angadreme, a seventh noble woman who felt called to the religious life and prayed for a miracle to avoid marriage. The answer to her prayers came when she was stricken with leprosy and immediately deemed unmarriageable. The disease was cured, we are told, the moment she received the veil from St Ouen. She became abbess at the nearby monastery of Oroër-des-Vierges. Her name has become associated with another local heroine, Jeanne Hachette, who saved Beauvais from capture in 1472. During the siege, a Burgundian managed to plant his banner on the battlements, when Jeanne, armed with an axe, flung him into the moat and tore down the flag. Like St Joan of Arc, her courage led to a revival in the morale of the defenders. The episode was remembered each year in a procession on the feast of St Angadreme, inaugurated by Louis XI, during which the women took precedence over the men and young girls fired a salvo of guns.

There is also the obscure, fifth-century St Maxentia, said to have been the daughter of a Scottish king, who fled across the Channel to preserve an oath of virginity that she had privately taken. She became a recluse near the river Oise but was eventually tracked down by her spurned lover (or, some say, a Spanish Moor) and beheaded when she resisted his advances.

A further connection with Britain can be found in one of its sixteenth-century bishops: Cardinal Odet de Coligny, member of one of the most influential French families of the time. In 1561 he caused much controversy by becoming a Calvinist. In 1563 he was excommunicated but continued to wear his scarlet robes, most famously on the occasion of his marriage, in 1564, to Isabelle de Hauteville, known as Madame la Cardinale. Travelling to England, he died mysteriously in a guesthouse at Canterbury in 1571. Most historians agree that he was poisoned by his *valet de chambre*, who may have been in the pay of Catherine de'Medici. He was buried in a temporary tomb in the cathedral at the south-east end of the Trinity Chapel, not far from that of Cardinal Pole. The 'Huguenot Cardinal' remains there to this day.

The glory of Beauvais, for me, was inside the cathedral: a large and elaborate astronomical clock, built by Auguste Lucien Vérité in the 1860s and designed to be 'a clock of exceptional beauty and instructive to the faithful'. Taking up a whole side chapel, it consists of 52 dials and some 90,000 parts. A study of its dials provides a great deal of information, including the time of sunrise and sunset, the age of the world, the current year, the saint of the day, the meantime of the moon's passing through the Beauvais meridian and flood times at Mont St Michel and Montorgueil Castle (Jersey). On the central dial is an image of Christ, 'the beginning and the end', the Master of Time.

This is not just a masterpiece of clock making but a meditation on time and eternity. At the top a different character appears at each quarter reflecting the ages of man: a child playing with a ball and standing on a stall, ready to fall; a youth reading a book; a strong warrior in the prime of life and an old man. There is even a periodic scene of moving figures and flames depicting the Last Judgment and the End of Time. The clock is a wonderful example of science in the service of religion and expresses in mechanical form the eternal truths pointed to by the soaring vaults and arches of this unfinished cathedral.

BEC (FRANCE)

Notre Dame du Bec

Standing on a crowded Northern Line train on the London Underground could not be further removed from the peace of a cloister, yet as the bored commuter studies the names of the stations there is an unexpected reminder of one of the greatest medieval abbeys.

I am thinking, of course, of the southern suburb of Tooting Bec, with land once owned by the abbey of Bec in Normandy. It was one of many English places with an association with Bec. Others include Ruislip (on the edge of west London), St Neots (Huntingdonshire), Wantage (Oxfordshire), Goldcliffe (Monmouthshire) and Stoke-by-Clare (Suffolk).

The abbey of Notre-Dame du Bec was established in 1034 by St Herluin, a Norman knight who turned his back on the world after a vow made during a seemingly hopeless melee which he thought he would not survive. He lived an eremitic life on his estate and, after attracting several disciples, founded a monastery at Bonneville under the Rule of St Benedict. The location, however, proved to be inaccessible and with little water and so in 1039 it was transferred to a pleasant valley by the banks of the Bec. The place now bears the name of both river and founder: Le Bec-Helloin. A splendid church was built and the monastic community quickly grew; a total of 136 monks were professed under St Herluin. Duke William of Normandy, the Conqueror, and his followers lavished the abbey with many gifts, hoping these would help their eternal salvation.

Bec became an intellectual and cultural powerhouse, with a distinguished school. Perhaps the most celebrated members of the community were two Italians: Lanfranc, a jurist, and St Anselm, the great theologian and Doctor of the Church. Lanfranc's pupils included the future pope, Alexander II. St Anselm, who succeeded St Herluin as abbot, likewise attracted many gifted students and during his time at Bec wrote his famous works, the *Monologion* and *Proslogion*.

The abbey left a huge legacy on the English Church, including three archbishops of Canterbury. Both Lanfranc and St Anselm were appointed to this primatial see, as was Theobald, the fifth abbot, who had a key role to play in the complex political disputes under King Stephen. Despite the best efforts of Canterbury, he was never canonised a saint although he numbered among his protégés the greatest of all medieval English saints: Thomas Becket.

The Bec community also provided three bishops to Rochester, including Gundulf, who mixed the vocation of monk and architect. He was responsible for the White Tower at the Tower of London, Colchester Castle and the cathedral and castle at Rochester. Monks of Bec also served as abbots at Battle, Bury St Edmunds, Canterbury, Chester, Colchester, Ely and Westminster.

The later history of Bec was less happy. Like so many churches, it was affected by the Hundred Years' War (during which time it was fortified) and damaged during the sixteenth-century Wars of Religion. In the seventeenth century there was a revival thanks to the Benedictine monks of St Maur, who were known for their historical scholarship, but the monastery was finally suppressed at the French Revolution. Little now remains of the medieval monastery, though the fifteenth-century St Nicholas Tower (Tour Saint-Nicolas) gives a hint of past splendour, as do several ranges of buildings from the seventeenth and eighteenth centuries.

In 1948 the site was re-settled by Olivetan Benedictines under Dom Paul Grammont. The former monastic refectory was transformed into a chapel and the abbey became famous for both its pottery and its ecumenical work, inspired by the venerable connections between Bec and Canterbury.

Today, the abbey appears to slightly downplay its history. On my visit there was little information in English and tourists seem to focus on the pretty village (said to be one of the most beautiful in France) as much as the abbey. But look hard enough and the past soon comes back to life: the tomb of St Herluin and triptych of St Anselm in the church, the presence of the *Rue de Canterbury* and restaurant *Le Canterbury* in the village, and the plaque listing the English bishops and abbots who came from Bec. As the 1907 *Catholic Encyclopaedia* put it, 'when we remember how deep and far-reaching has been the influence of its greatest scholar, Anselm, on later theology, we cannot but feel that though the old abbey may be in ruins the school of Bec still lives on, and all may sit at the feet of its famous masters'.

CAEN (FRANCE)

The Tomb of the Conqueror

Caen is memorable as the city of William the Conqueror. As Duke of Normandy it was his favoured residence; he surrounded it with strong walls, built a castle and, with his wife, founded two abbeys. It was near Caen that William won his first significant military victory in 1047 over a rebellious cousin; it was here, also, that he proclaimed a 'Truce of God' in 1061, prohibiting any act of warfare between Wednesday evening and Monday morning at the risk of excommunication.

The foundation of the twin abbeys at Caen involves a strange love story. William chose Matilda of Flanders as his bride: not only was she considered a beauty but an alliance with her father, the Count of Flanders, was politically advantageous. The pope, Leo IX, disagreed: he feared a Norman-Flemish alliance would threaten the German emperor, his chief supporter, and so he vetoed the marriage. He explained his decision by pointing to the couple's consanguinity—by blood they were fifth cousins and a further complication was that Matilda's mother, St Adela, had married William's uncle.

It seems also that Matilda was reluctant to marry Duke William, declaring she would never marry a 'bastard'. The Chronicler of Tours even claimed that William forced himself upon her in her chamber, seizing her by her plaits, dragging her around and beating her. Such behaviour, if it ever happened, undoubtedly made her more hesitant in entering marriage but she relented and, in defiance of the papal ban, the couple married at the end of 1051. It was left to another pontiff, Nicholas II, to give his blessing to the union at a later date. By the time he set out for England in 1066 he was able to carry with him a papal banner. In return for the sanction for his marriage, however, William and Matilda agreed to found two abbeys in Caen: the Abbaye-aux-Hommes, dedicated to St Stephen, on the east side of the city, and the Abbaye-aux-Dames, dedicated to the Trinity, on the west side. This has been described as 'the most magnificent atonement for sin ever offered by erring human creatures'.

The monastery for women was dedicated in 1066, shortly before the invasion of England, and William's daughter Cécile would later become its second abbess. When Matilda died in 1083, she was buried there; she also gifted the house with her crown and sceptre. Despite the rocky start to their courtship, it seems that William and Matilda grew fond of each other; her death plunged William into the deepest mourning.

The monastery for men, St Étienne, was dedicated in 1077 and, like its counterpart, built from Caen stone—allowing for a speedy construction. When William died in Rouen in 1087, just as the Domesday Book was completed, his body was embalmed and brought to the abbey by way of the river Orne. An unseemly quarrel interrupted the burial service. A local man named Asselin stood up and claimed his father had once owned the land in which William was about to be entombed and when the abbey was built had never received compensation. This led to a delay and, after negotiations, the man was offered 60 sous, with the promise of further repayments. As the king's body was finally lowered into his grave, however, it burst and not even the most skilled thurifer could cover the stench with sweet-smelling incense.

Nor was the body allowed to rest here in perpetual peace. In 1522 the tomb was opened; some have suggested that an attempt was being made to canonise William, who, despite his uncouthness, had been a great friend to the Church. An artist painted a portrait of the king, based on his well-preserved remains, and a copy of this survives in Caen to this day—William is shown dressed in the costume of the sixteenth century and looks suspiciously like Henry VIII. Then in 1563 the tomb was desecrated by Huguenots and the bones scattered. The same fate befell the tomb of Matilda. All that remains under the current slab at St Étienne is a femur of the Conqueror.

In June 1944, as Caen suffered bombardment after bombardment from the Allies, many of the citizens took shelter in the mighty Norman church. They not only had confidence in its mighty walls but hoped that the Allies would avoid damaging the burial place of William the Conqueror. There was also a local tradition that St Étienne would come to no harm as long as the kings of England were on the throne. More than 1,400 moved into the abbey, sleeping on worn mattresses and straw, the children playing in the cloisters. The parish priest, Mgr des Hameaux, did his best to raise morale, lead prayers and celebrate the sacraments.

Caen has rebuilt itself in peace meaning that, despite its destruction, it is an interesting and charming place to visit. A plaque in St Étienne proudly recalls how, on the sixtieth anniversary of the Normandy landings, a German cardinal visited St Étienne and led a service of thanksgiving, praying for reconciliation. The following year he was elected pope.

William the Conqueror has left his mark on Caen and the troops who fought there seventy-five years ago must have been aware of this heritage. A Latin inscription on the Memorial close to the war graves cemetery at Bayeux puts it well: 'We, once conquered by William, have now set free the Conqueror's native land'.

DOUAI, FRANCE

The British in Douai

Visitors to France tend to drive off the ferry at Calais and leave the Pays du Nord as quickly as they can on the way to Paris and other 'more interesting' destinations. True, the countryside around the port is flat, heavily industrialised and will never compete with Provence or Brittany for beauty. But look a bit deeper and there is much of interest.

A place that should definitely be more familiar to British visitors is Douai. The Place d'Armes is, like so main French town squares, impressive and the Hôtel de Ville renowned for its carillon of some 62 bells, the largest in Europe. There are two surviving medieval gateways and an impressive collegiate church. Most importantly, Douai was once the home of English, Scots and Irish Colleges, as well as houses of English Franciscans and Benedictines. The Downside community originated at St Gregory's, Douai, while in the nineteenth century the English Benedictines formerly of Paris settled at Douai, before establishing themselves at Douai Abbey, near Reading, in 1903.

It was at Douai that William Allen, the future cardinal, opened an English College on 29 September 1568. The town seemed a good location for such an enterprise: situated near the English Channel, the university had recently received its charter from Philip II of Spain and was already the home to many English exiles. The college was founded with the help of John Vendeville, Regius Professor of Canon Law at Douai and a future Bishop of Tournai. He had hoped to receive papal support for a mission amongst Muslims but, after he failed to secure an audience with the pope during a visit to Rome, he was persuaded to transfer his missionary energies from Barbery to Britain. He had also, interestingly, long been interested in the training of priests and his proposals were in part adopted by the Council of Trent, which decreed the foundation of diocesan seminaries across the Catholic world.

That is not to say that the college was founded with this purpose in mind. Initial priorities revolved around uniting the exiles and providing the resources for Catholic scholarship that could no longer be found at Oxford and Cambridge. The Jesuit Fr Persons affirmed that 'there was no intention at all (as I have often heard Dr Allen affirm) of the end of returning again into their country to teach and preach'. However, it is perhaps natural that the eyes of the exiles should begin to look longingly to the other side of the channel, especially as numbers increased and those who had completed their studies had little to do.

The college thus became a celebrated seminary, the first in the Anglophone world, and produced a new type of missionary: the 'seminary priest', highly trained in theology and controversy, and eager to return to his homeland, despite the obvious dangers. The first to leave Douai for England was Lewis Barlow—ordained in 1574 and back on English soil the same year. In 1577 Cuthbert Mayne became the first 'seminary priest' to be hanged, drawn and quartered. Nearly two-thirds were imprisoned at some point and a total of 116 were executed during Elizabeth's reign. These martyrs are remembered not only in their native country but in the shrine at the back of Douai's Collegiate Church of St Peter, which includes a relic of St John Southworth, whose body was found during excavations on the site of the English College in 1927 and sent to Westminster Cathedral.

The first years of the college were marked by financial difficulties and concerns surrounding security—it proved easy enough for the English authorities to plant spies and this led to the custom of students and staff adopting aliases (sometimes several of them). Further trouble was caused by the fact the Low Countries were a hothouse of religious politics. Indeed, for most of its history the college was affected by the seesaw of European politics and between 1578 and 1593 the college was relocated to Rheims.

What was life like at the English College in the time of Allen? As might be expected, there was daily Mass, weekly reception of Holy Communion, prayer using the method of St Ignatius Loyola and twice weekly fasting for 'the conversion of England'. The academic syllabus was partly influenced by the Jesuits and included a comprehensive grounding in scholastic theology (particularly that of St Thomas Aquinas) but the course was adapted to suit future missionaries in Protestant England. Much attention was paid to preaching, disputation and the study of Sacred Scripture, the chief 'weapon' used by Protestant controversialists. The timetable included daily Scriptural lectures, classes in the Biblical languages, readings from the holy book at meal times and regular debates on disputed points.

The college also sponsored a translation of the New Testament in 1582, made by Gregory Martin, Thomas Worthington, Richard Bristow, John Reynolds and, of course, Allen (all of them Oxford men). The volume included extensive notes and, although it was described as a translation from the Vulgate, use was clearly made of the existing English Bibles of John Wycliffe and Miles Coverdale. The Old Testament followed in 1609–10, which meant the complete 'Douai-Rheims Bible' was already available by the time the King James Bible was produced in 1611. Indeed, the New Testament of 1582 was one of the sources used by the translators of the King James. The text was later revised (essentially retranslated) by Bishop Challoner (1749–52) and others, and the Douai-Rheims remained standard among English-speaking Catholics up until the second half of the twentieth century. Indeed, at his presidential inauguration in January 1961 John F. Kennedy used his family's copy of the Douai-Rheims.

Think of Douai, then, and you think of the brave band of martyrs, who sacrificed everything to keep the Faith alive and celebrate the sacraments, and the pioneering translation of the Bible, which disproves the myth that Catholics were discouraged from coming to know and love the words of Sacred Scripture. As we raised our glasses in the Brasserie L'Abbaye on Douai's Place Carnot (roughly on the site of the English College), we toasted this little French town and all it had contributed to the Church.

DUBLIN (IRELAND)

Catholic Memories in Phoenix Park

The capital of the 'Isle of Saints' perhaps does not rank as one of Europe's great pilgrimage locations. True, there are shrines of the Jesuit, Blessed John Sullivan, and that great temperance hero, Venerable Matt Talbot, and a much-loved image of Our Lady of Dublin at Whitefriar Street. Moreover, University College, Dublin (UCD) originated as Newman's hoped-for Catholic University and occasioned his great classic, *Idea of a University*. Many make a pilgrimage to the magnificent library of Trinity College to view the Book of Kells, one of the glories of monastic manuscript production. Yet, at the time of writing, there is no Catholic cathedral on the Liffey; the solemn neo-classical St Mary's has acted as a pro (or temporary) cathedral since 1886.

One of Dublin's Catholic hearts can be found at Phoenix Park, a vast area of parkland that, before the Reformation, belonged to the Knights Hospitaller. In 1979 St John Paul II celebrated Mass there during his pastoral visit; the congregation is said to have comprised about a third of the country's population. When Pope Francis celebrated Mass in the park in August 2018 the crowds numbered a more modest 152,000.

These papal celebrations echoed the open-air Mass held there in 1932, when Dublin hosted the International Eucharistic Congress for the first time. The Irish Free State was then a decade old and five years later would officially become the Republic of Ireland; George V was still represented by a governor general and there was a new prime minister (or president of the Executive Council), Éamon de Valera. The Irish Church itself was confident and respected throughout society.

The Congress marked the 1,500th anniversary of St Patrick's mission to Ireland. Tributes were paid to the 'age of the saints' and the history of the Eucharist in Ireland; replica round towers were erected in Dublin, recalling the structures found in many early Irish monasteries. If the Irish had contributed much to the spread of the Faith in past centuries, great pride was also taken in the fact that many of the visiting prelates had Gaelic blood flowing in their veins. Cardinals Dougherty of Philadelphia, Hayes of New York and O'Connell of Boston, for example, were all Irish, while even Bourne of Westminster spoke with an Irish lilt (his mother was from a Dublin family). There were joyful reunions as priests from Irish families that had emigrated to America, Australia and elsewhere returned home and met with relatives, often for the first time.

Pilgrims flocked from all four points of the compass, those from the Eastern Churches attracting particular notice, as did Fr Philip Gordon of the Chippewa Tribe, Wisconsin, a convert to Catholicism, who went around in cassock and ceremonial headdress.

G. K. Chesterton, together with many other journalists, was present and later published his reflections in *Christendom in Dublin*. He was particularly struck by the street decorations: 'instead of the main stream of colour flowing down the main streets of commerce, and overflowing into the crooked and neglected slums, it was exactly the other way; it was the slums that were the springs'. Indeed, in this 'celestial topsy-turveydom' it seemed that 'the poorer were the streets, the richer were the street decorations'—a real testament to the depths of Irish devotion.

On 26 June around a million people attended the Congress Mass at Phoenix Park and use was made of the latest technology. 500 loudspeakers were positioned around the park and the city centre—the whole of Dublin became a sort of open-air cathedral—and a live message was relayed from Pope Pius XI himself (in Latin). The famous Irish tenor John McCormack, dressed as a papal count, sang Franck's *Panis Angelicus* at the offertory. Then, after the Mass and a short interval, the Blessed Sacrament was taken in procession to the city centre, where Benediction was given at a specially constructed altar on O'Connell Bridge.

The Congress served as a show-case not only of Ireland's deep faith but the nation's new-found independence. Government officials were closely involved in proceedings. De Valera, despite technically having been excommunicated for his support of the republicans during the 1922 Civil War, was a prominent participant and walked alongside the Blessed Sacrament in the great procession on the final day. Less edifyingly, the Congress gave him an opportunity to further the call for complete Irish independence: the Governor-General (James MacNeill) was deliberately not invited to the state reception welcoming the papal legate at Dublin Castle. Later that year MacNeill resigned and was replaced by De Valera's own candidate.

Politics and religion are often mixed. Indeed, participants at the Congress from Northern Ireland faced opposition when they returned home. As many as 500 Protestant loyalists were seen awaiting their arrival at the Central Train Station in Belfast, armed with bottles and other missiles. Likewise, buses were vandalised at Ballymena. But the Congress was overall declared a great success, both in terms of organisation and spiritual fruits. For those five days in June 1932, Dublin was truly the focus of the Catholic world.

ECHTERNACH (LUXEMBOURG)

Dancing for St Willibrord

The English are a rather reserved lot, especially when it comes to religion. It could be said they have a deep religious sense without seeming to be particularly pious on the outside. Indeed, they are famously awkward when it comes to openly talking about their inmost beliefs or showing too much emotion.

This 'national' characteristic is reflected in our saints—men and women, to a large extent, of practical wisdom, quiet holiness and unassuming courage. Their cults, where they have survived, are often low-key and moderate, partly as a result of the Reformation.

But there are the odd exceptions, especially when it comes to those English saints who are venerated in other countries. Take St Willibrord, for example—the apostle of the Frisians and patron of the Netherlands and Luxembourg, whose feast we celebrate on 7 November. He is buried at Echternach (Luxembourg) and every Whit Tuesday a curious procession takes place through its streets in his honour. As bands play the traditional *Springprozession* tune, the saint's devotees—numbering several thousand, four or five abreast and holding the ends of white handkerchiefs—jump from left to right and then take a step forward, gradually moving their way towards the basilica. It takes most of the morning for the pilgrims to arrive and, after they pay their respects at St Willibrord's shrine, Pontifical Benediction of the Blessed Sacrament is given. A dance in honour of a saint—it all sounds rather un-English, although perhaps there is a passing resemblance to our own Morris dancers?

Who, then, is this St Willibrord, honoured by the jumping Luxembourgers? He was born in Northumbria in 658 to a pious family; indeed, his father Wilgils went on to serve God as a hermit at a chapel dedicated to St Andrew 'in the headlands that are bounded by the North Sea and the River Humber'. The night St Willibrord was conceived, we are told, his mother had a dream of a moon increasing in size, indicating that her child would one day 'disperse the murky darkness of error with the light of truth'.

Educated at Ripon (under St Wilfrid) and then in Ireland, St Willibrord was subsequently sent as a missionary to the pagan Frisians in 690, along with twelve companions. This was at the request of St Egbert (Bishop of Lindisfarne) and with the support of Pepin II, King of the Franks, who had nominal authority in the area. St Willibrord went to Rome on two occasions to seek papal approval and on his second visit Pope Sergius I consecrated him as an archbishop at the church of Santa Cecilia in Trastevere. Back in Frisia, the new prelate built his cathedral at Utrecht.

St Willibrord established many churches and founded monasteries, including that of Echternach in 698, which became his favoured place of retreat. I have an old print of St Willibrord, showing him dressed in cope and mitre, holding a model of the abbey in one hand and striking a barrel of wine with his pastoral staff. It refers to a rather attractive tradition that St Willibrord inspected the monastic cells at Echternach to see if anything could be improved. In the cellar he found only a small quantity of wine and prayed over the cask, into which he thrust his staff. Imagine the amazement of the steward when the wine began to overflow—rather reminiscent of the wedding feast of Cana and showing the superabundance of God's grace thanks to the work of the Northumbrian saint.

Missionary work was time-intensive and full of danger. One Frisian leader, Radbod, was particularly aggressive. When St Willibrord found himself on the island of Heligoland, where his ship was forced to land due to inclement weather, he found himself in a delicate situation. The island was considered sacred but the saint decided to show the futility of the locals' superstition by doing all that was forbidden on the island—killing animals for food, disobeying the rule of silence and baptising converts in a holy spring. Radbod was (understandably) furious and took the saint and his companions' prisoner, casting lots to see which of them would be sacrificed to their offended god. St Willibrord himself escaped unharmed.

In 714 Radbod managed to assert his authority over those parts of Frisia that had been lost to the Franks and much of St Willibrord's work was undone: clergy were killed and churches torn down. Things improved five years later after Radbod was killed and St Willibrord was joined for a time by that other great Anglo-Saxon missionary, St Boniface. In his old age, St Willibrord resided at his beloved Echternach and died there on 7 November 739, aged 81.

What about the 'hopping procession of Echternach', which has been included in the UNESCO Representative List of the Intangible Cultural Heritage of Humanity? Pilgrims flocked to St Willibrord's shrine from a very early date but it is hard to know why and when the dancing began—especially since Whit Tuesday has no obvious connection with St Willibrord's life. Rather than being a continuation of some pagan practice, as some suggest, it was probably a mixture of Catholic piety and folk tradition, possibly influenced by medieval penitential processions and designed to protect participants from epilepsy or the plague through the saint's intercession.

It was stopped (as so many traditions were stopped) by the rationalist Emperor Joseph II in 1786 but revived after the French Revolution. Perhaps in the twenty-first century there is less of a penitential aspect, but the skipping Luxembourgers exude great joy and pride in their English patron and apostle.

KERRYTOWN (IRELAND)

A Hidden Shrine in Donegal

Situated in the north-west of Ireland, County Donegal is unjustly neglected, even by those who know the country well. Yet it is a place full of history and stunning landscapes. If the weather was warmer and more consistent, the beaches would surely be famous across the globe.

There are high peaks, too, such as Errigal, shaped like the triangular mountains that commonly appear in children's drawings and seeming much higher than its 2,464 feet. On ascending my legs felt as if I had scaled Everest and, such were the large areas of scree, the going down was harder than the scrambling up! It was interesting to meet other walkers, who were not only locals but enthusiasts from the Netherlands and Czechia.

On the west coast there is a small area known as the Rosses, cut off from the rest of the county by high ground and rivers. It is centred around Dungloe, famous for its 'Mary from Dungloe' festival, and boasts an airport at Carrickfinn, with one of the world's most impressive landings. In the midst of its wild boggy landscape there is a much-loved shrine of Our Lady at Kerrytown. It may not normally appear in lists of great Marian sanctuaries but it is of great importance to locals.

I happened to visit Kerrytown on the Feast of Mary's Assumption. In previous years I had celebrated the great day either in the parish or (on occasion) more famous and prestigious shrines but as I drove along the narrow country lanes, stopping to enjoy the ever-changing scenery and the stunning glimpses of sea and sky, I could think of no place I would rather be. The signs indicated we were nearing the shrine, yet there was no great basilica, no rows of devotional stalls. As we turned into a small lane, a low white building came into view. The sun had broken through the omnipresent clouds and the shrubs and heather seemed particularly lush.

The story of Kerrytown starts on the night of 11 January 1939. Two teenage sisters, Mary and Teresa Ward, went outside their house. The reason for this is unclear: did they want a sisterly conference or were they fetching something from an outhouse, perhaps turf for the fire or even (as some suggest) fresh supplies of home-made poitín for the small gathering the family was hosting?

Nevertheless, it soon became clear that something unusual was happening. A short distance away, to the right of the entrance, was a granite cliff face, which came to be known as 'The Rock' (calling to mind the tradition of Mass Rocks to be found across Ireland). Now it was illuminated by light and what appeared to be a large white statue of Our Lady, with a black crown that resembled a priest's biretta, stood at the centre on a ledge, with her hands upraised. Unusually, the vision lasted three hours and was witnessed not only by the two girls but their parents, James and Minnie, brother Charley and the O'Connell family, neighbours who were playing cards with the Wards.

The Ward family were hard-working and honest. James had seen action in the Anglo-Irish War as captain of the local unit or *cumann*. His grandmother, Peggy Boyle ('Miseog') was regarded locally as a wise woman and prophetess. 'One day', she said, 'large white birds would come down from the sky at the white beach and carry people away'—seeming to foretell the opening of Donegal Airport.

The Wards and O'Connells tried to keep news of these strange happenings to themselves but it was not long before crowds gathered at Kerrytown and the newspapers published reports. The parish priest of Burtonport, Fr John McAteer, was unimpressed. As with so many other apparitions, the priest's first reaction was one of scepticism; 'another wonderful ghost story'. He was not even afraid to condemn the sightings publicly from the pulpit. However, on the night of Shrove Tuesday reports once again reached him of a strange phenomenon at 'The Rock'. Aware that Archdeacon Cavanagh had famously missed Our Lady's visitation at Knock after ignoring his housekeeper, Fr McAteer decided to go and investigate for himself. He restored order to the excited crowd, suggested the recitation of the Rosary and, seeing nothing unusual, began to make his way back. After a few yards, though, he turned back and saw an oval of light and 'the majestic Lady, clothed on the outside in a white garment and inside this, from the waist up, in blue'. Her hair came down upon her shoulders, rather like Murillo's famous painting of the Assumption, and he thought her expression was one of 'severe censure', as if she was asking the priest 'Now, do you believe?' Soon the cry went up, 'The Big Priest sees! The Big Priest sees!'

Fr McAteer became a firm supporter of Kerrytown and stated privately that the evidence for the visions was superior to those of Knock and at least equal to other cases approved by Rome. In fact, he wrote, 'if you reject Kerrytown evidence, you may as well abandon all reliance on all human testimony'. He saw the Blessed Virgin once again in 1942 and later professed that he would be happy to take his evidence to court, 'whether in this world or the next'.

Kerrytown has never received official approval but a group of devotees keeps the shrine open. Miracles have been claimed as well as further messages and visions, involving not only Our Lady but St Joseph, St Patrick, St Anthony and other saints. Prayer groups meet regularly and Masses are sometimes celebrated. Pilgrims come from both sides of the border and, indeed, during the 'Troubles', many sought Our Lady's solace at Kerrytown.

On my visit there was certainly a steady procession of cars. Some prayed in front of 'The Rock', sitting on the bench nearby or visiting a covered area containing prayer requests, *ex voto* offerings and obituary cards. Others lingered by the rose garden and the spring of water known as 'St James's Well', for what Irish shrine would be complete without such a spring? The house was open and the fire had been lit in the main room, even though it was the middle of August: a prayer group was expected. Some of the original fittings remain inside, giving a picture of the simple life once led by the Ward family.

Mary exercises her maternal care throughout the Church Universal. She draws people to little Kerrytown, providing them with solace in this 'vale of tears' and giving them hope and peace as they continue their journey through life.

KINCASSLAGH (IRELAND)

Mass Rocks and Hedge Schools

The church of St Mary, Kincasslagh stands in an idyllic Donegal location. Its white walls dominate the graveyard, full of tombs of local families—Boyles, O'Donnells, Wards and others—which gently meanders down to the sea. The church itself—founded in 1856 and subsequently rebuilt after a fire—is in excellent condition, thanks in part to the generosity of the town's most famous son, the singer Daniel O'Donnell. His dulcet tones can even be heard there on red-letter days.

Yet there was a time when Mass was virtually outlawed in Ireland. We were reminded of this as we drove along a country road and saw a sign to the local Mass Rock. It was not much to speak of: a short path to a craggy piece of rock, with a ledge where the sacred mysteries were sometimes celebrated. We thought it might be fitting on a future trip to have an impromptu Mass there, with the non-practising member of our party acting as a sentinel, in case the priest hunters or red coats suddenly arrived.

Ireland is dotted with these Mass Rocks. Sometimes we think that British Catholics faced the harshest measures in the sixteenth and seventeenth centuries, when priests and laity were put to death simply for celebrating Mass or sheltering priests. Although the last martyrs, recognised by the Church, suffered in the 1680s, a new batch of penal laws were passed under William and Mary, and Queen Anne. In Ireland, Catholics could not hold public office, open a school, seek education overseas or own a horse above the value of £5. The Popery Act of 1703 stated that if the eldest son of a Catholic converted to Protestantism, he would no longer have to share his father's estate with his brothers—an obvious incentive to leave the Faith. Clergy were banished from Ireland in 1697 and then from 1704 only 'registered' priests were allowed to function. Those who refused went into hiding; anyone who attended Mass celebrated illegally was liable to pay a substantial fine.

Mass came to be offered in private homes, ruined churches, stables, and rocks in the open air. Portable shelters were sometimes erected over the altar, perhaps made of wickerwork, to protect the sacred vessels and the celebrant from the elements. A similar tradition existed in parts of Scotland. On the island of Eigg, for example, a cave by the sea, only accessible at low tide, was used for Masses and known as Uamh Chràbhaich ('cave of worship').

Education was also provided in remote rural spots by itinerant teachers and became known as 'Hedge Schools'. One such master was Paddy Corrigan, a Fermanagh native; 'dressed in his corderoy knee breeches with long stockings to match, and sporting a wide brimmed hat', he traced maps on the ground with his stick and was a firm disciplinarian; 'his normal mode of punishment was to hoist the delinquent on the broad of one of the high briars and while in that position to favour him with a judicious application of the birch'.

Priests still risked their life in their ministrations. Near another Donegal Mass Rock, at Buncrana—known as 'Ireland's Paradise'—can be found the tomb of Fr O'Hegarty. Ordained by the martyr Archbishop of Armagh, St Oliver Plunkett, in 1672, he faithfully ministered in the area and resided secretly in a coastal cave. According to a nineteenth-century historian, 'from this wild seclusion he was accustomed to steal, under the shadow of night, to carry the ministrations of his religion to the hearths of the faithful fishermen around the coast, and the hardy mountaineer farther inland. His retreat was unknown to all but his sister ... None of her family ever questioned her when she departed from her cottage in the grey dawn each morning to carry him the provisions for the day'. He was eventually betrayed in 1711 by his brother-in-law, who alerted the authorities; the priest was killed by one Captain Vaughan—his head cut off—and buried nearby. The locals treasured his memory and made pilgrimages to 'Fr Hegarty's Rock'; it was said that his head bounced several times (rather like St Paul) and made nine holes in the ground, on which no grass grew.

A series of Catholic Relief Acts from the late 1700s eased conditions for Irish Catholics. Churches and schools could be operated openly, and the government even granted money for a new seminary at Maynooth. Opposition could still be encountered from Protestant landowners. One priest in County Clare in the 1850s had such difficulties in building a church for his destitute congregation at Kilbaha that he constructed a portable chapel, that could be drawn on a cart like an omnibus. It became known as the 'Ark'.

Irish Catholics continue to honour the sufferings of their forbears and preserve local traditions of Mass Rocks and Hedge Schools. As a poem by Felix Kearney puts it:

> Our priests like wolves were hunted down,
> O God 'twas surely hard.

That from the right to worship thee,
Thy children were debarred,
But still they proudly bore thru cross
Those simple mountain men were proud to share
Thy Calvary
By the Mass Rock in the glen.

KNOCK (IRELAND)

Mary's Silent Vision

The evening of 21 August 1879 was—not unusually for Ireland—wet and miserable. The inhabitants of Knock, a small village in County Mayo, stayed indoors as much as they could. As the priest's housekeeper, Mary McLoughlin, walked past the church to visit a friend who had just returned from a trip, she noticed a group of illuminated figures on the church wall. Given the heavy rain, she didn't pause for long, assuming the priest had ordered some new statues. Others also saw the scene and identified the figures as the Eucharistic Lamb standing on an altar with a cross, Our Lady, St Joseph and St John—the latter was not immediately obvious, given he was holding a book and dressed as a bishop, but it reminded one of the seers of a statue he had once seen. The experience lasted two hours and fifteen people witnessed the apparition. When the hardworking parish priest, Archdeacon Cavanagh, was told of this, he thought nothing of it and continued to dry his clothes after a day of pastoral visiting. He would live to regret his decision.

It was an unusual occurrence, unlike the other major Marian apparitions of the nineteenth century. Nothing was said and the figures only moved slightly. Some claimed that the images had been created by a magic lantern, operated by a devious Protestant policeman, though attempts at recreating the tableau through this means failed. Nevertheless, the symbolism of the figures was later unpacked by theologians and thought to be beyond the invention of the average Irish villager. How fitting that the Lamb appeared beside St John, the only Evangelist to describe Jesus as the 'Lamb of God' and to go on to write of the vision of the Lamb in the Book of Revelation. How poignant that Mary should appear with her hands raised, like a priest at Mass and as she was sometimes depicted in early Christian art. How appropriate that St Joseph should be included, given his recent declaration by the pope as patron of the Universal Church.

Words, therefore, were unnecessary, given such profound imagery. The apparition stressed the links between Mary and the Eucharist; indeed, the name Knock means 'hill' and the apparition transported the faithful to Mount Calvary, which is made present at every Mass. At Knock, Mary leads in worshipping the Lamb; she is there not only as Mother but fellow disciple. Perhaps, also, the choice of Ireland for such a eucharistic message was recognition of the many sacrifices made by priests and faithful in time of persecution.

A committee was set up by the Archbishop of Tuam; pilgrims flocked to the place and miracles soon attributed to Our Lady. One of the miracles of Knock must surely be the nearby airport, which serves the west of Ireland and was the brainchild of Mgr James Horan, the parish priest. He left a strong mark on the shrine, building a new pilgrimage church (1976) and hosting the landmark visit of St John Paul II (1979). Two years later he told a RTE journalist: 'We're building an airport. And I hope the Department of Transport doesn't hear about it. Now don't tell them … We've no money, but we're hoping to get it next week, or the week after.' Money was not the only issue; many thought the site too foggy and boggy. Nevertheless, through the priest's determination, a government grant and an ambitious lottery draw, the airport was opened in 1985. It has been voted Ireland's favourite regional airport and Mgr Horan's life has even inspired a musical, *A Wing and a Prayer*. Thanks to him, pilgrims continue in great number to Knock to honour *Muire Máthair Dé*, Mary, the Mother of God, Queen of Ireland, including Pope Francis (2018) and President Joe Biden (2023).

LISIEUX (FRANCE)

The Little Flower

Stopping at Lisieux for a night, the hotel was opposite the beautiful gothic cathedral, a reminder of the historic splendour of the town. Sadly, like so many places in Normandy, it has been badly scarred by war. Two thirds of its buildings was destroyed by Allied bombardment in 1944 and this is reflected in the bland architecture in much of the centre.

Medieval Lisieux was a place of some importance and many notable characters were associated with it. Henry II and Eleanor of Aquitaine held court here and it is said that St Thomas Becket stayed in 1170. There is no historical proof for this, and, in fact, it seems unlikely given the critical attitude of the then bishop towards him, but the town treasures one of his chasubles.

A fifteenth-century bishop, Pierre Cauchon, was a prominent judge at the trial of St Joan of Arc at nearby Rouen and instrumental in her conviction of heresy. At the time he was Bishop of Beauvais but moved to Lisieux shortly after the saint's execution and is buried in the cathedral choir.

Lisieux, of course, is best known for the 'Little Flower'. She is present everywhere. Her image can be found on all sorts of nick-nacks in the shops. Her elegant family home of Les Buissonnets gives an insight into her middle class childhood. In the cathedral, a note proudly proclaims that the high altar was donated by her father, himself also a saint, and a wax effigy of St Therese can be seen kneeling in the confessional where she celebrated the sacrament for the first time. In the museum of the Carmel there are numerous mementoes, revealing not only the daily life of the community but her attractive personality—there are examples of the plays she wrote and her artistic work (the painting and illuminating of pictures served as an additional source of income).

The town is dominated by the basilica, which is the second largest pilgrimage site in France, completed in 1954 after a quarter century of construction. Despite the heavy bombing of the town, it was astonishing that the rising structure survived almost unscathed—the crypt was in fact used as a shelter for many of the townspeople in 1944, including the saint's two surviving sisters.

It was largely due to her spiritual autobiography, *The Story of a Soul*, that St Therese became so well known. This was formed out of several fragments of memoirs that she wrote under obedience to her superiors in her final years, as she suffered from the effects of tuberculosis. Ostensibly these would serve as her testament to the community and help write her obituary that would be sent to other Carmels.

The volume was published and widely distributed after her death and pilgrims soon flocked to Lisieux. During the First World War, the saint was popular among many soldiers, who asked for her intercession and tried to follow her 'little way'. A volume recounting the many graces obtained, *Therese of the Child Jesus: Her Life—After Her Death*, sold two million copies and was a bestseller in the trenches. The Carmel received thousands of letters of thanks and votive offerings, including a book on the saint with a hole in it after stopping a bullet and saving a soldier's life. She was eventually beatified in 1923 and canonised two years later.

St Therese desired to become a saint but was aware of her weakness and the example of the great saints, who seemed like mountains while she was a grain of sand. St Therese's 'revolution' was in realising that she was loved by God and that she could approach Him as a child, despite her 'littleness'. Indeed, it was precisely because of her 'littleness' that she could come to the Lord, who would then take her in His arms and raise her up the steep steps of holiness rather like the lifts she had seen in the hotel on her pilgrimage to Rome. Just as a garden was full of flowers and shrubs of different sizes, each with its unique character, so each person could blossom in their own way, knowing that God is a merciful and doting Father.

Her 'little way' has inspired thousands to follow the Gospel by seizing the modest opportunities that each day brings—not so much grand heroics but small acts of love and self-denial: 'the only way I can prove my love', she wrote, 'is by scattering flowers and these flowers are every little sacrifice, every glance and word, and the doing of the least actions for love'.

According to St Pius X, St Therese was 'the greatest saint of modern times'. This is, perhaps, a surprising epithet for a young Norman girl who died in the obscurity of Carmel at the age of only 24. In our minds, she belongs to the nineteenth century. The faded photos of her, especially before entering the religious life, firmly place her in that context, as does the ambience of her childhood homes at Alencon and Lisieux. Yet, had the saint lived into her nineties she would have experienced not only two world wars but the Second Vatican Council. Her last surviving sister, Celine, died in February 1959, the same month as the launch of the first weather satellite and the plane crash that killed Buddy Holly, Richie Valens and the 'Big Bopper'!

St Therese remains a product of her times but very much a saint for today, her simple and profound message revolutionary in its impact and able to help a new generation follow the Gospel.

LOURDES (FRANCE)

Ave Maria!

Like many readers, I have fond memories of my pilgrimages to Lourdes, especially the two occasions I was chaplain to the Westminster Jumbulance, on which my mother was a *malade* (or, as we like to say, a 'V.I.P'.). The journey was smooth but (as you might expect) sleepless. As we hurtled down the French motorway, I reflected on how a pilgrimage is a symbol of our passage through life. Often it seems like an endless coach journey—as we leave familiar territory, deal with suffering and anxiety, and try to work out where we are going. But even in the most challenging of circumstances, God sends us assurances of His presence, rather like the elation we all felt when we arrived in Lourdes first thing on a Saturday morning, greeted by some very familiar faces. Lourdes shows us how things should be, a place where barriers are broken down, where selfishness is obliterated by service, where hope overcomes despair.

As I was sitting by the River Gave, watching the crowds streaming through Our Lady's grotto, I thought of the significance of Lourdes as a place. International as the shrine is now, the town has seen many different regimes over the years—indeed at the end of the fourteenth century this was English territory. Edward III, Richard II and Henry IV were all kings of Lourdes.

It is often forgotten that Lourdes owes its name to a Muslim leader called Mirat. The Saracens invaded France in the eighth century and were decisively defeated at Tours in 732. As they shrunk away, they still held parts of the extreme south, including the fortress of Lourdes (the ancestor of the castle that dominates the town to this day). Charlemagne besieged Lourdes in 778 but Mirat refused to surrender to any man. His situation, however, was becoming desperate. According to legend, an eagle dropped a fish at his feet one day, which was interpreted as a bad omen. Shortly afterwards Charlemagne's chaplain, Bishop Roricius of Le Puy (where there was a famous shrine of Our Lady) met with Mirat and persuaded him to surrender to the Queen of Heaven. He was baptised as 'Lorus' (from which we have the name 'Lourdes'), knighted by Charlemagne and sent Our Lady of Le Puy a handful of grass taken from the banks of the Gave, as a sign of his vassalage.

Over a millennium before the apparitions, then, Lourdes was considered a fief of Our Lady, closely connected to the shrine at Le Puy.

And the handful of grass sent there by the newly baptised Lorus found an echo in Our Lady's command to St Bernadette to eat the grass at the grotto—a penance, yes, and a sign of her docility but a nod also to the Marian heritage of the place.

It was providential, too, that Our Lady should appear at the time she did—challenging the growing secularism of the period. She came not to a person of noble rank or education but to a simple peasant girl, aged fourteen. The encounter took place not in a church or a place of respectability but at the 'Old Rock' (Massabielle) on the edge of the town. This was used as a rubbish dump and regarded with superstition and fear. Locals tried to avoid it as much as possible.

Only at the sixteenth of the eighteen apparitions did the Lady identify herself as 'the Immaculate Conception'. Indeed, when St Bernadette first spoke of her experiences, her mother assumed that this was some demonic vision and forbad any further visits to Massabielle. When the young girl did go back, she went armed with holy water, as a protection from evil. It is hard to realise the sinister reputation of the grotto as one watches the faith of the pilgrims and soaks up the atmosphere of peace today. Massabielle proclaims to the world that the Lord comes to meet us even in the midst of pain and evil, that He stoops down to raise us up, that He comes to the darkest corners of our lives and illumines them with His light.

It is likely that the grotto, long ago, was regarded as a sacred place by the pagans. Some suggest that the spring formed part of their rites, though by St Bernadette's time it was neglected and silted up. Now the spring has been fully Christianised, bringing grace and healing to many. I made my way rather gingerly to the baths, accompanying a young man suffering from severe autism. It was edifying to watch eight attendants gently lift him into the water. I was asked to say the prayers, though moments earlier I myself had been in the water, unable to speak because of the cold and being led in prayer myself! Apparently, until a few decades ago, the helpers at the baths drank a sip of the water in which the sick had been bathed every day as an act of faith. Who knows what diseases lingered in the water—but there is no record of any attendant falling sick.

Lourdes is a place where faith is made tangible—the silence of the grotto and the candles of all shapes and sizes burning there, the torchlight and Blessed Sacrament processions, the heroism and hope shown by so many of the sick (and their helpers!).

By St Bernadette's death, hundreds of thousands were making the journey to Lourdes, helped by the opening of a railway in 1866 and the personal interest shown by Napoleon III and his family. After

France's defeat by Germany in 1870–1, Lourdes became a favoured place for rituals of national repentance and reparation. The evolution of the modern Lourdes pilgrimage, encouraged in particular by the Assumptionist Fathers who cared for the shrine, was designed to be a vibrant and confident expression of the Faith in an increasingly secular, scientific age. Pilgrims thought of themselves adopting the customs of their medieval forebears and, in doing so, flew in the face of fashionable opinion—enduring challenging conditions on their journey, drinking 'dirty' water from the miraculous spring or praying with their arms outstretched in the form of a cross, like the early Christians. In the on-going dialogue between science and religion, Lourdes also took on an important role. Pilgrimages to Lourdes are very much centred on the sick and it is widely accepted that cures have been granted through the intercession of Our Lady.

Indeed, in 1883 the Bureau des Constatations Médicales (Medical Bureau) was set up to study all reported cures and consequently strengthened religious belief through science, rather than in spite of it. During his stay in Lourdes in 1913, Mgr Robert Hugh Benson, the famous writer and convert, was given permission to spend many hours in the Bureau, observing the work of the doctors who were 'keen-brained as well as keen-eyed'. It seems that a hundred years ago cures were seen as part of the pilgrimage 'package', particularly during the Blessed Sacrament procession, while today we tend not to expect them to such an extent, though we always remain open to their possibility. Past generations were perhaps bolder in their faith. On one occasion, as Mgr Benson was watching the procession, he saw 'a sudden swirl in the crowd of heads beneath the church steps, and then a great shaking ran through the crowd; but there for a few instants it boiled like a pot. A sudden cry had broken out, and it ran through the whole space; waxing in volume as it ran, till the heads beneath my window shook with it also; hands clapped, voices shouted: "*Un miracle! Un miracle!*"' For Benson, 'the supreme fact of Lourdes' was that 'I had been present, in my own body, in the twentieth century, and seen Jesus pass along by the sick folk, as He passed two thousand years before'.

It is little wonder, given the popularity of the sanctuary, that there are many 'imitation grottos' around the world. There was one such 'little Lourdes' in the grounds of my school, St Joan of Arc in Rickmansworth; they can be found beside churches and in people's gardens. Some attracted pilgrimages in their own right, such as the Belgian shrine of Oostacker, near Ghent. In 1872 the owner of the local chateau, the Marquise de Courtbourne, placed a statue of Our Lady of Lourdes in a grotto in the grounds, which had recently been designed as an aquarium to house his collection of exotic fish. Such was the local interest that the grotto was soon opened to the public. Pilgrimages were organised and cures attributed to Our Lady's intercession.

The most sensational of these involved Peter de Rudder, a labourer whose leg had been crushed by a falling tree. He neglected his injury and it became infected; for eight years he was confined to his bed. Hearing of the grotto at Oostacker, de Rudder decided to make a pilgrimage. Arriving exhausted, he drank some of the water and lay in front of the statue of Our Lady. After a while, he felt a strange feeling in his leg and found he was able to walk. His leg had suddenly become whole and intact; the fracture and sores completely healed.

For those who believe, no explanation is necessary; for those who do not believe, no explanation is possible.

LANGUEDOC (FRANCE)

Cathar Country

Driving south from Toulouse airport, a sign announces that we have entered the Pays Cathare, 'Cathar Country'. This was rather unnerving—a region actually identifying itself with a medieval heresy. Were the guide books hiding something? Was the Albigensian Crusade still going on? Would I need a sword and shield to protect myself from random Cathar attacks? Perhaps it was for the likes of myself that the souvenir shops were crammed full of replica medieval weapons.

As a tourist brand, the Pays Cathare might seem harmless. Visitors are encouraged to drive from one Cathar castle to another, although many actually date from a slightly later period. At Mazamet you can visit the Musée du Catharisme. And at one restaurant I even spotted a Pizza Cathare, although, given the Cathars' austere diet, there were more tempting options on the menu.

For centuries the Cathars have become symbols of freedom of conscience, equality and regional independence. They have also been the subject of all sorts of wacky theories involving secret treasure, sun worship and UFOs. The subtext, of course, is that they were victims of a Church that was repressive and power-hungry.

The term 'Cathar', which only entered common use in the nineteenth century, has been variously traced to the Greek *Katharoi* (pure) or the old German *Katzer* (heretic), that is one who kissed the backside of a cat (*Katze*) in honour of the devil.

The Cathars were barely Christian, although they claimed to return to the true Christianity of apostolic times and they copied many of the structures of the Church, with their own 'bishops' and Councils. They rejected, amongst other things, the Trinity, the Incarnation, the Cross and the Sacraments, and professed belief in two gods: one good (master of the spiritual world) and one evil (master of the material world). For them it seemed to solve the problem of evil.

Cathars were divided into the 'perfect' and 'believers'. The first of these constituted, in a sense, a sort of Cathar priesthood, men and women who had received the pseudo-sacrament of *consolamentum*, a liberation from the world that ensured redemption. The 'perfect' abstained from meat and wine and from sexual intercourse, while 'believers', who formed the majority of Cathars, were not bound by such austerities and hoped to received *consolamentum* on their deathbed. Some have accused the Cathars of encouraging euthanasia, since those who had received the *consolamentum* on their deathbed were supposed to abstain from all food and drink until they were freed from their earthly bodies. However, the lack of sources, especially from the Cathars themselves, makes it hard to evaluate what the norm was.

Although the Cathars were known for their detachment from the world, the cause soon became mixed up with politics. 'Occitania'—the area in the south of what is now France where the Cathars flourished—was markedly different from the more northerly territories around Paris. One Norman chronicler said that the inhabitants of Languedoc were 'as different from the Franks as chickens are from ducks'. The law was strongly influenced by that of the Romans; women had a more prominent position in society; the literature was more secular and vernacular; and the locals spoke the *langue d'oc* (the language which says '*oc*' for 'yes') as opposed to the northern *langue d'oil* (the language which says '*oil*' or more latterly '*oui*' for 'yes').

The Cathars are still seen as a symbol of regional pride and, at the time, were sometimes protected by local rulers, such as Raymond VI, Count of Toulouse—a sort of medieval Henry VIII who had five, possibly six wives, including Joan Plantagenet (daughter of Henry II). It was not so much that he was an out-and-out Cathar but that he resented the aggression of the nobility from the 'north', who had their greedy eyes on his territory, and he was bound to some of the Cathars by ties of kinship and friendship.

It is little surprise that the Church was highly concerned by Catharism. At first preachers were commissioned to win back souls through peaceful means, including both St Bernard and St Dominic. Indeed, both would have appealed to the Cathars since they embraced an austere life of poverty, fasting and itinerant preaching. Unfortunately, the fruits of this work were limited and, following the murder of the papal legate (Blessed Peter of Castelnau) by supporters of Count Raymond at Toulouse in 1208, Innocent III called a crusade against the heretics.

It has to be admitted that the Albigensian Crusade (which takes its name from the Cathar stronghold of Albi) was hardly a glorious moment for the Church. The fact that the Cathars live on today in the public memory is largely because they were victims of so much bloodshed. One thinks of the massacre at Béziers in 1209, at which the Abbot of Cîteaux is supposed to have said 'Kill them all, God will know His own' (though many historians think this is apocryphal). Likewise in March 1244 around 220 Cathars were burned at Montségur, after the castle's capture. Moreover, the religious enthusiasm of the crusaders was soon sullied by baser motives. As historian Christopher Tyerman put it, the campaign 'degenerated from a genuine attempt to cauterise widespread heresy, which many saw as a dangerously infectious wound bleeding all Christendom, into a brutal land seizure'. By 1229 Languedoc had been conquered and subsumed into the kingdom of France. Of course, the Cathars and their supporters were guilty of atrocities as well: churches were destroyed, the Eucharist profaned and clergy attacked.

The twelfth century saw a change in the combat of heresy, with obstinate heretics being handed over to the 'secular arm' to be put to death. In 1045 Bishop Waso of Liège spoke for many when he said that 'we are not entitled to deprive heretics of the life which God has given them simply because we believe them to be in the clutches of Satan'. A century later, however, the mood had changed, due in part to the threat posed by the Cathars and other heretical groups. These involved not just a few eccentric individuals but whole regions; orthodoxy was endangered and with it public order and security.

The Albigensian heresy led to the set up of the Inquisition, which was administered by local bishops from 1184 and then placed under papal oversight in 1230, with the help of the Dominicans. Bernard Gui, the fourteenth-century Inquisitor made famous by *The Name of the Rose*, worked in the Toulouse area for fifteen years and presided over 42 burnings for heresy out of over 900 guilty verdicts. This is a shocking enough figure but modest compared to some of the statistics to be found in books and on the internet. As Jonathan Sumption points out in his excellent history of the Albigensian Crusade, the aggressive suppression of religious dissent did not originate in 'the theocratic ambitions of the Church' but rather in the actions of 'secular princes and lynch mobs', which was hardly surprising given that 'a medieval community was defined as much by its religion as by its political allegiance or geographical cohesion'.

The Cathars were eventually eradicated and the region solidly Catholicised. But their memory, mixed with all sorts of contemporary exaggerations and myths, shows no sign of fading away.

MONS (BELGIUM)

The Angels and Doudou of Mons

I have always had a soft spot for the Belgian town of Mons, even though John Terraine described it as 'one of the dreariest in Western Europe'. I visited the place several times as a child with my Belgian cousins, and remember climbing the impressive belfry and stroking the cast-iron monkey in front of the Hôtel de Ville, which is supposed to bring good luck.

I was too young, perhaps, to consider the town's historical importance. Inhabited as early as Neolithic times, it became an important commercial centre in the Middle Ages. Given its location in the 'cockpit of Europe' it is no surprise that Mons has seen its fair share of war. It was besieged no less than four times between 1572 and 1746, and heavily fortified by Marshal Vauban, the visionary military architect. The town went on to play a major role in the First World War: the site of the British Expeditionary Force's first battle and the scene, also, of some of its final shots in 1918. How strange it is that the first and last British casualties of that global conflict lie peacefully in the same little cemetery outside Mons!

The town's great annual festival is the Ducasse de Mons, affectionately known locally as the 'Doudou'. Each Trinity Sunday there is a dramatic re-enactment in the town square of St George's famous fight with the dragon—rather appropriate for a town with so many British associations. The dragon is about 33 feet long and his tail is covered with a mane made of horsehair; small models of it appear in many of the shop windows. The creature enjoys the help of various allies: devils armed with balloons (originally made from cow bladders) and wild 'leaf men' covered in ivy. Supporters dressed in white move the dragon around anti-clockwise, its long tail attacking St George as well as the vast crowds, who try to take parts of its main since this is believed to bring good fortune. The saint, meanwhile, is helped by bizarre dog-like creatures known as *chinchins*, who find themselves under constant attack from the balloon-wielding devils; nor are the crowd immune from the onslaught. St George wears a yellow jacket, riding boots and a cuirassier helmet, making him look as if he has just left the battlefield of Waterloo, and moves in a clockwise direction as he tries to kill the dragon with his lance. In a quirky modern take on the traditional story he finally shoots the fearsome beast with his pistol.

This raucous fight between good and evil was introduced by a local guild dedicated to St George and became part of an annual festival celebrating the town's escape from the plague in 1349. This was thanks to the intercession of the patron of Mons, St Waldetrude (or Waudru), a seventh-century abbess who belonged to a notable family of saints with wonderfully distinctive Frankish names. The daughter of SS Waldebert and Bertilla, her sister was St Aldegund and her children (through her marriage to St Vincent Madelgarius) were SS Landericus, Dentelin, Aldetrude and Madelberta. Before St George kills the dragon in front of vast crowds each year, the relics of St Waldetrude are processed through the streets of Mons in a magnificent eighteenth-century carriage, the Car d'Or, which is normally kept in the large church of Saint Waudru.

In the popular imagination, Mons is inextricably associated with angels. It was claimed that during the 1914 battle and the subsequent retreat, British troops were protected by angels. The problem is that no one has satisfactorily found first-hand evidence of sightings of them at Mons. Undoubtedly the battle was a decisive one. The British troops, despite being heavily outnumbered (as they had been at Agincourt), did their best in driving back the waves of Germans. The first Victoria Cross of the war was won beside the Mons-Condé canal by Maurice Dease of the Royal Fusiliers, an old boy of Wimbledon and Stonyhurst Colleges.

So, where did the story of angels at Mons originate? No survivors of the battle mentioned them in the immediate aftermath. Most have pointed the finger of blame at the Welsh writer Arthur Machen, who published a short story 'The Bowmen' in the *London Evening News* of 29 September. This concerned a British soldier who remembered in the heat of battle a vegetarian restaurant in London which he had visited, with plates bearing the figure of St George and the motto, Adsit Anglis Sanctus Georgius—May St George be a present help to the English. This became his prayer as he fired at 'the grey advancing mass', until he started hearing voices about him: 'Harow! Harow! Monseigneur St. George, succour us', 'Heaven's knight, aid us!' Soon, he saw visions of bowmen at his side; the soldier with his rifle was at one with the English bowman of Agincourt.

Thanks to a combination of Chinese whispers and wishful thinking, the bowmen became angels, and the fiction had become established fact, quoted in newspapers, sermons and church magazines. It could be said that the widespread belief in the Angels of Mons showed that, despite the materialism of the age, war-torn Britain still believed in the supernatural and looked to the intercession of the angels (and even saints) in a time of need.

MONT ST MICHEL (FRANCE)

In Honour of St Michael

One of my seminary professors in Rome liked to say that the Church does believe in extra-terrestrial intelligent life forms. We call them the angels. Catholic tradition gives a central role to the Archangel Michael in particular and he is depicted wearing many hats—as marshal of the heavenly army, conqueror of Satan, defender of the Church, helper of the sick and dying and guardian of purgatory. In the extraordinary form of the Roman Rite he is mentioned by name in the *Confiteor* (I confess) and the blessing of incense at the offertory, as well as in the prayers after Mass—'Holy Michael the Archangel, defend us in the day of battle'. His feast was known in England as Michaelmas, one of the quarter days of the year, giving its name to academic and legal terms.

In a special way St Michael came to be associated with mountain sanctuaries. The oldest of these is Monte Gargano in Italy, treated elsewhere in this volume. Then there is the incomparable Mont St-Michel, dramatically situated off the coast of southern Normandy. This was formerly one of the great shrines of Christendom; now the hordes of pilgrims have been replaced by an endless procession of tourist coaches which clog up the narrow causeway. Despite the crowds holding aloft their cameras, the church on top of the mount still manages to be a spiritual oasis, helped by the prayerful presence of the Fraternités Monastiques de Jérusalem.

According to legend, the Archangel appeared to St Aubert, Bishop of Avranches, in 708 and instructed him to build a church on the islet. The message was ignored until, on his third visit, he burned a hole in the bishop's skull with his finger—a reminder that angels are awesome, powerful spirits as opposed to the cuddly, almost comic creatures we find on Christmas cards. The chapel was duly built and consecrated on 16 October 709. It was designed as a replica of Monte Gargano and the bishop sent two clerics to the Italian shrine to gain relics; they brought back a piece of stone on which St Michael had appeared and even a piece of the angel's red cloak.

The island became popular with pilgrims and was cared for by a small religious community, later replaced by Benedictine monks in 965. By this time the mount was part of the Duchy of Normandy and the dukes took great interest in the site for strategic as well as spiritual reasons. The close connection between duke and monastery is clearly shown in the Norman invasion of England in 1066—the monks equipped three ships and four members of the abbey were eventually moved across the channel as English abbots.

Mont St Michel even appears in the Bayeux Tapestry, which begins by documenting the alliance between William and Harold that the latter eventually betrayed (in the eyes of the Normans). Indeed, the two men fought together in Brittany and passed Mont St Michel, where Harold is shown saving two Normans from the infamous quicksands. The treacherous nature of reaching the island was an important part of the pilgrimage. It is widely believed that the traditional garb of a medieval pilgrim originated at Mont St Michel: the staff was used to test the path across the sands, the horn to call for help and the cockle shell a souvenir picked up to show that the dangerous journey had been completed.

As the Middle Ages progressed Mont St Michel became a fortified abbey. This was a feat of medieval engineering and the building work spanned five centuries, transforming the inhospitable rock into a miniature town, crowned by *la merveille* (the marvel). The abbey was several times besieged by English forces but it was never captured. Unfortunately, once the building work was finally completed in 1520 the monastic community was beginning to show signs of decline. At the French Revolution, Mont St Michel became a prison and in the late nineteenth century designated a national monument, made more accessible by the construction of a causeway across the quicksands and the high tide that cuts off the islet from the mainland.

This part of France has close connections with Cornwall, on the other side of the waters, and the majestic Mont St Michel is echoed in St Michael's Mount (near Penzance), which, according to tradition, is the site of an apparition of St Michael in the fifth century (competing with Monte Gargano for its antiquity). The little Cornish island was granted to Mont St Michel in the eleventh century and a contingent of Norman monks set up home there and build a church. This connection was severed in 1383, during the Hundred Years' War, and the priory became independent for a brief time before being dissolved in 1424. The remaining years up until the Reformation saw the Mount being supervised by the Bridgettine community of Isleworth (Middlesex), one of the great religious houses of pre-Reformation England.

There is one final English connection: St Michael's Abbey, Farnborough (Hampshire), built as an imperial mausoleum for the tombs of the exiled Napoleon III and his family. Around the time of the First World War the Bishop of Coutances and Avranches (the successor of St Aubert) hoped to restore Benedictine life on Mont St Michel and a rescript was issued by the Holy See in 1917 authorising him to do so as soon as circumstances would permit. In the meantime, the Abbot of Farnborough was appointed Apostolic Administrator, with the right to add to his title that of Abbot of Mont St Michel. This honour would remain until a new abbot might be elected in the restored monastery. It is for this reason that the arms of the Hampshire abbey incorporate the pilgrim shells of Mont St Michel and the present-day abbot on high days uses the beautiful Mont St Michel pectoral cross and crozier. He told me that he found these old privileges very useful when he was trying to jump the ice cream queue on the Mont on one recent visit!

OUDENBOSCH (THE NETHERLANDS)

The Dutch St Peter's

Write a list of the world's most Catholic countries and it probably wouldn't include the Netherlands. It comes as a surprise, then, to discover the country's rich Catholic heritage, especially in the area just north of the Belgian border. Nowhere is this clearer than the town of Oudenbosch in North Brabant.

As the visitor approaches, he may begin to doubt the accuracy of the sat. nav. or even his or her eyes, for the large domed church on the horizon looks suspiciously like St Peter's in Rome. This is no accident. The Basilica of SS Agnes and Barbara has a façade based on the Lateran and a dome and interior modelled on St Peter's, complete with a copy of Bernini's famous *baldacchino*.

All this is thanks to the vision of a remarkable Cistercian, William Hellemons, who was parish priest at Oudenbosch between 1842 and 1884. He had entered seminary as a youth, after working for a tobacconist, and then felt the call of the monastic life. Joining St Bernard's Abbey at Bornem, he continued his formation in Rome. That is where the seed was planted for his great project in later life. He lived at S Croce in Gerusalemme, the view out of his bedroom window taking in the splendours of St John Lateran, and it was in this church that he was ordained in 1833. Would it not be wonderful, he thought, to bring the glories of Rome to the colder climes of his homeland?

As pastor of Oudenbosch, Fr Hellemons could not be accused of laziness. He invited Franciscan sisters to run a school for girls and helped establish the Institute of the Brothers of St Louis (named after St Aloysius Gonzaga), who looked after the boys. Conscious of the need for a larger church, he then began his project to build a Roman basilica. In 1863 he sent an architect to the Eternal City to begin research: Peter Cuypers, who would build over a hundred churches as well as civic buildings like Amsterdam's Rijksmuseum. He dutifully made his sketches, though he thought the monk's vision too ambitious and personally preferred the gothic to the baroque style. However, money began to be raised and work started in 1865.

The church was also designed as a monument to the Dutch men who had volunteered for the Pontifical Zouaves. As the forces of nationalism and liberalism questioned the existence of the Papal States and chipped away at the pope's sovereignty, the Catholic youth of the world took arms to defend his territories. The temporal power was seen as a necessary guarantee of the pope's authority at a time of revolution and secularism. A regiment of Pontifical Zouaves was founded in January 1861, modelled on the elite corps in the French Army that had originated in the Algerian highlands. Volunteers came from all over the world and included 329 from Great Britain and Ireland, 2,964 from France, 1,634 from Belgium and (the largest group of all) 3,181 from the Netherlands.

Their cause was, ultimately, doomed but these troops showed much heroism, not only on campaign but in countering brigandage in the Roman campagna and helping the victims of a cholera epidemic that hit the town of Albano. Some of the Zouaves fell ill themselves and died. They also won a notable victory against the forces of Garibaldi at the battle of Mentana on 3 November 1867.

Fr Hellemons was an enthusiastic supporter of the Dutch Zouaves and made Oudenbosch a point of assembly for the many new recruits—including 22 men from the parish. Here they would spend their last night before travelling to Brussels for their army medical and then on to the Papal States by steamer. When the Zouaves returned home after the Fall of Rome in 1870, Oudenbosch continued to act as a magnet for the associations of veterans that were founded. The last survivor died as late as 1941. Children would dress up as Zouaves for processions and pageants and a Zouave Museum was founded—the only one in the world. It contains a collection of 'Zouaviana' gathered together by a Brother of St Louis who taught history at the school in Oudenbosch. It makes an interesting visit and provides resources for historians and those tracing Zouaves in their family tree.

The Basilica of Oudenbosch was ready for consecration in 1880. Sadly, Fr Hellemons could not enjoy his life's work for long, dying at the age of 74 in December 1884. But his legacy lives on to this day—a reminder of the historical links between the Netherlands and the Holy See, and an impetus for renewal in the Dutch Church.

PARAY-LE-MONIAL (FRANCE)

City of the Sacred Heart

Given it is one of France's most popular shrines, on the hot August day I visited Paray-le-Monial the streets and churches were almost deserted. A few pious ladies joined us at the Mass we celebrated in the Chapel of the Apparitions at the Visitation convent and the sacristy contained a little babble of priests and sisters. But, compared to the mass pilgrimages that would be taking place at Lourdes, Paray was a ghost town.

The shrine is indeed understated. There are few shops selling 'pious articles' and limited amounts of the usual kitsch—no flashing lights or illuminous statues. Surprisingly, perhaps, there is a dearth of information available (especially in English) and it would be possible to visit the town without realising the significance of the apparitions that took place there in the 1670s, which did so much to define modern Catholicism.

Paray differs from most other major sanctuaries in that it would still receive many visitors had providence not chosen it for a special purpose. Without their shrine, few would include Lourdes, Fatima or Walsingham on a travel itinerary. Paray, however, has its magnificent eleventh-century basilica, which is one of the architectural wonders of the region. Built as a priory of Cluny, the great Benedictine abbey nearby, the church was based on its mother house, which at the time was the largest church in Christendom and remained as such until St Peter's was rebuilt in Rome in the sixteenth century. Cluny did not survive the French Revolution and so a visit to Paray gives a taste of its lost splendours, though on a much smaller scale.

Though the chapel at the Visitation Convent is not a place of startling beauty it is one of great spiritual significance. It was here that the Lord revealed the secrets of His Heart, burning with love for humanity, to St Margaret Mary. Thanks to the gentle direction of the Jesuit priest, St Claude de la Colombière, who is buried nearby at the 1930s chapel of La Colombière, the private revelations received by the nun gradually became known around the world. Indeed, English pilgrims to Paray are proudly recall that when St Claude was sent to London to serve as chaplain to the duchess of York, the court of St James's became one of the first places where the new devotion was preached. Mary of Modena would later petition the pope for an Office and Mass of the Sacred Heart to be used by the Visitation Order.

The Sacred Heart became imprinted on the history of France. The Lord asked St Margaret Mary to send a message to Louis XIV: 'I want My Heart to reign in his palace, to be painted on his standard and engraved in his arms, to make him victorious over all his enemies, and by placing at his feet these proud foes, to make him victorious over all enemies of the Holy Church'. Neither the 'Sun King' or his immediate successors consecrated France to the Sacred Heart, although shortly before his execution Louis XVI succeeded in doing so privately. The emblem of the Sacred Heart was used by those who resisted the Revolution—such as the rebels in the Vendee—and can still be found on badges and car stickers to this day.

The unassuming Chapel of the Apparitions has had another wide-ranging legacy. A French woman, Marie-Marthe Tamisier, was at Mass there on 29 June 1873 when she was inspired to start a series of mass pilgrimages in honour of the Blessed Sacrament, especially to the shrines commemorating eucharistic miracles. Strongly influenced by the work of St Peter Julian Eymard, the 'Apostle of the Blessed Sacrament', she had long been devoted to this mystery and felt that her vocation as a lay woman was to honour it in any way she could. The pilgrimages quickly grew into the idea of holding regular international eucharistic congresses at different venues, with papal approval, where there would be splendid liturgies, processions, periods of adoration and lectures. The first was held at Lille in 1881, with the theme: 'The Eucharist Saves The World'; 800 took part, including a Franciscan priest from England.

The nineteenth century was, indeed, an age of congresses, whether they were political, scientific, cultural, commercial or religious. Made possible by developments in technology—especially the advent of the railways—they were a modern way of bringing people together. Eucharistic congresses were held most years leading up to the First World War. Although most took place in France and Belgium, there were notable Congresses in Jerusalem (1893), London (1908) and Montreal (1910). Tamisier's contribution was only fully acknowledged after her death in 1910. Eucharistic congresses have become a regular part of Catholic life and so spread the fires of God's love across the world.

PARIS (FRANCE)

The Churches of Paris

From the top of Monsieur Eiffel's tower, the city of Paris stretches out below. On a fine day you can trace the Seine with its tree-lined boulevards and book-stalls, work out the different arrondissements, and locate favourite restaurants.

It is easy to see how Paris began essentially as a collection of well-fortified islands centred around the Île de la Cité. Not only was it easily defended but had easy access via the Seine to both the sea and inland. A plaque near the cathedral marks 'Point Zero', the marker from which all distances to the capital are measured within France.

Paris is a city of churches, which can be divided into two categories. There are, firstly, those that originated from the age of faith. On a fine day the cathedral at Chartres can be spotted from the Eiffel Tower. Closer to home are the large edifices of Saint Eustache and Saint Sulpice, and Saint Denis, the resting place of the French kings and the birthplace of the gothic. There is the charming Saint Severin, built on the site of the saint's hermitage, beloved by the university students who have left numerous plaques giving thanks for examination results, and Sainte Chapelle on the Île de la Cité, with its wondrous stained glass, built by St Louis to house a relic of the Crown of Thorns.

Chief among them is, of course, Notre Dame, sitting on the river like a majestic ship. Construction began in 1160 and was completed nearly two centuries later. It has seen many great events. James V of Scotland married Madeleine of Valois there in 1537, though the poor bride died six months later from consumption. James later remarried and his daughter became the most famous 'Queen of Scots'. In 1431 Notre Dame saw the only coronation of an English king as King of France: Henry VI, son of the victor of Agincourt. Rheims could not be used since it was in French hands. In early December Henry, who had just turned the venerable age of ten, made his solemn entrance into Paris riding a white horse. It was, says one of his modern biographers, 'one of the finest succession of pageants and tableaux fully recorded in the fifteenth century'. Most French rulers were crowned at Rheims, though Napoleon famously held his coronation at Notre Dame in 1804 in the presence of Pius VII—although the emperor placed the crown on his own head.

Notre Dame was also well known for its musical tradition: a group of composers associated with the church developed the polyphonic style in the Middle Ages, while more recently the cathedral has boasted a celebrated *grande organ* and organists such as the composer Louis Vierne.

Many will remember watching the fire rip through the cathedral in Holy Week 2019. On reflection, it was remarkable how the Notre Dame fire captured the headlines. After all, no-one lost their lives; there seemed to be no evidence of foul play; and, in the end, most of the treasures were saved, including the magnificent rose windows and the relic of the crown of thorns acquired by St Louis. Even the beehives on the roof survived.

Some might say that there were more urgent headlines that day or that the millions of euros already raised for the restoration should have been devoted to the poor and the hungry. However, the point is that Notre Dame is more than a building; it is an icon, representative of values and traditions that transcend mere stones and timber. This mythic status was, of course, accentuated in the nineteenth century by Victor Hugo and his story of the hunchback, the cathedral effectively becoming one of the characters in the novel. Around the same time, the cathedral was restored by Viollet-le-Duc, the 'French Pugin', who added the famous gargoyles and the spire.

Paris, of course, has a secondary narrative: the centre of revolution, secularism and anti-clericalism. Who can forget the martyrs who suffered under the guillotine's blade, especially during the Reign of Terror (1793–4), and the enthroning of the Goddess of Reason at Notre Dame. Two archbishops of Paris died in subsequent revolutions: Denis-Auguste Affre, shot while standing on a barricade while negotiating a truce during the 1848 Revolution, and Georges Darboy, who stood before a firing squad during the Paris Commune of 1871.

Despite the bloodshed and desecration, nineteenth-century France also saw an astonishing religious revival, with new devotions and religious congregations, especially for women (with an active rather than contemplative charism). In Paris Our Lady appeared to St Catherine Laboure, a Daughter of Charity, in her convent chapel on the Rue du Bac in 1830 (another year of revolution) and requested the creation of miraculous medals, which brought comfort to many. Six years later, in another part of the city, the Abbé Dufriche-Desgenettes received the inspiration to form an arch-confraternity of the Immaculate Heart of Mary at his church of Notre Dame des Victoires. By 1870 there were 22 million members spread across the world, including St Therese of

Lisieux and St John Henry Newman; the church has thousands of ex votos giving thanks for the Blessed Virgin's intercession.

With revival came a sense of the need for reparation. From a Catholic perspective, Paris had brought much evil into the world and France's disastrous defeat by Germany in 1870–1 was seen by many as divine punishment. Not only had the Revolution unleashed many negative forces but the war had necessitated the removal from Rome of the French troops defending the Holy Father and, as a result, papal Rome was occupied by Italian nationalists. As early as 1870 it was proposed to build a church in reparation, dedicated to the Sacred Heart. The result, of course, was the Sacré Cœur, designed by Paul Abadie and situated on Montmartre, the 'Hill of Martyrs'—the site of St Denis's martyrdom and the birthplace (in 1534) of the Society of Jesus. Here, in the midst of fashionable cafes and artistic circles, prayers were offered 'which alone can deliver our Sovereign Pontiff from captivity and reverse the misfortune of France'. Alas, the church was completed in 1914—another dark year for France—but perhaps the nation's faithful had realised by now that what was important was not physical comfort but spiritual greatness and fidelity.

ROCHEFORT (FRANCE)

The Hulks of Rochefort

'Rochefort', my travelling companion exclaimed as we looked at the map of the area around our hotel at La Rochelle. 'Isn't that the name of a famous cheese? Why not stop off there and taste the local produce?' On arriving forty minutes later, we soon realised that *fromage* was not the heart of its tourist industry and, after a little hurried research, that the cheese in question was Roquefort and came from a completely different part of France.

The excursion, however, was not a wasted one. Holidays are full of serendipitous discoveries and Rochefort was worthy of our attention for a number of reasons. Developed in the reign of Louis XIV as an important naval base on the estuary of the river Charente, just off the Atlantic, most modern visitors come to Rochefort not to eat cheese but to see the impressive Arsenal and dockyard areas. There are several maritime museums and a replica of the *Hermione*, the frigate that took General Lafayette across the ocean to help the American revolutionaries fight the British in 1779. It was near Rochefort, moreover, in July 1815 that Napoleon finally surrendered himself to the British aboard *HMS Bellerophon* in the aftermath of Waterloo. A bizarre commemoration of this can be found in the Tourist Information Centre, where bottles of Napoleon's reconstructed *eau de Cologne* can be purchased.

It was in the church of St Louis that we found clues to an impressive part of Rochefort's ecclesiastical history. Being a seventeenth-century 'new town', there were no legends of saints going back into the mists of time, as with so many French towns. At its foundation, Rochefort was designed not only to be a powerful naval base but a Catholic port in contrast to nearby La Rochelle, with its history of Protestant semi-independence and revolt against the French Crown (with English aid).

During the French Revolution Rochefort produced a crop of Catholic martyrs, beatified in 1995. On 12 July 1790 the Civil Constitution of Clergy was passed by the National Constituent Assembly, with radical implications for the French Church. Religious Orders were suppressed, diocesan boundaries redrawn, papal authority limited and church offices became elected. The clergy were required to take an oath of allegiance recognising the Civil Constitution. About half refused, especially after the pope condemned the legislation, and these became known as 'refractory priests' or 'non-jurors'. Initially they were able to continue their ministry, though in time they were replaced by 'official' priests who had signed the Civil Constitution. Church and society had become bitterly divided and from November 1791 refractory priests began to be arrested in large numbers. They were imprisoned and threatened with deportation.

Given its important naval base, it is no surprise that Rochefort was one of the centres that these priest prisoners were brought in April 1794: 829 of them, to be exact. The idea was to put them on two former slave ships, *Les Deux Associés* and *Le Washington* (slavery had been abolished by the revolutionary government in 1794—one of its more positive acts of legislation) and deport them to the colony of Guyana. They were crammed into the old ships and had to survive in dire conditions and poor diet; a large pot of broil was their daily food.

The prisoners must have been surprised when the ships weighed anchor just off the Île d'Aix in the Charente estuary. A British blockade and the poor conditions of the frigates meant that the journey to Guyana was impossible. The priests would stay there, marooned off the Atlantic coast, for ten long months. Conditions got worse and many of the men succumbed to starvation, maltreatment, scurvy and typhus. Two-thirds of them died and eventually a hospital was set up in tents on nearby Île Madame.

Life on this small island must have been a welcome relief after the cramped ships. However, 254 priests died within two months and the able-bodied acted as nurses. One prisoner made a crucifix using a seaman's knife, which was devotedly kissed by the sick and dying. It is still treasured today, though the ravages of time has caused it to be called the 'Christ without arms'. There was a spirit of faith and fraternity and one survivor even wrote: 'if we are the unhappiest men, we are the happiest Christians'.

In November 1794 the tents of the makeshift hospital were blown and the surviving prisoners returned to the dreaded ships. However, the 'Reign of Terror' was over and conditions were easing; by February 1795 the priests were transferred to Saintes and freedom.

The priests were soon forgotten as France rebuilt itself after the Revolution and endured the changing regimes of the nineteenth century. In 1863 the new *curé* of St Nazaire sur Charente, Abbé Manseau, crossed to the Île Madame. He noticed one of his flock kneeling in a field and went over to ask him what he was doing. 'What sir!', the man replied, 'you do not know that it is here that the saints are buried'.

And so, the memory of the 'Martyrs of the Hulks of Rochefort' was revived. A large cross of pebbles was made at the spot where many of the priests were buried. Since 1910 an annual pilgrimage is made on foot each August in their honour. On 1 October 1995 St John Paul II beatified 64 of their number, along with 45 victims of the Spanish Civil War. Some were diocesan priests, others Benedictines, Canons Regular, Carmelites, Carthusians, De la Salle Brothers, Dominicans, Eudists, Franciscans, Jesuits, Sulpicians and Trappists.

We gingerly drove to the Île Madame across the Passe aux Boeufs, the natural causeway exposed at low tide that links it to the mainland—so-called because at one stage cattle were left to graze on the island. We stood by the cross of pebbles and prayed for the intercession of these brave men, that we too would have the courage of our convictions amidst the challenges of our times.

'S HERTOGENBOSCH (THE NETHERLANDS)

The Sweet Mother of 's Hertogenbosch

The shrine of the 'Sweet Mother' at 's Hertogenbosch in the Netherlands is nearly fifty miles south of Amsterdam. The name is one that is likely to cause non-Dutch-speaking readers to stop in their tracks, which is why the town is often abbreviated to 'Den Bosch'. It is a pleasant market town, surrounded by twelfth-century walls and lush water meadows, and best known as the birthplace of the Renaissance artist Hieronymus Bosch.

Devotion to Our Lady is centred round the cathedral, dedicated to St John, which is one of the finest medieval churches in the country. Over the centuries it was almost continually being enlarged and the confusion caused by the building work perhaps contributed to the way the wonder-working statue of Our Lady was discovered. On Maundy Thursday 1380, we are told, an apprentice mason found the much-damaged image lying among a pile of stones in a builder's shed. Judging it to be worthless, he was about to chop it up for firewood when the architect suggested it could be added to the altar of repose—for the custom in those days was to place as many religious statues as possible around the altar. This caused considerable surprise among the faithful, who thought the image ugly and unworthy for such a setting and after the Triduum it was placed discreetly in a side chapel.

Unfortunately, Our Lady's troubles were not over. Labourers working in the church smeared the statue with yellow paint and added charcoal eyes—seemingly as a joke. However, a mantle was soon placed over the image, making it look more presentable, and the missing figure of the Christ Child was found nearby, being used as a doll by some children. Experts have subsequently questioned whether the Christ Child really did originate with the Lady statue but the two figures seem to fit quite well and certainly date from roughly the same period.

In 1381 a woman who saw the statue commented that it was deformed. Later that night Our Lady appeared to her in a dream, saying: 'Why do you call me ugly who am beautiful, and dwell in eternal heaven. I tell you to have recourse to me so that you may overcome your sufferings and gain heaven also'. The startled woman quickly made amends and arranged to mend and repaint the statue. Another lady who had jested that 'the Madonna has jaundice' fell ill shortly afterwards and also paid for the further restoration of the image. Miracles were soon being claimed and, when the church was damaged by fire in 1382, one of the spectators cried out 'Save yourself, Sweet Mother!' A man and a woman rushed in to rescue the statue and ever since the image was affectionately known as the 'Sweet Mother' or the 'Sweet Dear Lady' (Zoete Lieve Vrouw).

Devotion quickly grew. The favours attributed to Our Lady's intercession were soon being collected in a book called *The Miracles of Our Dear Lady at 's Hertogenbosch,* a confraternity was founded in her honour (of which the artist Bosch was a member) and, when the prestigious Chapter of the Golden Fleece met at the town, several European monarchs visited the shrine—including the Emperor Maximilian, Ferdinand of Castile and our own Edward IV. A yearly procession was made with the statue around the town, accompanied by fireworks, illuminations and much rejoicing, and not even the worst Dutch weather would prevent this from happening—for on one occasion the procession had been cancelled due to inclement conditions and (it was said) the following day it was observed that Our Lady's dress was covered with mud. It was assumed that she had made her journey around the town on her own.

The wars and religious troubles following the Reformation led to a difficult period for the shrine and the statue was eventually moved to Brussels for safety and did not return until 1856. However, Our Lady was not forgotten by the people of Den Bosch. They still visited the site of the shrine in the cathedral to pray and silently followed the route of the traditional procession, as individuals or in groups. The situation for Catholics in the Netherlands shared many similarities with the English recusants—they were banned from high office, had to practise their Faith discreetly and came under the Roman Congregation of Propaganda Fide (in other words, Holland was seen as mission territory). The hierarchy was not re-established until 1853, shortly after that of England and Wales.

Thus, it was illegal for processions to be organised. It was relatively safe for individuals to follow the processional route in Den Bosch but things got riskier during one cholera epidemic, when hundreds revived the old tradition—on one occasion, it is said, the king came incognito to watch with great puzzlement what his Catholic subjects were doing.

Today conditions are somewhat easier, although the Dutch Church is facing many challenges of her own. However, the shrine of 'the Sweet Mother' at the back of St John's Cathedral seemed to be very popular on the day of my visit and the statue was surrounded by a sea of flowers and candles. May she continue to protect her children with her mantle, through all the highs and lows of the path through life.

TROYES (FRANCE)

The Champagne Cork City

The French city of Troyes, declares the promotional literature, is 'shaped like a champagne cork'—rather fitting given that it lies in that ancient province. Situated a hundred miles south-east of Paris, Troyes is characterised by timber-framed buildings, a patchwork of canals and the local speciality, Andouillette sausage. It was originally a Roman settlement, Augustobona, situated near the Seine and on the Via Agrippa, the road stretching from Milan to Boulogne. It grew prosperous in the Middle Ages as a centre of power for the counts of Champagne and the site of an important fair.

Troyes is one of many French places that sets bells ringing in the mind of the historically minded visitor. I was vaguely aware of reading about Chrétien of Troyes, a medieval writer of chivalric romances concerning Lancelot, Yvain and Perceval; some even say he 'invented' the novel. Then there was the Treaty of Troyes of 1420, one of the high points of English influence in France. Signed in the aftermath of the battle of Agincourt, it stated that Henry V of England and his heirs would inherit the French throne after the death of Charles VI. Part of the deal was that Henry should marry Charles's daughter, Catherine of Valois. The marriage was duly celebrated at Troyes in May 1420, in the church of Saint-Jean-au-Marché.

It seemed a masterstroke for the English. However, both Henry and Charles died two years later, within months of each other, leaving the new-born Henry VI as King of England and France. A further treaty at Amiens in 1423 between England and Burgundy confirmed the terms of the Treaty but, unsurprisingly, the disinherited Dauphin claimed his father's throne and fought for his rights, with the help of St Joan of Arc. Thanks to her efforts, the Dauphin was crowned as Charles VII at Rheims (once it had been recaptured) in 1427. Despite this, the English Crown continued to claim the throne of France, at least on paper, until the reign of George III.

The Gospel was preached in the area at an early date, as seen by the witness of martyrs such as St Patroclus and St Sabinien, and one of its fifth-century bishops is considered the main patron of Troyes: St Loup (or Lupus). He is chiefly distinguished for saving the city from Attila the Hun in 451, although the barbarian was so impressed by the bishop that he had him accompany his army as a hostage. When he was eventually released, so the legend continues, he was accused of cooperating with the Huns and had to leave Troyes and live as a hermit for two years. Just as interesting for the visitor from over the Channel is that he accompanied St Germanus of Auxerre to Britain in 429 to counter the Pelegian heresy, as we examine elsewhere.

There are not many towns north of the Alps that can claim a pope but Troyes is one of them: the birthplace of Jacques Pantaléon, born in 1185 and elected as Urban IV in 1261. He was the son of a humble cobbler who studied at the local cathedral school and then at the Sorbonne, where his talents were recognised and rewarded with patronage. He went on to become Bishop of Verdun, papal legate to Poland and, in 1255, Patriarch of Jerusalem. He was visiting Rome on business in 1261 when the pope died and he found himself elected at the resulting conclave.

Pope Urban never forgot Troyes and built the magnificent church of St Urbain on the site of his father's shop. The windows include much eucharistic symbolism, which calls to mind one of the pope's great achievements. Admittedly, much of his pontificate, which lasted only three years, was spent dealing with the troubled political situation in the Italian peninsular and beyond, but we can still be grateful to this pope from Troyes for instituting the feast of Corpus Christi for the Universal Church on 8 September 1264, shortly before his death. He had been impressed by the revelations of St Juliana of Mont Cornillon, calling for a eucharistic feast, and the miracle at Bolsena, when at Mass a host began to bleed in the hands of a priest who doubted the Real Presence. Urban commissioned St Thomas Aquinas to write the liturgy for the Feast. Every time we sing the *O salutaris* and *Tantum ergo*, we should think of this pontiff, the son of a cobbler of Troyes.

YPRES (BELGIUM) & KYLEMORE ABBEY (IRELAND)

The Irish Dames of Ypres

Think of Ypres and images of utter desolation immediately come to mind—the ruins of the Cloth Hall, one of Europe's finest gothic buildings, or the bloody battle of Passchendaele in 1917. Before the Great War, though, it had a different reputation. 'To most people', a Benedictine monk wrote in 1908, 'it is perhaps best known as the episcopal city of the well-known Bishop Jansenius, whose name has been linked with a notorious heresy; but for Irish people it possesses a higher and truer interest owing to its associations with the historic convent which has found shelter within its walls for well-nigh two centuries and a half': the Royal Irish Abbey of Ypres.

These *Dames irlandaises* or *De iersche damen* traced their origin to the English Benedictine convent established at Brussels by Lady Mary Percy, daughter of the earl of Northumberland, in 1598. Numbers grew and daughter houses were founded at Cambrai and Ghent, which in its turn went on to establish communities at Dunkirk, Pontoise and, in 1665, Ypres. This foundation was unable to attract enough vocations and so in 1682 it was made into an Irish community. Such was its success that, at the request of James II, the nuns briefly moved to Dublin in 1688, though they soon had to return to Flanders after the king lost his throne during the 'Glorious Revolution'.

The 'Irish Dames' continued to provide a centre for the Irish community across the Channel, many of them Catholic and Jacobite. Some of these exiles fought for the French king during the Wars of the Spanish Succession and at the battle of Ramilles (1706) captured a flag which was hung in the nun's choir and was regarded as one of the abbey's great treasures. There is some confusion over its provenance—some sources say it was the Irish Brigade's banner which was lost to the English and then recaptured in the fierce fighting. Others say it was taken from the 'enemy', perhaps from the regiment that later became known as 'The Buffs' (Royal East Kent Regiment). The flag became the stuff of legend, as seen in Thomas Davis's song *The Flower of Finae*, concerning 'Sweet Eily MacMahon, the Flower of Finae' and her sweetheart, Fergus O'Farrell, who died in the battle:

> In the cloisters of Ypres a banner is swaying,
> And by it a pale, weeping maiden is praying;

That flag's the sole trophy of Ramillies' fray;
The nun is poor Eily, the Flower of Finae.

The nuns also educated generations of girls, including (very probably) Venerable Honora 'Nano' Nagle, who went on to become a pioneer of Irish education and foundress of the Presentation Sisters.

By 1914 the Irish Dames could look back with pride at its long history and its claim to be the only religious house in the Low Countries to survive the storms of the French Revolution and Napoleonic Wars. However, the First World War would prove to be a challenge of a different magnitude. Six weeks after its outbreak, intelligence reached Ypres that the Germans were approaching and restrictions were introduced; the Divine Office was recited in the chapter house rather than the choir, the sisters 'placing a double set of curtains on the windows to prevent the least little glimmer of light from being seen from the outside'.

On 7 October 1914 the sound of guns made the abbey shake while the nuns went about their spiritual reading. Soon the Germans were marching through the streets, followed shortly afterwards by the British (who had won the First Battle of Ypres). 'The contrast between the reception of the two armies was striking', wrote one sister. 'On the arrival of the Germans, people kept in their houses, or looked at the foe with frightened curiosity; now, everyone lined the streets, eager for a glimpse of the brave soldiers who had come to defend Ypres'.

The nuns had to deal with much uncertainty and shortage of provisions, but they did their best to contribute to the war effort. First and foremost were the prayers and Masses offered for the preservation of the town and for the dead. 'Instead of distracting us', we are told, 'the roar of the battle only made us lift up our hearts with more fervour to God; and it was with all the ardour of our souls that we repeated, at each succeeding hour: *Deus in adjutorium meum intende! Domine, ad adjuvandum me festina*!' ('O God, come to our aid! O Lord, make haste to help us!'). The nuns also distributed food to those who had fled their homes, offered their school buildings for use as a hospital and made badges of the Sacred Heart for the soldiers, which the local children helped distribute.

The Germans were not content to give up on the strategically important town and a heavy bombardment fell upon Ypres. The Blessed Sacrament was now removed for fear of desecration and the Divine Office began to be recited in the cellar, amid cases filled with potatoes and turnips. Several elderly nuns, including the lady abbess herself, left Ypres for places of safety. However, it soon became apparent that the situation was hopeless and that the whole community should find refuge elsewhere, 'leaving everything under the protection of the Mother and the Son'—indeed, the statue of Our Lady of the Angels was placed in an outside niche since it had survived undamaged through an earlier siege in 1744. The nuns went sadly about 'looking—perhaps for the last time—at the dear old scenes, which we had thought to leave only when death should knock at our door'. As they departed for the unknown, there was a providential delay in opening the door that led out of the enclosure; as the right key was fetched a shell landed nearby that would have injured some of the party as they left for safety. Over the subsequent weeks the abbey buildings were almost entirely destroyed.

After many adventures, the brave nuns found refuge in England: first at Oulton Abbey (Staffordshire) and then Highfield House in Golder's Green. They must have been relieved, however, to eventually reach Macmine House in Wexford, which had been prepared for them by public subscription. In 1920 they bought Kylemore Castle, Connemara—a magnificent, crenelated property situated beside a lake and built by Mitchell Henry, a Manchester-born surgeon, financier and MP.

What could be more natural than for an Irish community to be situated in such a quintessentially Celtic landscape of mountains, water and bogs? At the time, of course, the move from Ypres seemed strange and traumatic: 'we had left our country, home, and all, to shut ourselves up in the peaceful solitude of Ypres Abbey; and here we were, forced to retrace our steps and to return temporarily to the world which we had willingly given up'. Yet, there was far more space at Kylemore than at Ypres—indeed, the Archbishop of Tuam suggested they consider the surrounding mountains rather than the monastic walls as their enclosure. There was a ready-made neo-gothic church, too, inspired by the medieval English cathedrals and built as a mausoleum for Mitchell Henry's wife, who had succumbed to 'Nile fever' during a holiday to Egypt. The nuns opened a school, which closed in 2010, and looked after the farm and large estate, which made them largely self-sufficient. Today the abbey enjoys fruitful partnerships with the Universities of Galway (in the field of biodiversity) and Notre Dame, and is still a major employer and visitor attraction in the area. In recent years the once-autonomous community has joined the English Benedictine Congregation—a return, it could be said, to its historical roots.

CENTRAL EUROPE

Austria, Germany, Switzerland

ABSAM (AUSTRIA)

Icon of Faith

Absam, a village near Innsbruck (Austria), is the home of a miraculous image of Our Lady that has been compared to that of Guadalupe—'not made by human hands'. It is an unusual story, beginning on the evening of 17 January 1797, when eighteen-year-old Rosina Buecher was quietly sewing at home. She suddenly noticed an image on the pane of a window: the face of a beautiful young woman, her head leaning to one side. She called over her mother who also saw it and they deduced that it must be that of the Blessed Virgin Mary. It was almost as if she was peering in through that 'window in the wall', assuring them of her maternal presence and leading them to her Son.

At first, though, they thought it was a portent of some great misfortune. Perhaps Rosina's father and brother, who were both working in the local salt mines, had been involved in some dreadful accident? Luckily, before long, the two men returned home safely. It was decided that the priest should be called.

The window was eventually sent away for examination. The sceptical authorities tried to rub the image off, wash it away with water and even use acid. If they had succeeded they would have established once and for all that the mysterious image was man-made, a hoax produced by the pious family. But Our Lady's face could not be removed and its origins remained undetermined. It was even discovered that when dipped into water the image momentarily disappeared only to return once it was dry.

The small pane of glass was eventually returned to the Buecher family and, at the request of the villagers and the local priest, taken to St Michael's church for safe keeping and veneration. Crowds of pilgrims began to arrive and graces reported through the intercession of 'Our Lady of Absam'. As was the custom, many of these favours came to be depicted in *ex voto* paintings, which were placed in a specially constructed chapel just outside the church. There, to this day, you can examine the several hundred pictures that hang there, showing soldiers, farmers with their animals, families and the sick all kneeling in gratitude at the feet of Our Lady's image.

Absam also became a popular place for weddings. One such couple, who wished to tie the knot in the presence of the Blessed Virgin and travelled to Absam from Bavaria for this purpose in July 1885, was Isidor Rieger (a baker) and Maria Tauber-Peintner—the maternal grandparents of Benedict XVI.

1797 does not seem that far removed from our present day; a time when many were indifferent to the faith thanks to the prevalent secularism and rationalism. The Church was, moreover, threatened by the aftermath of the French Revolution and its soldiers were already making their way towards Rome. Absam was one of several Marian occurrences at this time of tension; indeed, a number of Marian images in and around Rome were seen to move their eyes as the French troops approached.

We too sometimes approach faith like those Tyrolese sceptics who tried to remove the image of Our Lady and explain away the supernatural with rationalist arguments. Sometimes we, like them, see religious beliefs in terms merely of human philosophy and discard the devotion of the people as old-fashioned and superstitious. A visit to Absam allows us to see the primacy of grace, to rediscover the joy of believing and to communicate our faith with conviction and enthusiasm.

AMORBACH AND ELSEWHERE (GERMANY)

Bavaria Sancta

It is not often that I start a baptism with the words *Ich bin ein Engländer*, a phrase borrowed from the war films of my childhood. However, the occasion seemed to justify it—I was in Bavaria, officiating at the baptism of Jan, the son of a friend, and I felt I should apologise for not being able to speak in the local tongue. Of course, being German, most of the congregation spoke near-perfect English and made me feel very much at home during the celebrations afterwards.

The baptism was held in the medieval Kapelle Amorbrunn, a small pilgrimage chapel in the outskirts of Amorbach. The place derives its name from the local patron, St Amor, believed by some to be an Irish or Scottish monk who brought the Faith to this area. He founded an abbey in the town in 734 and left behind him a holy well. The waters are said to cure eye diseases and promote fertility. Indeed, perhaps the saint's most illustrious client was the Empress Maria Theresa, who gave birth to her first son in 1741 after drinking St Amor's water. He later became Joseph II (no friend to the Church) and the Austrian empress went on to have a total of sixteen children, including Marie Antoinette. In memory of this great favour granted to the Habsburgs, special *Kaisermessen* (Kaiser Masses) were offered at Amorbach up until the end of the Austrian monarchy in 1918. Pilgrims still ask for St Amor's help. My friends paid a visit to the chapel last year and, shortly after drinking the water, found that they too were expecting a child!

The vibrant Catholicism of southern Germany is reflected in many different ways. Instead of saying *Guten Tag* (Good Day) Bavarians greet each other with *Grüß Gott* (God bless). Villages have road signs advertising Mass times. Fire stations are often decorated with a painting of St Florian, a fourth-century Roman soldier who was martyred by being thrown into the River Emms and consequently was popularly invoked against fire and flood. Whether in town or country, one is never far from a church; on one holiday with my friend Jan we drove around the Upper Palatinate, Bavaria's rural backwater, and counted how many *Wallfahrtskirchen* (pilgrimage churches) we could discover.

Bavarian Catholicism is colourful and festive—processions and pilgrimage, *Lederhosen* and beer. There are many local traditions and festivals. One of my favourites is observed at the Marian shrine of Bogenberg every Pentecost and originated with a vow made by the farmers of Holzkirchen in the fifteenth century. The Blessed Virgin assisted them in getting rid of a scourge of bark beetles and so, each year, the villagers carry a large candle to the shrine. The journey involves walking 46 miles while carrying a wooden pole 40 feet long, with a candle attached. From the town square of Bogen the candle is carried up the hill in an upright position. Strong young men take turns to achieve this feat. They are very careful not to drop the candle, because this, according to a popular belief, would mean imminent disaster in the area.

The most striking element of Bavarian Catholicism is the splendour of the baroque architecture of even the smallest village church or hilltop shrine. To a large extent this was an unexpected blessing to come out of the Thirty Years' War (1618–48). The widespread destruction of churches necessitated their re-building in the latest style. The baroque and rococo are not for everyone—nineteenth-century writers were particularly dismissive of them—but once they are understood, they will be seen as powerful instruments in preaching the Catholic faith. Walking into baroque churches such as these provides a feast for the senses and food for the soul: angels and saints point upwards to a vision of Paradise; light interplays with darkness; the invisible is made visible. The Christian is fully aware of the cosmic drama in which he or she plays a not insignificant part.

ANDECHS (GERMANY)

Holy Treasure

As a child I was very fond of the delightful Church Mouse stories, written and illustrated by Graham Oakley and featuring a long-suffering church cat called Sampson. I have not been aware of any communities of mice in the parishes I have served though I do have one of Sampson's cousins residing in the presbytery with me. However, I was amused recently to see a mouse on the steps of the altar at the pilgrimage church at Andechs in southern Germany. Unfortunately, it was not real, but a sculpture placed there eight years ago when the church was being restored. It forms a tribute to a fourteenth-century mouse that had an unexpected impact on the history of Andechs.

According to tradition, Mass was being celebrated in the partially ruined castle of Andechs on 26 May 1388 when a mouse scurried across the altar and left behind a scrap of paper that it had been carrying (or perhaps chewing). Once Mass was over, the priest examined the fragment and realised it was a relic certificate. The mouse's liar was promptly investigated and a trunk duly found containing the Heiliger Schatz ('Holy Treasure'), an extensive collection of relics that had once made Andechs famous—including three sacred hosts, a thorn from Christ's crown, part of the True Cross and Charlemagne's 'victory cross'.

Today Andechs is a Benedictine monastery perched on a hill-top with stunning views (on a clear day) of Munich and the Alps. However, as Bavarian abbeys go, it is not a very ancient foundation, only dating back to 1455. Originally the site was the stronghold of the counts of Andechs-Merania. The semi-legendary founder of this dynasty, Blessed Rasso, is said to have brought a valuable collection of relics to Andechs in the tenth century. He is supposed to have been a giant of a man, over two metres high, which is why in many images he is shown stooped or kneeling. In later years the number of relics grew so that it became the largest collection north of the Alps. So valuable were the treasures that, even today, to unlock the relic chapel you need to turn three keys simultaneously, each of which is kept by a different person.

The Andechs family even produced some saints themselves. St Hedwig was born at Andechs in 1176, the daughter of one of the counts, and later got married there to Henry the Bearded, the future High

Duke of Poland. Another saintly scion of the family was St Elizabeth of Hungary (St Hedwig's niece), whose bridal gown and cross form part of the Andechs relics.

Of the relics, the three sacred hosts especially require an explanation. Two of them are believed to have been consecrated by St Gregory the Great. A woman in the congregation made fun of belief in the Real Presence and St Gregory prayed for a sign. Suddenly a bleeding cross appeared on one of the hosts, on another a bleeding finger. A similar miracle occurred during the pontificate of St Leo IX, the first German pope, when a bloody 'I' appeared on the host he held in his hands. The three miraculous hosts were eventually brought to Andechs and kept in a special triple monstrance. This is carried in procession each year on the fourth Sunday after Pentecost, the Feast of the Three Holy Hosts.

Despite its sacred connections, Andechs was a castle that was prone to attacks from the count's enemies. In 1246 it was completely destroyed and, as we have already seen, the relics (which had obviously been hidden) were only discovered by the happy intervention of a mouse a century and a half later. Andechs became known as the 'Holy Mountain' and pilgrimages were directed first by the Augustinians and then, from 1455, by the Benedictines who had moved to the site.

The subsequent history of the monastery resembles that of many other German houses, having to withstand the effects of the Reformation, the Thirty Years' War, devastating fires and a period of dissolution in the nineteenth century. However, there were moments of revival and in the eighteenth century the church was redecorated in the flamboyant rococo style, aiming to make it a very visible piece of Heaven on earth, surrounding the faithful with swirling angels and interceding saints in the frescoes and stucco.

Kloster Andechs is well known not only as a centre of pilgrimage but as one of the most famous Bavarian breweries. It is no surprise that monasteries brewed beer. In an age when water was often dangerous to drink, beer was a stable part of the diet and a monastery, with its large community and tradition of hospitality, needed its own supply. Many households made their own beer but it was the monks who developed and perfected the science of brewing, which was carefully recorded and handed down the generations. In modern times monastic beers have become an important source of income and the brewery at Andechs was recently renovated. The website has a rather wonderful description of its opening in July 2006: after the blessing, the abbot served the first litre of Andechser Spezial Hell, the typical Andechs festival beer, directly from the new storage tanks. For an hour, over

200 guests could enjoy free beer at the foot of the Holy Mountain. As if in anticipation of the occasion, the weather turned into a pleasantly hot summer day that elevated spirits around the monastery brewery'.

A visit to Andechs, with its holy relics, rococo church and state of the art brewery, presents us with a very attractive expression of Catholicism, fully life-affirming and festive and not at all prudish or puritanical. It is summed up in the Andechs motto, found on its bottles and beer steins: *Genuß für Leib & Seele … seit 1455*; 'Benefit for body and soul … since 1455'. Amen to that.

CHUR (SWITZERLAND)

British Saints in Switzerland

Guidebooks tend to be full of dates but the one I was using contained a rather startling one. As I admired the impressive Reichenbach falls, I was told that here on 4 May 1891 Sherlock Holmes met his nemesis Moriarty and fell to certain death in the 'creaming, boiling pit of incalculable depth' below. Indeed, every year on 4 May a pilgrimage is made to the spot by admirers of the detective of Baker Street. Luckily for them, Holmes managed to survive his fall and make a comeback—but that is another story.

I was spending a three-day holiday in Switzerland and a friend was taking me on a driving tour. What soon became apparent was that Holmes was not the only 'Brit' to attract pilgrims in Switzerland.

Take one of the prettiest Swiss lakes, the Thunersee, not far from the scene of Holmes's titanic struggle. Local place names such as 'Beatenberg' and 'Beatenbucht' point towards the local patron, St Beatus, who settled at this spot and evangelised the area in the early centuries of Christianity. He was, says one version of the story, a Briton who had been baptised by St Barnabas, during that apostle's supposed sojourn across the English Channel, and then ordained by St Peter in Rome, before being sent out to preach the good news.

Arriving by Lake Thun, the saint climbed up to a nearby cave to encounter a fearsome dragon (an earlier version of Moriarty, perhaps?). He raised his cross and spoke the name of the Holy Trinity, at which the terrified dragon jumped into the waters below. The monster is still remembered by the dragon heads that can be seen on some of the lake's boats. St Beatus, meanwhile, is chiefly remembered in the caves that bear his name (St Beatus-Höhlen), where the saint lived until his death in 112 at the age of ninety and where tourists can admire all manner of stalactites and stalagmites. Formerly pilgrims came here, though at the Reformation the Protestants ordered the caves to be bricked up. Until 1947 St Beatus was actually one of the patrons of Switzerland.

If the story of a first-century British hermit bringing the faith to distant Switzerland seems extraordinary, it is not the only example of such a tradition. Having paid our respects to St Beatus, we drove to Chur, not far from the Royals' favourite skiing resort of Klosters. This magnificently situated cathedral town claims to be the oldest continuously inhabited city north of the Alps. There is evidence of human settlement here more than a millennium before Christ and the Romans arrived in 15 BC, establishing the town as Curia Rhaetiorum ('Curia' later developed into 'Chur').

Walk to the cathedral and everywhere you will see the image of a saintly king—above the main door, on the fine gothic reredos, in stained-glass windows and wall frescoes. Meet St Lucius, the second British saint we encountered in Switzerland. According to St Bede, he was the British 'king' who asked Pope St Eleutherius to send missionaries in 179 so that his people could be educated in the Faith. He established St Peter-upon-Cornhill in the heart of London as his cathedral and, finally renouncing the crown, travelled overseas to preach the Gospel. The traditional collect in the Roman Missal describes him as *beato Lucio Regi, Episcopo et Martyri* ('the blessed King Lucius, bishop and martyr'). As a missionary, he founded churches in Bavaria and Switzerland, before settling at Chur. Here, he encountered opposition from the pagans and, after hiding in a cave that is still known as Luciuslöchlein, was captured with his sister, St Emerita, who had also renounced her life of privilege. She was burned alive and he was beheaded.

There are many problems with the historicity of the St Lucius story but it is not impossible that British Christians spread the Faith in this part of the Roman Empire. Recent research has shown that Britons were displaced by the Romans from northern Britain to what is now Switzerland during St Lucius's lifetime.

The British saints linked to Switzerland do not end there. If St Beatus and St Lucius might lack the support of firm historical documentation, there is no doubt that St Columban and his Irish monks brought the Faith to the area at the end of the sixth century. St Columban ended his days at Bobbio in Italy but one of his disciples gave his name to one of the most famous Swiss monasteries: St Gallen—founded in 612 and for centuries an important centre of scholarship and book production. Another of St Columban's monks, St Sigisbert, founded a monastery at Disentis in the canton of Grisons. Some suggest that the story of St Beatus originated with the arrival of one of these Irish monks in the area of Lake Thun and that, over time, the sixth century he was transformed into a first-century hermit.

Switzerland's main pilgrimage site is Einsiedeln, where we stopped for prayers and a bite to eat. Inside the abbey church, decorated in a swirl of rococo pink, we prayed at the image of the Black Madonna. The monastery here was founded by St Meinrad (pilgrims can buy a bottle of the local *Meginrad* liqueur in the shop), who, as far as I could see, had no British connections. However, beside the sanctuary I saw a list of previous abbots, including one 'St Gregory of England'. He was a tenth-century version of St Lucius—claimed even as the brother of King Æthelstan, though disappointingly not mentioned in scholarly biographies of this first English monarch. St Gregory's alleged blue blood would certainly explain Otto I's decision to make him Prince of the Holy Roman Empire, a title claimed by all subsequent abbots up until the early nineteenth century. Apparently St Gregory received the monastic habit in Rome, where he was staying as a pilgrim, and visited Einsiedeln on his return to England. He was so impressed by what he saw that he joined the community and, as third abbot, it flourished and grew.

Switzerland is not a very large place—about the size of Wales or Israel. It is not merely a land of chocolate, fondues and watches. Whatever the exact historical details, English and Irish saints were involved in the evangelisation of this mountainous area, even as early as the first century. British Christianity is not only ancient in its origins but, from the very beginning, evangelical and outward-looking.

COLOGNE (GERMANY)

St Ursula and her Eleven Thousand Companions

The Dom or cathedral of Cologne is Germany's most visited landmark and a glory of gothic architecture. All is not as it seems, however. The structure, with its towering spires, was only completed in 1880—over six centuries after construction began—and was for four years the world's tallest building.

There is no doubting the cathedral's antiquity. There has been a Christian church on the site since the fourth century and the cathedral contains many treasures. Most famous are the relics of the Magi, the Three Kings, obtained by the Emperor Frederick Barbarossa in 1164 and enshrined in a gilded reliquary. There is the tomb also of an eleventh-century local saint, Irmgardis, but my attention is always fixed on the chapel of St Ursula, one of the most universally popular saints in the Middle Ages.

It seems historically certain that a group of Christians suffered at Cologne and that, at least by the fifth century, a church was built in their honour. But beyond this, there is little we can be sure of. A seventh-century sermon mentions Vinnosa rather than Ursula as the chief martyr, and suggests that the group were Britons, returning from a pilgrimage to the Holy Land. St Ursula is first named as the leader of these martyrs in a calendar dating from the ninth century.

The number of martyrs seems to have fluctuated. The earliest liturgical books mentioned five, eight or eleven. When Wandalbert of Prüm compiled his martyrology in the mid-ninth century, he referred to several thousand. By the tenth century the number of virgins had been fixed at eleven thousand, with Ursula as their leader. The usual explanation for this is that the abbreviation XI M.V. (*undecim martyres virgines*—eleven virgin martyrs) was misread as XIM V (*undecim millia virginum*—eleven thousand virgins). Or perhaps the tradition of eleven martyrs, mentioned in the first calendars, got mixed up with Wandalbert's reference to 'thousands'. Others have ingeniously suggested that one of Ursula's companions was called St Undecimillia or Ximillia, thus creating the confusion.

During the ninth century, the familiar story of St Ursula and her companions began to be formed. Over time, there were many variations, but the basics remained the same. St Ursula was the beautiful daughter of a British king. A pagan prince asked for her hand in marriage, but St Ursula, who had taken a vow of chastity, was warned in a dream (made famous in Carpaccio's painting) to delay the matter for three years. During this time, she went on a great pilgrimage, taking with her ten noble women, each of who had a suite of one thousand virgins. Finally, after visiting Rome, the virgins were massacred by the Huns in Cologne.

Another version held that the Emperor Maximian (or Maximus) sent a group of Britons to colonise Armorica, under the leadership of a prince called Cynan Meiriadog. He appealed to the King of Cornwall, Dianotus, to provide wives for the settlers. The king responded generously by sending his ravishing daughter, Ursula, together with 11,000 noble maidens and 60,000 women of a commoner class. Their ships were blown north by a storm, and the women suffered slavery and martyrdom among the barbarians.

In his 1818 poem, *Don Juan*, Lord Byron wrote of Cologne as

> A city which presents to the inspector
> Eleven thousand maidenheads of bone,
> The greatest number flesh hath ever known.

Those 'eleven thousand maidenheads of bone' were discovered at Cologne in the twelfth century, when an ancient burial ground was excavated. This boosted the cult of St Ursula and was supported by the visions of St Elizabeth of Schönau. The fact that many of these bones belonged to men and children rather than young maidens did not deter the authorities since they were quickly identified as members of St Ursula's entourage: bishops, cardinals, even a certain Pope Cyriacus. Although he does not appear in the official records, he was claimed as a British-born pope, who received St Ursula into Rome and resigned his office in order to follow her on her great pilgrimage.

The majority of the relics are still kept in Cologne in the magnificent Goldene Kammer ('Golden Chamber') at the church of St Ursula. This chapel contains over 120 reliquary busts, dating from the fourteenth to the seventeenth centuries and ranged on shelves on all four sides. Additional skulls are wrapped in red cloth in glass cupboards and, above the shelves, thousands of bones serve as wall decorations.

Following the discovery of their bones, St Ursula's companions took on a life of their own. As well as a pope, the happy band supposedly included the Empress of Byzantium and the Queen of Sicily. Relics of the various companions were distributed across the Catholic world and stories and cults began to develop around them. Thanks to the visions of a nun called Helentrudis the world first learnt of St Cordula (a name meaning 'little heart'), who was so terrified by the massacre of her companions that she hid in a ship. The next morning, she repented of her cowardice and presented herself to the Huns, who promptly dispatched her into eternity. Her feast was thus kept separately, on 22 October.

Others also survived the massacre, at least initially. SS Cunegund, Mechtund, Chrischona and Wibrand were later martyred in Switzerland. St Cunera, a cousin of St Ursula, was supposedly saved from the massacre by King Radbod, who took her to his castle at Rhenen and made her one of his chief counsellors. His queen became jealous and ordered her to be strangled and buried in the stables. Soon, a bright cross could be seen shining over her grave and her body was given an honourable burial. The queen meanwhile was punished and eventually flung herself from a high precipice.

In 1493, while on his second voyage across the Atlantic, Christopher Columbus 'discovered' a group of small islands east of Puerto Rico. The largest he named after St Ursula and the others her Eleven Thousand Companions. The modern flag of the British Virgin Islands shows the figure of the virgin martyr surrounded by eleven lamps and two green branches. St Ursula's Day (21 October) is still kept there as a public holiday.

St Ursula was demoted from the Universal Calendar in 1969 but that does not mean she has disappeared completely. Churches and schools still bear her name and in 2005 she was named as one of the patrons of World Youth Day at Cologne. Although much of her story owes more to legend than fact, St Ursula and her companions still have the power to fascinate and inspire.

DRESDEN (GERMANY)

Like a Phoenix from the Ashes

As you stand on the banks of the River Elbe, the city of Dresden is a spectacular sight. With its baroque buildings and world-famous museums, it has been called the 'Florence of the Elbe' and 'the Jewel Box'.

Two churches are particularly prominent on the skyline. Despite being a traditionally Protestant city, it is a surprise to find that one of these is Catholic—the Hofkirche. Its origins are intriguing. In 1697 the Elector of Saxony (whose Court was in Dresden) was elected King of Poland, on the condition that he become a Catholic. Since Augustus 'the Strong' was seen as an *ex officio* champion of the Reformation and the head of the Protestant Estates within the Holy Roman Empire, this caused widespread shock. Had circumstances been different the new polity of Saxony-Poland-Lithuania, stretching from Dresden to Kiev, would have become a major European power and may even have limited the rise of Prussia. However, political division, economic hardship and military defeat meant that Augustus never fulfilled his potential. Interestingly, though, his dynasty remained staunchly Catholic and, fast forwarding to modern times, the last Crown Prince of Saxony decided, after the kingdom had been dissolved in 1918, to become a Jesuit priest.

The electorate—and later kingdom (by grace of Napoleon)—of Saxony itself, however, remained solidly Lutheran. As a result, plans for the building of the Hofkirche by Augustus the Strong's son, Augustus III, were kept in great secrecy. Situated next to the palace and connected by a bridge it became a symbol of the dynasty's new-found faith and today is the city's Catholic cathedral. It also served as a balance to the other dominant church on the city's skyline—the magnificent domed Lutheran Frauenkirche, known as the 'Protestant St Peter's'.

Modern visitors to Dresden have to remind themselves that the historic centre, despite its 'oldie worldie' character, was almost completely obliterated during the controversial Allied bombing of 13–14 February 1945, on the eve (appropriately enough) of Ash Wednesday. Indeeed, lingering below the cobbles are painful memories; as Sinclair McKay memorably puts it, 'this is the macabre truth of Dresden: every vision of beauty carries a split-second awareness of the most terrible violence'.

Dresden had, up until this point, been virtually unaffected by bombing raids; indeed, such was the city's presumed safety that it was nicknamed the *Reichsluftschutzkeller* ('the air-raid shelter of the Third Reich'). Rumours emerged that there was an unofficial agreement to spare Oxford and Dresden or even that Churchill's aunt lived in the area. It was perhaps because of this that the city had an insufficient network of shelters.

In a situation of 'total war', the bombing of Dresden aimed to demonstrate Allied air power, damage industrial, transport and military targets, and undermine German morale. The raid destroyed fifteen square miles of the city centre and caused a huge number of civilian casualties—while some Nazi sources claimed 200,000, the real figure was probably between 20 and 30,000, including many nameless refugees. Their ghosts still haunt those who walk Dresden's streets. The blazing flames, the gutted buildings, the civilians roasted and suffocated in the cellars, the bodies of the drowned in the huge reservoirs set up in the Markt and elsewhere, where safety had been sought from the flames. The cityscape made into a moonscape, the fiery hell of human making.

The Frauenkirche itself was thought to be invincible. It had survived earlier hostilities; when the city was besieged by the Prussians in 1760, cannon balls bounced off the dome. And, interestingly enough, the church at first seemed to have survived the 1945 bombing, for it proudly stood in the midst of the resulting firestorm, while several hundred people huddled together in the crypt, hoping that this would guarantee their safety. However, the fire soon penetrated the shattered windows and, with temperatures rising to an astonishing 1,000° C and above, the dome collapsed on the morning of 15 February.

For decades, the Frauenkirche lay in ruins in the centre of Dresden. The Communist leaders of the German Democratic Republic showed little enthusiasm to rebuild this relic of the past, although such was the level of popular sentiment that the rubble was never completely cleared away and the site became a 'memorial against war' and the scene of official ceremonies of remembrance. Plans to restore the church only began to emerge with German Unification.

It took fifteen years to rebuild the church, thanks to a massive fundraising effort and the work of many specialists. Whereas the cathedral in Dresden's twin town of Coventry was rebuilt in a modern style, the Frauenkirche was lovingly restored according to the original plan. The result is admirable and the only give-away sign that this is a recent building is the brightness of the stone, although there are, here and there, darker areas where the original blocks have been used.

The magnificent dome, one of the largest north of the Alps, was constructed in just eight months and in June 2004 a golden cross was placed on its top. This had been presented by the Duke of Kent in 2000 on behalf of the people of Great Britain as 'a sign of reconciliation and lasting freedom'. It was made by the son of a Bomber Command veteran who had been involved in the bombing and had subsequently become a pacifist. A further sign of reconciliation is the Coventry Cross of Nails that can be found on the church's altar, made from nails taken from the ruins of the medieval cathedral.

Dresden has risen like a phoenix from the ashes. It is not just a beautiful history full of art and history but a symbol of hope in a war-torn world.

EICHSTÄTT (GERMANY)

St Walburga and her Miraculous Oil

It is easy to forget that much of Germany was brought to the Faith by British monks and nuns from the eighth century. One of these missionaries was St Walburga, remarkable not only for her life but also for the miraculous oil that seeps from her shrine in the beautiful Bavarian town of Eichstätt.

According to tradition, Walburga was born in Devon around 710, the daughter of St Richard, often referred to as 'King' of Wessex, and 'Queen' Wuna, as we have already seen. It was a family of saints, a pedigree that would serve her well in the future: her uncle was the great St Boniface, 'Apostle of Germany', and her brothers were St Winnebald (an abbot) and St Willibald (later Bishop of Eichstätt).

Walburga received a solidly Christian upbringing. The family said their daily prayers before a wooden cross that was erected on their land and, in 720, she entered the double monastery at Wimborne (Dorset). Under the direction of St Tatta, the abbey had gained a reputation of learning and holiness, and it would prepare Walburga for her missionary years in Germany. Around the same time, her father and two brothers embarked on a pilgrimage to Rome and the Holy Land. However, her father developed a fever and died at the Italian town of Lucca.

During this period St Boniface was busy consolidating the Church in Germany, establishing monasteries and bishoprics. Winnebald and Willibald eventually joined their kinsman in great apostolate and in 750 St Walburga herself travelled to Germany. She may have stayed in Antwerp, where she is venerated as a patroness, and then settled at the monastery of Tauberbischofsheim, under the supervision of another relative, St Lioba.

It must have been a great joy to be near her brothers, after many years of separation, and Walburga later moved to Heidenheim, where Winnebald had founded a monastery. After his death in 761, Walburga's surviving brother, Willibald, now Bishop of Eichstätt, appointed her abbess, with government over both the monks and nuns. She was also skilled in medicine and did much to look after the sick and dying.

When Walburga died on 25 February 779, she was buried at Heidenheim and venerated as a saint. However, the monastery did not survive long and devotion to St Walburga waned to such an extent that in 870, as workmen were restoring the church, the saint's tomb was desecrated. The outraged saint appeared to the local bishop, complaining that her remains were being trampled upon 'irreverently by the dirty feet of the builders'. Shortly afterwards, the north wall of the church collapsed, which was widely interpreted as a sign from heaven. The body of the saint was quickly exhumed and moved to Eichstätt, where her cult was revived. Since 1035 the shrine has been cared for by Benedictine nuns. During its long existence, the abbey has founded many daughter-houses, including Minister Abbey in Kent.

What about her 'holy oil'? When the saint's tomb was opened in 893, 'the workmen found the venerable bones of our holy mother Walburga moistened as if with a film of spring water, so that they were able, as it were, to press droplets of dew-like liquid from them'. This 'oil' (*Walburgisöl*) has been constantly flowing from Walburga's shrine, between the months of October and February, for over 1,200 years. Chemical tests have revealed that the 'oil' is actually natural water, although its contact with the bones of the saint justifies its use for pious purposes and is a powerful example of Church's treasury of sacramentals—visible things that lead us to the invisible.

The 'oil' is collected from a shaft built under the tomb and the abbey contains an impressive collection of glass phials used to contain the substance, some of them dating back to the sixteenth century and covered in damask and brocade. The nuns see it as their special apostolate to distribute the oil—both locally and around the world—and to deal with the many prayer requests that are sent to the abbey. The walls of the chapel containing the saint's tomb are covered in hundreds of *ex voto* paintings, depicting favours granted, especially concerning escapes from disease and accidents and successful childbirth. The baroque altarpiece in the main church, next to the shrine, depicts St Walburga in glory, with angels pouring drops of the holy oil over a group of the faithful.

The saint is largely unknown in England, though one of the most impressive churches of the 'Second Spring' is dedicated to her: St Walburge's, Preston. Designed by Joseph Hansom, the inventor of the eponymous cab, its majestic spire is the third tallest in the United Kingdom and constructed from sleepers that once served the Preston and Longridge Railway—making it typically Victorian! The unusual dedication is explained by a cure attributed to the oil of St Walburga, which was applied to the injured leg of one Alice Holderess, maid at St Wilfrid's Presbytery. And so, when a new church was built in Preston, it bore the Saxon saint's name.

KLOSTERNEUBURG (AUSTRIA)

St Leopold

Just north of Vienna, standing on the Danube, is the impressive abbey of Klosterneuburg. It boasts a magnificent church, extensive monastic buildings, Austria's oldest wine estate and priceless works of art, such as the famous twelfth-century Verduner Altar. At its heart, though, is the tomb of a Margrave of Austria who since 1683 has been the country's patron: St Leopold 'the Good'.

St Leopold was a member of the Babenburg dynasty, the dominant ruling house in Austria before the Habsburgs, and a keen supporter of the pope in the on-going Investiture Controversy, which saw a clash between secular and ecclesiastical powers over such matters as the appointment of bishops. As well as consolidating Babenburg territory and promoting peace, St Leopold is chiefly remembered as a founder of *Stifts* (the Austrian word for monastic foundations)—Heiligenkreuz, Mariazell, Seitenstetten and (indeed) Klosterneuburg, beside which he built a new castle (Neuburg).

The legend of the founding of Klosterneuburg is a particularly charming one. St Leopold married Agnes, who was an influential lady in her own right as the daughter of the Emperor Henry IV and widow of Frederick I of Swabia. On the day of their wedding, a gust of wind blew the veil from her head as the happy couple were standing on a balcony of their hilltop castle at Leopoldsburg. A careful search was unable to retrieve it but Leopold made a vow that if he found the veil he would thank the Lord by building a church on the spot. Nine years later (in 1114) it was discovered in an elderberry tree during a hunting expedition. Our Lady appeared and ordered the building of what would become Klosterneuburg.

The *Schleierlegende* ('Legend of the Veil') is picturesque but full of historical inaccuracies. At the time of the wedding there was no castle on the Leopoldsburg and there was already a settlement at Klosterneuburg and a chapel dedicated to Our Lady. The legend is only first mentioned in written form in 1371 and been much celebrated in art. Yet the essential truth is that Klosterneuburg owes its foundation to Leopold and Agnes—and, given it is the story of a noblewoman's veil, perhaps Agnes played an equally important role. The veil and parts of the elderberry bush are still kept in the monastery's *Schatzkammer* (Treasury).

The monastery was founded for a provost and twelve canons. The second provost was St Leopold's own son, Otto, who went to Paris to continue his studies. Otto and a number of his companions unexpectedly decided to join the recently formed Cistercians, whereupon the undoubtedly disappointed St Leopold entrusted Klosterneuburg to Augustinian Canons. They have remained ever since and the community has a long and distinguished history. Over the years, religious life has been affected by the various wars that consumed Austria: the two Sieges of Vienna, the Napoleonic occupation and the Nazi regime, during which the Stift was actually suppressed. The monastery serves a number of local parishes and, in the first half of the twentieth century, became an important centre of the Liturgical Movement, especially through the teachings of one of the canons, Pius Parsch. In an attempt to unlock the treasures of the Church's liturgy for the period, he introduced practices such as Mass facing the people and vernacular responses decades before Vatican II. In more recent years the monastery's pastoral oversight has extended to Norway and America.

Klosterneuburg has always retained close links to the Habsburgs, who saw themselves as the successors of St Leopold and the Babenbergs. The Treasury contains the Archducal Crown of Austria, presented by Maximilian III in 1616 so that it could rest near the bones of St Leopold. Anyone removing it from the monastery for non-official purposes faced excommunication. In the eighteenth century Charles VI tried to make Klosterneuburg into an Austrian version of the Escorial—part monastery, part palace. By the time of his death in 1740 only an eighth was complete, including the Marble Hall and Imperial Rooms, which can still be seen today.

St Leopold was canonised in 1485 and his feast (*Leopoldifest*) falls each year on 15 November. Up until 1776 the emperor and his court made a pilgrimage to the abbey that day and distributed meat, bread, wine and medals to the poor. A more unusual custom is the *Fasslrutschen*, which involved sliding down a giant barrel that can hold 12,000 gallons of wine!

MELK (AUSTRIA)

Austria's Irish Patron

One of Austria's top tourist destinations is the Benedictine abbey of Melk. With its spectacular position, perched over the River Danube, and magnificent architecture, built on the grand baroque scale, it is easy to see why.

Melk has long been a place of importance. Founded by the ruling Babenburg family on the site of a former castle in the eleventh century, the monastery quickly became a centre of study, education, art and book-production, its library inspiring the late Umberto Eco to write *The Name of the Rose*. In the fifteenth century Melk gave its name to a monastic reform movement which spread around the region; one of the local houses that joined was the Scottish monastery (*Schottenstift*) in Vienna. The Abbot of Melk himself was a figure of some power and influence, both as a landowner and president of the clergy in the Estates (representative assembly) of Lower Austria.

After being damaged during the Siege of Vienna in 1683, plans were made to rebuild the monastery. This was largely due to the bold vision of Berthold Dietmayr, elected as abbot at the young age of 30, and his architect, Jakob Prandtauer. Many of the monks opposed the grandiose plans and the huge expense—the whole project came to 725,000 florins—but the abbot was able to cover costs and argued that structural weakness made the rebuilding necessary. The result served to give glory to God, the emperor, the Benedictine Order and Dietmayr himself.

The visitor used to British monasteries might be surprised to find such features as an imperial staircase and an emperor's hall (*Kaisersaal*) at Melk. Members of the imperial family were frequent guests and the abbey was a useful first stop on any journey towards Germany and the west. Emperors came regularly and, in 1770, Marie-Antoinette stayed with her brother Joseph as she left Austria for her marriage to the future Louis XVI. On this occasion a play was performed for her, during which she was recorded as looking rather distracted, as well she might. Twelve years later, hospitality was provided for another notable guest, Pius VI, during his rare papal visit outside of Italy.

The church was itself a pilgrimage site with its relic of the True Cross, the lance of St Maurice and the bodies of two catacomb saints, Clement and Frederick, dressed in their bejewelled baroque finery.

The most precious treasure, however, was the body of an Irish saint who became patron of Austria: St Coloman (or Colman).

We know very little about Coloman's early life, except that he came from Ireland (or possibly Scotland). Later tradition identifies him as a king's son and he is often shown in pilgrim's garb, with a crown at his feet. Around 1012 the saint embarked on a pilgrimage to Jerusalem, as many did at the time despite the perils of travel and the unstable situation in the Middle East. He followed an old route along the Danube, which would have taken him through Hungary, recently converted to Christianity. Unfortunately, the region around Vienna was volatile, with ongoing conflict between the Austrians, Bohemians and Moravians. St Coloman, with his strange language and habits, was captured at Stockerau on suspicion of being a spy. He was first tortured to extract information. At St Stephen's Cathedral in Vienna, a small stone can be seen in what is now the gift shop 'on which the blood from the sawing of the bones of the martyr, St Coloman, was poured'.

Unable to defend himself, owing presumably to the barrier of language, he was hanged on 13 July 1012. His body remained hanging for eighteen months and, unlike the bodies of two thieves put to death with him, it remained intact: it was said that his hair and nails continued to grow and that the dead wood on which he was hanged bloomed.

Perhaps the people of Stockerau found out his real identity and began to regret their action, or perhaps they were overawed by the miracles that were being claimed after contact with his body, for a cult of 'Coloman the Martyr' quickly spread. The Margrave of Austria soon heard of it and moved the relics to Melk to rest beside the tombs of the Babenburgs. Thus, this obscure Irish pilgrim became a heavenly vehicle in the complex politics of eleventh and twelfth-century Austria, as the Babenburgs sought to consolidate their power. He became a dynastic patron and patron of Austria until he was replaced by St Leopold in the seventeenth century.

His remains are still enshrined at Melk, now ornamented by a Baroque altarpiece, with the saint kneeling at the foot of a rather striking obelisk. Many churches are dedicated to him in German speaking lands, including a famous pilgrimage church in Schwangau (Bavaria), not far from the picture postcard castle at Neuschwanstein. It is believed that St Coloman passed through the area on his way to Austria and that he rested, preached and even pastured cattle there. This perhaps explains the colourful celebrations on the Sunday nearest to his feast (13 October), the Colomansfest. The little church is surrounded by several hundred horses and decorated carriages. After

Mass, the devotees of the saint ride around the church three times to receive his blessing, followed by the inevitable feast of beer and meat.

Is this simply a charming story from a distant age, based on limited historical facts and marked by Austrian folklore? On their website, the monks of Melk draw out St Coloman's significance for the twenty-first century: 'In our times, where listening to each other has become increasingly difficult, he can be seen as a contemporary saint, as he, stranger in a strange land, was not understood. Whoever is different, looks or speaks differently, makes himself suspicious and causes fear can easily become the victim of prejudice'. The Irish pilgrim continues to challenge a millennium after his violent death.

MUNICH (GERMANY)

Catacomb Saints

Walk into St Peter's church in central Munich and you will see a sight that is common throughout German-speaking lands but remains unnerving to Anglo-Saxon eyes: a glass casket containing the skeletal remains of St Munditia. What is particularly striking is the way the relics have been arranged. The bodies of saints are often shown lying, as if sleeping, meekly waiting for the Day of Resurrection—like our own St John Southworth in Westminster Cathedral. But St Munditia is half reclining, her body decorated with red and green gemstones and a rather garish tunic, her bejewelled teeth forming a startling grin and the glass eyes staring boldly at modern visitors.

St Munditia is thought to have been martyred in Rome at the beginning of the fourth century; apparently, she was 'beheaded with a hatchet'. Beyond that little is known of her, except that her body came from the Roman catacombs and brought to Munich in 1677. Hers is one of many such sets of relics north of the Alps—known in German as the *Katakombenheiligen* ('catacomb saints').

The 'migration' of these relics was a consequence of the rediscovery of the catacombs at the end of the sixteenth century, thanks largely to the work of Antonio Bosio, the so-called 'Columbus of the Catacombs', who produced his influential *Roma Sotteranea*. In 1645 the English diarist John Evelyn visited the catacombs and wrote: 'we crept on our bellies into a little hole, about twenty paces, which delivered us into a large entry that led us into several streets, or alleys, a good depth in the bowels of the earth, a strange and fearful passage for divers miles, as Bosio has measured and described them in his book ... Many skeletons and bodies are placed on the sides one above the other in degrees like shelves, whereof some are shut up with a coarse flat stone, having engraved on them *Pro Christo*, or a cross and palms, which are supposed to have been martyrs'.

The catacombs were not only of interest to antiquarians; they were an important monument to the courageous witness of the early Christians and an inspiration to contemporary Catholics, trying to defend the Faith at a time of religious division. Indeed, the catacombs demonstrated the antiquity of the Church, the centrality of Rome and the power of the Communion of the Saints. Increasingly the relics found there were viewed from the perspective of the religious polemics of the day.

Although the Vatican tried to carefully certify any bones that were to be venerated by the faithful, it is clear that the provenance of many of these catacomb martyrs was somewhat dubious. Ancient Romans they may have been, but were they necessarily Christian martyrs? The Anglican bishop and theologian, Gilbert Burnet, wrote in horror that 'the Bones of the Roman Slaves, or at least those of the meaner sort, are now set in Silver or Gold, with a great deal of other costly Garniture'.

It was believed by many that any Christian burial in the catacombs was most probably that of a martyr; after all, was not the Tiber swollen by the blood of the martyrs in those violent times? So it was thought. On one famous occasion, a diplomat asked St Pius V for a relic of the early martyrs and the Pontiff bent down and gave the man a handful of Roman soil, saying that the very dust of the Eternal City contained the blood of the martyrs!

Whereas it was hoped that the catacomb relics would be 'weapons to fight against the heretics', their presence in churches provided ammunition to the Protestant apologists and enlightened sceptics. The authorities were honest enough to give generic names to these saints whose real names were often not known. At Wardour Castle in Wiltshire, for example, two Roman martyrs lie beneath the high altar: St Primus and St Secundus, given to the Arundell family by Alexander VII. Likewise, a framed reliquary in my possession has a number of large fragments of bone with names such as 'S. Romani', 'S. Dulcedinis' and 'S. Felicitatis'. In some churches you might even encounter 'S. Anonymus' or 'S. Incognitus', reminiscent perhaps of the 'Tomb of the Unknown Soldier'.

The catacomb saints were especially popular in Central Europe, where many churches had been destroyed during the Thirty Years' War and new supplies of relics were needed to replace those destroyed by both military action and the zeal of Protestant iconoclasts. The Swiss Guards and the religious Orders (notably the Jesuits), with their contacts in Rome and beyond the Alps, acted as agents in translating them. On their arrival, the bones would be arranged by religious women (including some of the English convents in France and Flanders) and artists. The bones were carefully arranged and embellished by costumes and jewels.

As already mentioned, the effects could often be startling: St Felix sits in a baroque throne in his chapel at the Augustinian monastery at Gars am Inn (Germany). St Pancratius stands in a rather flamboyant suit of armour at the Swiss village of Wil, one skeletal hand grasping his sword and martyr's palm, the other pointing towards Heaven. St

Valentin at Bad Shussenreid (Germany), like several others, has had wax added to the skull, making the relics look eerily lifelike.

By the late eighteenth century many felt embarrassed by these relics and their doubtful provenance. 'Enlightened' monarchs, such as Emperor Joseph II, ordered the destruction of many, fearing they encouraged superstition, while the ripples of the French Revolution claimed many more. Thus, the bones of St Munditia in Munich were covered up in 1804. However, it is interesting how many can still be seen in churches today—stored securely in some lumber room or vault and then put back on public display decades later, a unique part of the Church's wide-ranging patrimony.

St Munditia's glass eyes still make contact with the devout and the curious today, just as they did three hundred years ago. Many put their trust in her prayers, especially those trying to find husbands! Even if the details of her life are unknown and her appearance somewhat garish, St Munditia is representative of that great 'cloud of witnesses' interceding for us before the Throne of the Lamb.

NUREMBERG (GERMANY)

The Iron Virgin

Mention the German city of Nuremberg to anybody and they will start talking of rallies and trials. It's a great pity because Nuremberg, with its castle, walls and famous Christmas market, is highly picturesque and well worth a visit. However, despite its many charms, the city has been rather overshadowed by its connections with the darker side of history.

In addition to its sinister Nazi associations, tourists are encouraged to visit a medieval prison and torture museum, where they can see the famous 'Iron Virgin of Nuremberg'. Such displays are pretty commonplace these days in historic sites. The sub-text seems to be: 'come and see how cruelly people treated each other in the past and how lucky we are to live in an age of enlightenment!' There is, of course, some justification to this approach but the tourist industry too often exaggerates historical fact and shows a simplistic and patronising view of the past. And often, mixed into the pot, is a critique of that institution which has survived down the centuries: the Church.

The 'Iron Virgin of Nuremberg' is a case in point. This terrifying instrument of torture stands over two metres tall and has a female head, supposedly that of the Blessed Virgin although the face does not resemble the standard Marian depictions. The victim was placed inside and as the doors were shut, the spikes on the inside penetrated the body while cleverly avoiding the major organs. Added to the physical pain was the panic of being enclosed within the machine, with no light or sound reaching the prisoner. Sometimes the doors were closed gradually to increase the pain.

That, at least, is the legend. It makes an effective subject for lovers of horror but it has little basis in fact. Scholars doubt whether the fearsome instrument was actually used at all and suggest that the existing models were created in the nineteenth century from various antique artefacts so that they could be displayed in sensationalist exhibitions, which met the craze for 'gothic horror'. A fraudulent history was written, claiming (for example) that a coin forger had been executed by use of the Iron Virgin in August 1515 and that it was used by the Inquisition. The original was probably first exhibited in 1802 but was destroyed in the Allied bombing of 1944. However, a copy 'from the Royal Castle of Nuremberg' had been made previously and sold to the Earl of Shrewsbury in 1890, along with other instruments of torture. It was displayed around the world, including the Chicago World's Fair of 1893.

Machines like the Iron Virgin not only attracted the crowds into museums (and made a nice profit along the way) but demonstrated the progress of modern times and the perceived dangers of Catholicism. Instruments of torture were often mentioned as evidence of the Church's bloody past. For non-Catholic Victorian readers it served as a warning; after all, the Catholic community was quickly growing and many felt threatened. Memories of the 'Fires of Smithfield' and 'St Bartholomew's Day Massacre' were still fresh in the collective Protestant consciousness. The Catholic Truth Society even thought it necessary to publish a pamphlet on the Iron Virgin in 1898, written by Fr Herbert Lucas SJ, to counter these accusations.

Where did the idea of the Iron Virgin come from? The myth may have been influenced by a real torture device, the Schandmantel ('cloak of shame'), which enclosed a prisoner but had no spikes. Further inspiration may have come from antiquity. According to St Augustine, for example, the Roman general Marcus Atilius Regulus was put to death by the Carthaginians by being placed in 'a tight wooden box, spiked with sharp nails on all sides, so that he could not lean in any direction without being pierced'.

Horrific torture did indeed exist in the past but its use was less common than we often assume and often subject to strict regulations. It is ridiculous to caricature our forebears as sadist tyrants who spent their spare time devising ingenious instruments of pain for their dark dungeons. Having said that, history shows the cruel depths to which human beings can descend and, sadly, we are unable to take the moral high ground. Although the Iron Virgin was never used by the Inquisition, it may have been used by the regime of Saddam Hussein. A crude copy of the machine was found at the palace of Uday Hussein, the dictator's eldest son, and was allegedly used on Iraqi soccers players for losing matches. Perhaps our times are not as 'enlightened' as we like to think.

OBERNDORF (AUSTRIA)

The Town of Stille Nacht

Oberndorf sits on the Austrian-German border, on the Salzach river. Across the water is the Bavarian town of Laufen, with its square castle which, during the Second World War, held prisoners brought here from the Channel Islands.

Snow-covered Oberndorf is the sort of scene you find on Christmas cards, with its little village church. It might come as no surprise, therefore, that on Christmas Eve 1818, the carol *Silent Night* was sung here for the first time. The initial performance was a duet, sung by the assistant priest, Fr Joseph Mohr, who took the tenor line, and the teacher and organist, Franz Gruber, who sang bass. According to Gruber, the song was met with 'general approval by all', the little congregation being largely made up of shipping labourers and boat builders.

Fr Mohr was a native of Salzburg, who was brought up by a single mother and was named after his godfather (as was the custom with unmarried parents at the time)—although according to his baptismal record, his godfather was Joseph Wohlmuth, the last official executioner of Salzburg. Mohr was ordained a priest in 1815 and had written the words to the carol the following year, while stationed in the parish of Mariapfarr. On arriving at Oberndorf, he asked Gruber to set his text to music. Mohr accompanied the carol on the guitar, commonly used in those parts as a folk instrument—which might come as a surprise to anyone who thinks that such practices only began in the 1960s!

The carol quickly became popular and was made known by travelling singers, rather like the von Trapp family of a later date. For example, one such group, the Strasser family, sang the carol at Leipzig in December 1832, while the Rainers included it in a performance given before the Russian tsar and Austrian emperor. By the 1840s it had become a firm favourite of Frederick William IV of Prussia. It was around this time that the melody was slightly altered to the tune that we know so well today.

Myths began to grow around *Silent Night*. It was said, for example, that Mohr was inspired to write the words after visiting a new-born child that Christmas Eve or that emergency measures had been required since an impertinent mouse had eaten through the organ bellows at Oberndorf, necessitating a new carol that could be played with guitar. Others claimed the melody was written by Haydn, Mozart or Beethoven.

Mohr died in 1848, having gained no riches through his famous composition. His final appointment was to Wagrain, now an Alpine ski resort, and he left what money he had to the children and elderly people of the parish. He was described as 'a reliable friend of mankind, toward the poor, a gentle, helping father'. Gruber, meanwhile, continued to produce arrangements for his masterpiece and ended his days at Hallein, where his house is now a Silent Night museum.

Silent Night is remembered as a carol of peace. It was written, let us not forget, in the aftermath of the Napoleonic Wars, which had left its impact on Oberndorf. Originally part of the Principality of Salzburg and forming a suburb of Laufen across the river, the two towns were cut off by a new border. At the time the carol was performed, the locals were struggling with the economic depression that so often follows war. Little wonder that Mohr longed for the peace and comfort that Christ alone gives.

During the unofficial Christmas Truce of 1914 the carol took centre-stage. Some German troops began decorating their trenches near Ypres with evergreens and placed candles in the trees. Henry Williamson of the London Rifle Brigade, who would later go on to write *Tarka the Otter*, remembered: 'then about 11 o'clock I saw a Christmas tree going up on the German trenches. And there was a light. And we stood still and we watched this and we talked, and then a German voice began to sing a song—[*Stille Nacht], Heilige Nacht*. And after that, somebody, 'come over, Tommy, come over'. And we still thought it was a trap, but some of us went over at once … And very soon we were exchanging gifts'.

Christmas can so often be anything but silent or peaceful, yet the carol encourages us to escape the commotion and embrace the stillness of that holy night.

WIESKIRCHE (GERMANY)

The Church in the Meadow

The Wieskirche, about twelve miles north-east of Oberammergau, is one of the most astonishing churches I have visited. It is in an idyllic location, with the alps in the background and a flowery meadow (*Wiese*) nearby. On one visit I had a late breakfast of white sausages and beer in a nearby café—this, combined with the view, seemed to be a little piece of heaven!

The church grew around a statue of the Suffering Christ, depicted as He was being scourged, which had once been kept at the Norbertine monastery of Steingaden but had found its way to Wies. As I write this, I have a little metallic figurine of the image on my desk, a little reminder I picked up at the gift shop. The statue is not a masterpiece but on 14 June 1738 it was seen to shed tears by the farmer's wife, Maria Lory. Despite the best efforts of the canons, news spread and pilgrims came. A temporary chapel was built in the meadow and by 1745 work was begun on a more permanent structure. It was opened in 1754.

What a church this is! The outside is pretty enough but like many churches in this part of the world. Nothing quite prepares you for the moment you open the door. The church interior seems to be alive with saints and angels, everywhere you look there is movement, gradually leading the eye upwards to the ceiling—designed not to look like a roof but rather an open heaven, with the figure of the Risen Christ in the centre. The church is a swirl of whites and pinks and the Zimmermann brothers who created it were masters not just of art but of light, with a clever use of windows so that all the details can be enjoyed.

The most striking element of Central European Catholicism is the splendour of even the smallest village church or hilltop shrine. To a large extent this was an unexpected blessing to come out of the Thirty Years' War in the seventeenth century: the widespread destruction of churches necessitated their re-building and the development of a creative new style, bursting with colour and life. Baroque and rococo churches are not for everyone. Victorian writers were particularly dismissive of them but once they are understood, they can be seen as powerful instruments in preaching the Christian faith.

In his famous book on the *Baroque Churches of Central Europe*, John Bourke wrote:

> To the aspiring soul and the struggling sinner are opened up visions of the saints in light and the Godhead in glory. The Church Militant here on earth looks upward and sees portrayed the shining splendour of the Church Triumphant. And indeed the effect of the greatest of these paintings, seen in favourable light, is overwhelming—the richness and variety of the colouring, the marshalling of the figures in their groups and ranks, the illusion of great depth and height produced by a combination of subtlest perspective drawing and skilfullest gradation of colour from full and glowing reds, blues, greens and browns at the base of the picture to the fine, intense blends of white and yellow in the mystical blaze at the summit. The link between the visions in these frescoes and the worshipper in the church is formed by statuary and the altar paintings. A great multitude of figures and groups surrounds the visitor in one of these churches. He sees saints and prophets and Fathers of the Church at decisive points of vantage, significantly poised and with their appropriate attributes. He sees angels and *putti* flying, sitting, leaning, supporting, listening, adoring, pointing, reproving, on altar and pulpit, organ and confessional, making jubilant music, bearing emblems of the Betrayal or the Crucifixion, bringing messages from on high, in charge of the mounting horses of Elijah's fiery chariot, attending the crucified and awaiting the risen Saviour, up-bearing the Virgin at her Assumption.

The Wieskirche is, I think, a supreme example of this. Over a million pilgrims come here each year, some on foot, to see the image of the Suffering Christ and enjoy the church's artistic magnificence. The fusion of colour and light has earned it the name, 'Lord God's Ballroom', but its charm is also in its natural setting, with green meadows, majestic summits and pure air. A pilgrimage worth making!

WÜRZBURG (GERMANY)

St Kilian

Many places across Europe (and beyond), as we have seen, still honour Irish monks and hermits who first brought the Faith to the region. Perhaps the most spectacular story concerns St Brendan and his disciples, who may have reached the shores of America (the 'Isle of the Blessed') in a small wooden boat in the sixth century.

There are many other examples and a tourist will often stumble across an Irish saint during a vacation on the continent. The German city of Würzburg, famous for its white wine, sold in the distinctively rounded bottle (*Bocksbeutel*), is a prime example of this. While absorbing the Franconian culture, it is impossible to escape the local patron saint: an Irish bishop called St Kilian. His benign presence is everywhere in Würzburg—the cathedral (Kiliandom) is dedicated to him and his shrine can be found in the nearby Neumünster, his statue is on the main bridge, and the first week of July is devoted to the Kilianfest. Even the local Gaelic Athletic Association Club is named after him.

Next to nothing is known of St Kilian's early life. He may have originated in Mullagh, County Cavan, where there is a church dedicated to him, and he may have been connected to the great monastery of Iona. In 686, having discerned the call to leave Ireland and take up his cross, St Kilian journeyed to the continent together with eleven companions. They sailed down the Rhine, and then branched off along the Main, until they reached the town of Würzburg, where they found a potential target for their mission—Gozbert, the local pagan ruler.

St Kilian then travelled to Rome in order to gain support for his missionary work. He had an audience with Pope Conon, an elderly Sicilian who reigned briefly between October 686 and September 687. The band of missionaries then returned northwards and dispersed themselves over the region. The saint returned to Würzburg, together with the priest Colman and the deacon Totnan. Gozbert was duly baptised in a large wooden tub, together with many of his subjects, but the situation became increasingly tense when the saint turned his attention to the prince's personal life. Gozbert had followed the pagan custom of marrying his brother's widow, Geilana (or Geila). St Kilian denounced this marriage as invalid and persuaded the duke to leave his wife. When Geilana discovered the nature of the bishop's conversations with her husband, she plotted his murder. Legend says that she hired members of the castle staff to kill Kilian, Colman and Totman while the duke was away on a military expedition.

On 8 July 689 the three apostles were beheaded and their corpses secretly buried at the scene of the crime together with their sacred vessels, vestments and books. A stable was hastily constructed over their tomb. Their bodies were soon found, however, when a blind priest was unexpectedly cured at their burial place. The legend goes on to say that the plotters were punished for their evil deeds: the murderers met miserable deaths and Geilana, initially denying any knowledge of what had happened, ended her days possessed by an evil spirit and gripped by insanity. This convinced Gozbert of the truth of Christianity and he remained a fervent believer until his death.

Scholars have tried to deconstruct the legend of St Kilian—suggesting that Christianity existed in the area long before his arrival and doubting his visit to Pope Conan. They also question the circumstances of his martyrdom, which bears a strong resemblance to other lives of the saints. However, the fact that an Irish missionary worked in the Würzburg area and eventually died for his Faith seems beyond reasonable doubt.

The Celtic connections continued after St Kilian's death. Many Irish pilgrims made their way to Würzburg to venerate the shrine of their compatriot. In 1059 the great Irish chronicler Marianus Scotus was ordained priest at St Kilian's tomb. During the twelfth century, an Irish monastery was founded at Würzburg, in the shadow of the Marienberg fortress, which may have acted as a hospice for Irish pilgrims. This Abbey of St James was confusingly referred to as the Schottenkloster, since the Irish were generally known as *Scoti*. Its first abbot was St Macarius, a well-known scholar, who made the monastery a celebrated centre of manuscript production.

Between 1595 and 1803, the monastery was in the hands of Scottish Benedictines; the body of St Macarius was rediscovered and translated to a new shrine in 1615. He won new fame and news of his miracles even reached the Stuart Court in London. In 1688, Queen Mary of Modena (wife of James II) gave birth to a son, James Francis Edward (later known as the 'Old Pretender'). However, the baby suffered from poor health and the doctors expected him to die, like Mary's other children. The queen asked for a relic of St Macarius, which was brought over from Würzburg and placed on the infant's head. From that moment onwards, the infant grew stronger and it is said that, in later life, he always carried a relic of St Macarius on his person. The baby's survival alarmed many of the king's opponents, since he now had a Catholic heir. It could indeed be said that an indirect result of the intercession of St Macarius of Würzburg were the events of 1688, whereby the Protestant William of Orange forced out the Catholic James II.

Würzburg is unusual in boasting so many links with the Celtic Christian world and St Kilian deserves to be remembered as one of the great Irish missionaries. The Irish Church may be going through some dark, uncertain days but let us not forget that it has been instrumental in shedding Christ's light across the world.

EASTERN EUROPE

Bulgaria, Croatia, Czechia, Hungary, Montenegro, Poland, Romania, Slovenia

AUSCHWITZ (POLAND)

The Metropolis of Death

It was wet and windy the day we visited Auschwitz. Appropriate, though, for it matched the despair and tragedy that the stones scream out. The red-brick buildings, originally built as barracks, do not at first look particularly sinister. Unexpectedly there is even grass and trees—but the birds do not sing in this 'Metropolis of Death'.

As I walked around, the full scale of the horrors of the Holocaust began to dawn: piles of spectacles, brushes and shoes; suitcases with the names and date of birth of their owners (some of whom shared a school year with my parents); most sickening of all, a room full of human hair. There were photographs too of those who were brought here—gazing at the numbed visitor and pleading them not to forget.

In this dreadful place at least a million people were exterminated: Jews as well as Poles, those with physical or mental limitations and suspect political beliefs, those who simply did not fit in. This was evil on an industrial scale. One wonders how the guards could have quietened their consciences. Surely, they were family men, surely they could not be indifferent to the misery before their very eyes? Auschwitz survivor Primo Levi wrote: 'monsters exist, but they are too few in number to be truly dangerous. More dangerous are the common men, the functionaries ready to believe and to act without asking questions'.

No visitor to Auschwitz can remain indifferent. Everyone walks around as if in a nightmare. Some will understandably be angry: Where was God in all this? Why was such evil allowed to prevail? There is no easy way to answer these objections; perhaps they are unanswerable. But I remembered the powerful words of Rabbi Jonathan Sacks: 'people sometimes ask me: 'Where was God in the Holocaust?' But the real question is: Where was humanity? God's voice has been heard since man first walked on earth — in the words, "You shall not murder"; in the words, "Do not oppress a stranger"; in the words, "Your brother's blood cries to me from the ground". God wasn't silent in the Holocaust ... But when God speaks and we don't listen, even God can't save us from ourselves'.

Another hint at an answer lies in the dreaded Starvation Cell in the basement of Block 11. This is where St Maximilian Kolbe died, having given his life for that of another man. It took the Franciscan a fortnight to perish but he encouraged the nine others sentenced with him to pray and sing hymns. It is one of the few places in the camp where there is religious symbolism—candles and a plaque left in his honour.

The other famous Christian martyr of Auschwitz is St Teresa Benedicta of the Cross (Edith Stein), the Jewish convert and philosopher who became a Carmelite nun. Her fate was that of so many others. In August 1942 she was transported from Holland in an over-crowded train. At Auschwitz, the new arrivals were quickly divided into two queues by an SS Doctor. One queue were considered fit for work, the other went immediately to the gas chamber. Of the 559 people who arrived on 9 August, about 350 were sent off to their deaths, including the saint. With her was a sister, Rosa, who was also a Christian convert and a Third Order Carmelite. In the convent in Holland where Edith spent the last period of her life, she worked as the porter. When the Nazis came to take them away, Edith held Rosa's hand and said 'Come, let us go for our people'. St Teresa Benedicta was able to send one last message to her prioress: 'I am content now. One can only learn the *Scientia Crucis* [the knowledge of the Cross] if one truly suffers under the weight of the Cross. I was entirely convinced of this from the very first, and I have said with all my heart: Hail, Cross, our only hope'.

There were other Catholic martyrs linked to Auschwitz. Blessed Katarzyna Celestyna Faron, a Polish Sister Servant of Mary Immaculate, had worked as a teacher and ran an orphanage before being arrested by the Gestapo. She arrived at Auschwitz on the Feast of the Epiphany 1943 and, like so many prisoners who avoided the gas chambers, was assigned to manual labour. She developed typhoid fever and tuberculosis but remained steadfast in her Faith, receiving much consolation when Holy Communion was smuggled to her by a prisoner priest on the Immaculate Conception. As she lay dying, she prayed on a rosary made of stale bread and offered her sufferings for the conversion of a priest she knew. She finally died on the morning of Easter Sunday 1944.

We should also not forget the German Trinitarian nun, Angela Maria Autsch, known as the 'Angel of Auschwitz'. She had been arrested after a careless incident while buying milk. In greeting an acquaintance, she mentioned that the allies had recently sunk a German ship off Norway and said that Hitler was a calamity for Europe. Word of this soon reached the Gestapo; she was sentenced to imprisonment in Innsbrück before being moved to Ravensbrück and finally Aushwitz. She showed great compassion for her fellow inmates, sharing her rations (which was strictly forbidden) and giving them comfort. Autsch finally died just before Christmas 1944—not in the gas chambers but of a heart attack during an allied air raid on the camp.

Auschwitz represents one of the lowest points in human history. Yet, despite the cold brutality, hope was never completely extinguished. And surely it can be no coincidence that just fifty miles away from this hellhole stands the shrine of the Divine Mercy. Evil has not had the final word. Love ultimately triumphs.

BRAN (ROMANIA)

The Legend of Dracula

The medieval Romanian fortress at Bran is billed to tourists as 'Dracula's Castle'. It certainly looks the part, with its turrets, towers and picturesque courtyard, all mounted on a rocky precipice, and the surrounding shops make the most of the connection. Bran is not mentioned in the novel *Dracula*, though Bram Stoker may have been inspired by an illustration he saw of the castle in a book on Tranyslvania. The famous Romanian who actually lived there was much more recent: Queen Marie, a granddaughter of Queen Victoria, who numbered the castle as one of her favourite residences. Confiscated under Communist rule, the castle was returned to her family in 2009 in the person of her grandson, Archduke Dominic von Habsburg.

Ever since Stoker published his novel in 1897, Dracula and his fellow vampires have been a constant presence not only in Romania but in literature, movies and TV. The vampire has appeared, as Van Helsing says in the novel, 'everywhere that men have been ... He have followed the wake of the berserker Icelander, the devil-begotten Hun, the Slav, the Saxon, the Magyar'.

Vampires were believed by many to have existed, especially in central and eastern Europe. There was a spate of reports from peasant communities in these remote areas in the seventeenth and eighteenth centuries that attracted the attentions of rulers and 'enlightened' thinkers. The Holy Roman Emperor, Charles VI, launched a public inquiry after rumours of vampirism led to mass hysteria in the village of Medvegia, near Belgrade, in 1731. Horace Walpole wrote that George II 'had no doubt of the existence of vampires, and their banquets on the dead' and the Benedictine scholar, Dom Augustine Calvet, included many of these stories in his *Treatise on the Apparitions of Spirits and on Vampires or Revenants of Hungary, Moravia, et al.* (1751).

Dracula is full of explicitly Catholic imagery. The count prefers the darkness to the light and for this reason is a creature of the night. He recognises the power of Catholic sacramentals, shunning the cross and rosary, holy water and, indeed, the Eucharist. There is that strange scene, deeply upsetting for Catholics and left out of most of the movies, where Van Helsing crumbles consecrated hosts and sprinkles them around him as a screen of protection. He claims a special permission to do so although in our eyes it seems a sickening desecration.

What is beyond reasonable doubt is that the inspiration behind Count Dracula really did exist: Vlad III 'the Impaler' (1431–76). He was ruler of Wallachia, to the east of Transylvania, and is still regarded there as something of a hero—which explains why *Dracula* was only translated into Romanian in 1990.

The name 'Dracula' has a Catholic origin. Around 1430 Vlad's father, who bore the same name, was inducted into the prestigious Order of the Dragon by Sigismund, King of Germany and Hungary (later Holy Roman Emperor). He had founded the Order on 12 December 1408 as a military order, similar to the Hospitallers and Templars. Its members included the chief nobles of the kingdom, as well as foreign allies such as Henry V of England and Vlad of Wallachia. With St George as its patron, its members aimed to fight the Turks, defend the kingdom of Hungary and protect the Catholic Church from heresy—although the Order was also open to Orthodox Christians such as Vlad. Members of the order wore a badge of the dragon, with the words *O quam misericors est Deus* (O how merciful is God!) and *Justus et Pius* (Just and Faithful), and a green cape worn over a red garment. On Fridays and in Passiontide they wore a black cape in honour of the Lord's passion. Next time you see Count Dracula, remember that the black cape originated in a Catholic order of knighthood.

However, the dragon was also a symbol of evil and on his return to Wallachia Vlad became known as 'Dracul' (Romanian for 'devil') and his son 'Dracula' ('son of the Dracul/devil').

Vlad 'Dracula' is remembered for his cruelty; political enemies and criminals invariably ended up being impaled and raised aloft in public places and some sources number his victims in the tens of thousands. Numbers may be exaggerated by German propaganda but it seems that Vlad was proud of the order achieved by his reign of terror; a golden cup was even placed in the central square of his capital, Târgoviste, for the use of thirsty travellers and was never stolen during his rule.

Vlad spent much of his life fighting the Turks. When Pope Pius II called for a new crusade at Mantua in 1459, following the capture of Constantinople six years previously, Vlad was one of the few to show any enthusiasm. There are many tales of his heroic exploits. In 1462 he captured the fortress of Giurgiu by disguising himself as a Turk and ordering the gates to be opened in fluent Turkish (for he had spent a period in Ottoman captivity). Soon afterwards there was a significant—though inconclusive—battle at Târgoviste. The sultan withdrew, having passed many of his men impaled on stakes by Dracula. Yet Vlad's tactics could be surprisingly modern—he was one of the first European leaders to use gunpowder and was not afraid to try 'biological warfare', sending people infected with the plague, leprosy and other deadly diseases into the midst of the enemy.

Dracula lost power to his younger brother but managed to escape from his castle into the mountains. To cut a long and complicated story short, he spent some time in captivity but eventually regained his freedom—some say through conversion to Catholicism—and (in 1476) his throne. After a few months, however, he was dead, reportedly killed by a Turkish assassin who then sent his head as a trophy to Constantinople. His body was probably buried in a nearby monastery that he had established—a reminder that Dracula founded over fifty churches and religious houses.

Vlad 'the Impaler' is indeed a complex figure, variously regarded as a heroic defender of Christendom and a bloodthirsty villain. We may never know the whole truth but it is clear that his legend will never die.

BUDAPEST (HUNGARY)

A Hungarian Coronation

Budapest really consists of three previously separate towns: Buda, Óbuda, and Pest, which were formally united in 1873. Much of Pest was rebuilt in the nineteenth century, including the magnificent neo-gothic Parliament building and St Stephen's Basilica. Buda feels more ancient: with the castle district, royal palace and Gellért Hill—named after the city's patron saint, who was flung into the Danube in a sealed barrel in 1046 after preaching the Gospel to the Magyars. There are popular baths and spas too, a remnant of the century and a half that the area was under Ottoman rule.

One of the great sights of Buda is the Mátyás Church, named not after the Evangelist but King Matthias Corvinus, who embellished it. He is remembered as a just monarch who brought the Renaissance to Hungary, gathering together one of the finest libraries of the period, the Bibliotheca Corviniana. Sadly, this was dispersed and much of it taken to Istanbul after the Ottoman defeated of the Hungarians at the battle of Mohács in 1526. Indeed, between 1541 and Buda's liberation in 1686, the Mátyás Church functioned as a mosque. The church subsequently underwent baroque and then neo-gothic renovations.

Walking round the church, my mind wandered to the dramatic ceremonies that had been witnessed by its venerable walls. This was, after all, where Hungarian coronations took place, the last being that of Blessed Charles (or Karl) Habsburg on 30 December 1916, in the midst of a world war. This event is not only interesting because it involved the earthly crowning of a future saint but because it was, in many ways, the last of the great European royal pageants.

The old Emperor of Austria and King of Hungary, Franz Joseph, died on 21 November 1916 after 68 years on the throne and was succeeded by his pious great-nephew, Archduke Charles. His coronation as King of Hungary was hurriedly organised since, according to the Hungarian constitution, the Austrian emperor only became King of Hungary once he had been crowned. In time of war and economic crisis there was, obviously, an urgent need for an active ruler who could enact any necessary laws. In particular the royal assent to the annual budget had to be obtained before the end of the year.

Preparations were quickly made. In the vivid language of historian Gordon Brook-Shepherd, 'bank vaults were opened for family tiaras;

wardrobes scoured for court dresses and trains which had languished for decades in moth-balls; and the old coaches were pulled out from the backs of stables and made roadworthy again'.

Finally, the great day arrived; it was cold and the streets of Budapest frozen. The royal couple arrived at the Mátyás Church in the Hungarian state coach, drawn by eight white horses, for the coronation ceremony, which took place in the context of Mass and lasted some three hours. At its heart, of course, were the king's vows to protect the Christian Faith, the Church and Hungary and then the placing of the Crown of St Stephen on his head. Made up of two medieval crowns—one Latin (given by the pope himself), the other Byzantine—it had a distinctive crooked cross, since it had been damaged in the seventeenth century. Judging from photographs, it was clearly too large for the young king. The crown had incredible historical and spiritual significance for Hungarians; it summed up Magyar kingship and nationality and, for this reason, it still appears on the country's coat of arms; indeed, it continues to be regarded as a 'legal person' and is carefully guarded in the Paliament's Domed Hall. It was said to have dated back to the time of St Stephen of Hungary and bore witness to his conversion and his gift of the kingdom to the Blessed Virgin Mary. Indeed, such was the pleasure of the pope that he gave St Stephen and his successors the title of 'His Royal Apostolic Majesty'.

As the crown was placed on the new king's head, recalled Count Miklos Banffy,

> a shaft of light shone through the window above the altar, a pale wintry ray but sunlight nevertheless, transforming the scene into a magical shining picture … The combination of the sunlight from outside and the electric glow of the chandeliers banished all shadows, metamorphosing the multiplicity of ritual hieratic garments … into one translucent, crystalline, unreal, angelic mist'. Indeed, 'in that resplendent, unreal, fairyland atmosphere no-one noticed the passing of time … there was music and song; and incense rose in clouds and dissolved in the high vaulting of the church.

The most dramatic part of the coronation ritual occurred outside. The newly crowned Charles IV mounted his horse and, while still wearing the sacred crown, had to gallop up the coronation hill (Diszter). This was made up of soil taken from each of the sixty-three counties of the kingdom. Once successfully on top of the ritual mound, he brandished the great coronation sword to all points of the compass, showing his resolve to protect Hungary and the Faith from their enemies.

According to Banffy, 'suddenly the mounted figure of the king emerged from the forest of banners in the square. Up the little balustraded hillock he rode. Then with the sword he slashed the air as a groom turned the charger's head to north and east and south and west, to the four corners of the world. A few moments the steed was once more led down into the crowd and the figure of the king lost to sight among the ceremonial banners. Not long afterwards ... with the joy of a job well accomplished, he emerged from the crowd ... waved a greeting to his wife ... and then quickly galloped away towards the palace'. He must have been deeply relieved that the crown had not fallen off.

Watching the grainy footage of the coronation, it may seem like a sad pantomime performed by a dying monarchy. The horrors of revolution, counter-revolution and Soviet control lay in the not-so-distant future. Blessed Charles, meanwhile, died in exile at the young age of 34, leaving behind a widow and eight children (the last of whom died in 2011). He had spent his brief reign pushing for peace; in the words of Anatole France, he was 'the only decent man to come out of the war in a leadership position, yet he was a saint and no one listened to him. He sincerely wanted peace, and therefore was despised by the whole world'.

His Christian faith was at the heart of everything he did; he attended Mass and prayed the rosary daily, went on pilgrimages whenever he had the opportunity and saw his family as a true domestic church. The crown he wore that day in Budapest was no empty piece of regalia. It called to mind his God-given vocation as a Christian monarch and formed a link with the great St Stephen. The seemingly quaint ceremonial bore witness to a deeply Christian concept of government, centred round the Gospel, and a devout if tragic monarch.

CZĘSTOCHOWA (POLAND)

Our Lady of Częstochowa

In a country of many holy places, the shrine of Our Lady at Częstochowa is Poland's spiritual capital. The city itself is not the most attractive place and, rather like Walsingham, public transport options are limited. Yet millions come here each year to venerate the 'Queen of Poland'.

The famous icon was traditionally attributed to St Luke, painted on the top of a table made by Jesus the Carpenter. Like many other venerable images, tradition has filled in the gaps in our knowledge and tells how it was discovered in Jerusalem by St Helen and kept for many centuries in Constantinople. We know for sure that the image, which is similar to many other Byzantine icons, was given to the Pauline monastery at Jasna Gora ('Bright Hill') in 1382 by its founder, Duke Ladislaus of Opole.

There are two things that you immediately notice about the image. Firstly, that the face is dark, one of the so-called 'Black Madonnas'. This is in contrast to the rich, colourful 'robe' normally placed over it; those that are not in use are displayed in the museum, one of which includes not only a fragment of the plane that crashed near Smolensk in 2010, killing the Polish President and 95 others, but meteorites, making it truly 'out of this world'. The dark appearance of Mary's face probably originated from age, dust and soot. But it was seen as appropriate because of the verse in the Song of Songs, where the 'Beloved' says 'I am dark but beautiful' (*Nigra sum sed formosa*). Some have suggested that this expresses Mary's closeness to the Lord. When something is very close to the source of light, it will appear dark. So with Mary, as she sits beside the Light of the World. And that is the point of the icon: Mary is pointing to her Son, leading us to Him; 'to Jesus, through Mary'.

The image is also damaged. Just before being given to Jasna Gora, it was caught up in a Tatar attack and the Virgin's throat was struck by an arrow. Likewise, the image was desecrated in 1430 by robbers (often described as Hussite heretics), one of whom struck the image several times with his sword. Though the perpetrator died on the spot, the sword cuts can still be seen. Restorers have tried to cover them up but they have never disappeared. In artistic terms it may seem like an unfortunate blemish but, in truth, it deepens the power of the image—this is a Mother who suffers and fights battles alongside her children. The image of Częstochowa, warts and all, has become intertwined with Polish history. She bears the country's wounds as well as its triumphs. We see this in her subsequent history.

In 1655 the Swedish troops besieged Jasna Gora during the 'Second Northern War'. This conflict between Sweden (one of the superpowers of the seventeenth century) and Poland-Lithuania and her allies is little known in this country but Poles refer to it as 'the Swedish Deluge'—a term popularised by Henryk Sienkiewicz in his 1886 novel *The Deluge*. Crossing the Polish border in July 1655, Charles X Gustav of Sweden quickly took Warsaw, Poznań and Kraków. However Częstochowa unexpectedly proved a harder nut to crack. This was due to the spirit of its defenders and the fact that the monastery and shrine, located in a strategic position near the Silesian border, had become something of a 'Marian Fortress' (*Fortalitium Marianum*) in previous decades, with walls, earthworks and bastions.

During the siege, Jasna Gora was defended by 20 Polish nobles, 160 soldiers and 70 of the monks who had had previous military experience, under the leadership of the prior Fr Augustyn Kordecki. They faced a mighty Swedish army of over 2,000. However the defenders sang hymns to Our Lady in the midst of battle and on one occasion a cannon ball, about to strike the shrine chapel, 'turned back toward the enemy camp, as if it had been touched by an invisible force, spreading a terrible fire through the air'. The Swedes eventually withdrew and, the following year at Lvov, King John II Casimir placed the Polish-Lithuanian Commonwealth under the protection of the Blessed Virgin as 'Queen of the Polish Crown and of his other countries'.

In 1683 the Turks were decisively defeated at Vienna, thanks largely to the intervention of the Poles under Jan III Sobieski. He prayed at Częstochowa before the campaign and returned there in thanksgiving afterwards. More recently in 1920, when the Russians invaded Poland, Our Lady of Częstochowa was invoked by the defenders of Warsaw and some reported seeing in the skies above; the resulting victory was known as the 'Miracle on the River Vistula'. During the Soviet occupation, she retained her popularity in Polish hearts. In 1956 Cardinal Stefan Wyszyński wrote a new set of national vows while in captivity, renewing the ones made at Lviv in 1656. A million pilgrims attended the ceremony and, as a bishop proclaimed the vows at Częstochowa, Wyszyński made them in his cell before a copy of the icon. Ten years later the shrine was at the centre of the millennium celebrations of the country's conversion to Christianity.

Pilgrims flock to Jasna Gora as individuals, groups or as part of walking pilgrimages, such as the one made annually from Warsaw.

Pilgrims have included St John Paul II, Benedict XVI and Francis, all of whom left the prestigious papal gift of the 'Golden Rose'. Pius XI and St John XXIII also visited before their elections, and St Paul VI was only prevented from making a pilgrimage by the Communist authorities.

Our Lady of Częstochowa is still known as 'Queen of Poland'. In 1979 St John Paul II said that she 'has revealed her maternal *solicitude* for every soul; for every family; for *every human being* living in this land, working here, fighting and falling on the battlefield, condemned to extermination, fighting against himself, winning or losing'. At Częstochowa 'we have always been free'; 'you need to lend an ear to this sacred spot to hear the heartbeat of the nation in the heart of the Mother!' He noted that 'the Poles are accustomed to link with this shrine, the many happenings of their lives: the various joyful or sad moments ... They are accustomed to come with their problems to Jasna Gora to speak of them with their heavenly Mother, who not only has her image here ... but *is specially present here*'.

As we prayed in the shrine chapel, surrounded by the singing of Polish hymns and rows of *ex votos* and rosaries on the walls, we reflected that this image belongs not just to Poland but to Christians everywhere. Mary is our Mother and the scars on her face are a sign of our own scars—the scars of failure and bitterness, of sickness and bereavement, of disappointment and betrayal. We pass them to Mary so that she can hand them to her Son. *Totus tuus, Maria.*

DUBROVNIK (CROATIA)

City of St Blaise

The charming walled city of Dubrovnik—the 'Queen of the Adriatic' and for centuries the capital of the Republic of Ragusa—is also the city of St Blaise. He is best known as the saint whose speciality is diseases of the throats. Many of us gratefully received his blessing on his feast, hoping our throats would be preserved from the perils of the winter. Indeed, in Spain tonsillitis is sometimes referred to as the 'curse of St Blaise'.

However, little is actually known of St Blaise. He seems to have been Bishop of Sebastea (Armenia) who was martyred under Diocletian, on or around 3 February 316. He was beheaded, some say after being tortured by wool combs (hence his patronage of wool-combers). One legend has him trying to escape his persecutors by hiding in a cave, where he befriended various wild animals. He was eventually found by hunters, who handed him over to the authorities, but as he was led away he tamed a wolf that had carried off an old lady's pig. She visited him in prison, bringing food and candles. It was in prison also that St Blaise cured a boy who had a fish bone stuck in his throat. These two later episodes are memorialised each year by the blessing of throats while candles are held under the recipient's chin: 'Through the intercession of St Blaise may God deliver you from all evils of the throat and every other evil'.

But how did devotion to St Blaise or 'Sveti Vlaho' reach the city of Dubrovnik? On the night of 2 February 971 one of the cathedral canons, Stojko, was returning from a walk when he noticed that the church doors were wide open. Venturing inside, he saw an old man who identified himself as St Blaise and said, 'I come to warn you of great danger for the city'. Beyond the city walls, in the darkness of the Adriatic, a Venetian fleet was anchored with the intention of taking the city by surprise. Stojko raised the alarm, defences were heightened and the Venetians withdrew.

It is little surprise that St Blaise quickly became the city's protector and the identities of both became virtually indistinguishable. His patronage was not simply a matter of devotion; there was a political dimension as St Blaise became a symbol of freedom against the threats of Venetians, Turks or any other enemy. Dubrovnik enjoyed the status of a self-governing city state for much of its history. As recently as the

1990s, it continued this tradition by withstanding a nine-month siege from the Serbians and Montenegrins. No wonder St Blaise seems as popular as ever.

Since at least 1190 his feast in Dubrovnik has been celebrated with much pageantry, being recognised by UNESCO in 2009 as an example of the Intangible Cultural Heritage of Humanity. There are brass bands and church bells and volleys from the *trombunjeri*, the city's distinctive musketeers. After a Solemn Mass, there is a procession down the city's main street, the Stradun, with the relics of the saint's head, larynx, foot and right hand. Added to this is the other great spiritual treasure of Dubrovnik: Christ's swaddling clothes.

St Blaise is popular in other countries too—in Italy, France and, indeed, England, especially given his association with wool-combers. In Cornwall there is a village named 'St Blazey' and even a tradition that the saint made a visit to the West Country, teaching the locals the secrets of the wool trade! In London there is a medieval wall painting of the saint at All Saints, Kingston-upon-Thames, and in Bromley you can find St Blaise's Well—in the Middle Ages there was a chapel here and pilgrims could obtain a papal indulgence. The blessing of throats enjoyed a modern renaissance through the efforts of the Rosminians at St Etheldreda's, Ely Place, from about 1876 and since has spread to churches throughout the land.

ESZTERGOM (HUNGARY)

The Hungarian Relics of Becket

May 2016: it was the most English of events, with the ceremonial splendour of Westminster Cathedral and William Byrd's famous setting of the *Mass for Four Voices* honouring a martyred archbishop of Canterbury. It had a distinctive Hungarian flavouring, with the Mass being celebrated by the Primate of that country, Cardinal Péter Erdő, in the presence of the President, János Áder. The front section of the cathedral contained representatives of the Hungarian community, staff from the embassy and presidential bodyguards scanning the packed congregation. And so 'Becket Week' began, designed to strengthen relations between the two countries and honour the twelfth-century saint.

At the heart of proceedings was a relic—a fragment of bone from St Thomas's arm, venerated for centuries at Esztergom, the ecclesiastical centre of Hungary. To this day, a small hill behind the cathedral is known as 'St Thomas's Hill'; a 1595 engraving of the siege of that city identifies it as 'Thomasberg'. A provostal church was built there, dedicated to the English martyr, with a chapter of six canons. The chapel was destroyed during the Ottoman occupation of the city in the sixteenth century but a new chapel was built near the site in 1823, dedicated to Our Lady of Sorrows.

The origins of the Hungarian cult of St Thomas are obscure but most likely originated with Archbishop Lukács of Esztergom, who may have known the saint personally and lived a remarkably similar life, even though a martyr's crown eluded him. Like Becket, he fought hard for the Church's rights and prerogatives against undue state interference, constantly stressing the primacy of the spiritual power. After the death of Géza II he refused to crown his younger brother, László II, and supported the claims of Stephen III, the dead king's son. He interdicted a fellow bishop who had unlawfully performed the coronation. After a brief imprisonment, Archbishop Lukács stormed into the royal chapel and confronted the king publicly. Further conflicts led him to refuse to crown, in turn, Stephen IV and Béla III. It is no wonder that St Thomas, who had shown similar resilience in challenging royal authority, quickly became one of his patrons.

Another early promoter of the cult was Margaret of France, who had been married to Henry the Young King, son of Henry II and, for a time, co-ruler. His coronation was, perversely, one of the contributing factors leading to St Thomas's martyrdom—the archbishop fiercely condemned the ceremony, for he was then in exile and it was his prerogative to crown a monarch. He even excommunicated those bishops that had taken part, further strengthening the stalemate between king and archbishop. Margaret went on to marry Béla III after the young king's death and kept the martyr's memory with great reverence.

St Thomas was canonised in 1173 and his body translated to a new shrine at Canterbury in 1220. On that occasion there was at least one Hungarian bishop present, who may have taken relics back with him. The earliest surviving inventory of Esztergom Cathedral only dates from 1528, but this confirms that the relics were present there before the destruction of St Thomas's shrine in Canterbury at the Reformation. They also survived the Turkish occupation.

The martyr's cult declined, especially with the destruction of the chapel on 'St Thomas's Hill', and many simply assumed that this location took its name from the apostle. It was not until 1930 that a scholar rediscovered the connection with the English saint. Devotion enjoyed an unexpected revival during the Communist era, Christians honouring St Thomas for his fearless struggle against the tyranny of his day. From the 1970s a candle lighting service took place each 29 December, St Thomas's day, with the veneration of his relics.

The story of St Thomas does not just belong to England but to the whole Christian world. His legacy carried on to this day and his battles on behalf of the Church's freedom continue to be fought. During the Mass at Westminster Cathedral, I thought of another great Hungarian event to be held there—the visit of Cardinal József Mindszenty in July 1973. I was not privileged to be there but my father was and he often spoke of the excitement of seeing a living martyr, who had suffered so much behind the Iron Curtain. On this occasion, Cardinal Heenan spoke in strong terms: 'We who live in liberty must not rest while men and women of any religion are persecuted'. Mindszenty followed in the footsteps of St Thomas (and, indeed, Archbishop Lukács) as a champion of religious liberty and truth. Declared a 'Venerable' in 2019, his tomb can be found in the crypt of the basilica at Esztergom.

GYŐR (HUNGARY)

Hungary's Irish Madonna

It was only on a whim that we decided to visit the northern Hungarian city of Győr. Driving back from a day trip to Bratislava, across the Slovak border, we had an hour or two to kill. The guide book suggested that Győr was a place of moderate interest, situated halfway between Vienna and Budapest. But guide books do not always tell the whole truth.

The historic centre was full of unexpected delights—picturesque streets, magnificent squares, even a baroque monument showing angels holding the Ark of the Covenant. This was erected in reparation after the Blessed Sacrament was attacked during the Corpus Christi procession in 1727. The cathedral itself contains one of the great relics of Hungary: the head of St Ladislaus, second only to St Stephen in fame as a saintly king.

The reliquary bust had been moved to a smaller chapel near the Bishop's Palace due to restoration work in the cathedral. And next to it was the city's other great sacred treasure. It was one of those 'eureka' moments when the inter-connectedness of Catholic Europe is vividly demonstrated and I could hardly believe my eyes. Here, in a little-known corner of Transdanubia, there is a living devotion to 'the Weeping Irish Madonna'.

There was even a lavishly illustrated hardback book in English detailing the history of the devotion to this 'Consoler of the Afflicted'. I felt obliged to buy a copy, though I wondered how many had flown off the shelves of the little shop this past year. It seems that Irish pilgrims do indeed make their way to Győr—making me feel ashamed of my ignorance—and the connection is much celebrated: 'many parallels have been drawn between Hungary and Ireland', the publicity said, 'two nations submitted for centuries to foreign dominance, which degraded true life to mere survival ... Both countries dedicated to the Virgin Mary'.

The west coast of Ireland seems a long way from Hungary, for the story of the 'Weeping Madonna' begins in Galway. The Bishop of Clonfert, Walter Lynch, a member of one of the county's leading families, fled overseas in 1651 in the face of Cromwell's forces. The escape was full of drama: English artillery fired on the ship as it left Irish shores, Lynch was wounded, as was one of his episcopal companions who died a few days later. Those who survived reached the island of Inisbofin and appealed to the pope himself: 'we spend our days in the woods so that the sword of our persecutors does not find us ... Famine, thirst, and frequent sickness are the ordinary guests of ours, hard stone our pillow, rain or moist fog our cushion'. Eventually the refugees reached the comparative safety of Flanders. Lynch remained there for a time before moving on to the imperial city of Vienna.

Bishop Lynch had one great consolation. He had taken with him a much-treasured painting of Our Lady with her divine Child. It was not Irish in origin—probably acquired by the Lynch family in Spain, Portugal or France—but it had hung in a place of honour either in Clonfert or Galway. Indeed, in the church of St Nicholas, Galway, where the family have their vault, there is an empty stone frame that some believe once contained the 'Weeping Madonna'.

In Vienna, Bishop Lynch met the Bishop of Győr, János Püsky, who invited him to his city. The Bishop of Clonfert was duly appointed a canon, worked as an unofficial auxiliary bishop and finally found some security. He did not forget his Irish diocese, however. In 1661 he decided to appoint an Irish priest also living in Győr, Thomas Burke, as his Vicar General and sent him back to Clonfert. The Chapter refused to accept him and an ugly exchange of letters followed between Győr and Clonfert, leading to the excommunication of Archdeacon Kelly. Bishop Lynch realised that he himself needed to travel to Ireland to restore order. Alas, before he could set out on the risky journey, he died unexpectedly and was buried in Győr Cathedral. His beloved image of Our Lady was placed nearby.

Fast forward to 1697. It was a difficult year for Irish Catholics, seeing the passing of several penal laws, including 'An Act for banishing all Papists exercising any Ecclesiastical Jurisdiction and all Regulars of the Popish Clergy out of this Kingdom'. Meanwhile in Győr, it was noticed early on the morning of St Patrick's Day, while Mass was being offered in the cathedral, that the Irish Madonna wept tears of blood. 'Immediately the multitude swarmed about the place', we read, 'the wall was dry, and the image not only continued to weep, but was wet with sweat of blood. The drops were wiped with pure white cambric, but the image painted on the canvas wept again'.

There was an episcopal investigation and soon a new altar was commissioned for the miraculous image. Veneration spread through Hungary and copies of the image were erected in many churches in the surrounding area and even as far afield as the Bavarian village of Ringelai. During the Communist era Our Lady of Győr took on a special importance, especially during the 250th anniversary celebrations. 'O Mary!', read the prayer composed for that occasion, 'once again turn thy tear-covered eyes towards our suffering Church and our Hungarian Fatherland beset by such great distress. Have mercy on us!'

It was only during the bicentenary celebrations of 1897, however, that contact was made with the Bishop of Clonfert. Since then there has been growing Irish interest in the devotion and the organisation of pilgrimages. Churches have been dedicated to Our Lady of Győr, 'Consoler of the Afflicted', in Donnycarney, Dublin (1969) and Fahy, Clonfert (1970).

Our Lady thus provides an unexpected link between the peoples of Hungary and Ireland, who turn to her as a Heavenly Consoler as they faced the afflictions presented to any nation through the course of history.

LJUBLJANA (SLOVENIA)

Here be Dragons

As capitals go, Ljubljana is surprisingly compact. Topped by a castle and traversed by the Ljubljanica river, it is a city of bridges and colourful baroque churches, of green spaces and a mountainous backdrop. The ubiquitous dragon—the city's symbol—calls to mind the beast killed nearby by Jason and the Argonauts, who is supposed to have founded the city. The defeated monster is now seen as its protector, and is found everywhere: on heraldry, souvenirs, buildings, pavements, and, of course, the popular Dragon Bridge. There is even a Dragon Carnival each year.

Slovenia traverses western and eastern Europe. For much of the second millennium a large part of it was under Habsburg rule, as part of Carniola—one of those territories that English-readers occasionally come across in history books and vaguely understand as being somewhere east of Vienna. At the Reformation, Ljubljana (or Laibach) was an example of a majority Protestant population that was won back to Catholicism through the policies of the Habsburgs and the efforts of the religious orders. This is evidenced by the city's sanctuaries, such as the pink Franciscan church, the old Jesuit church of St Joseph or the Ursuline church, with its impressive facade.

Walking round the picturesque city centre, it is easy to forget the faultlines in Ljubljana's more recent history (as with the rest of the former Yugoslavia). There have been periods of oppression and bloodshed. Remembered with special affection is Anton Vovk, the great nephew of the famous Slovenian poet, France Prešeren. Appointed as auxiliary bishop in 1945, he courageously stood up to the post-war Communist regime in Yugoslavia. It was a time when clergy were regularly arrested and interrogated—339 Slovenian priests between 1945 and 1961 received prison sentences and four were executed. The authorities undertook an intensive effort to 'de-christianise' the population, banning religious gatherings and processions, confiscating books, seizing ecclesiastical property and limiting religious education. Special collections were forbidden and the people were only allowed to support priests that belonged to the Association of Catholic Priests of SS Cyril and Methodius, which had been set up by the government and caused a division between ordinary and so-called 'patriotic' clergy.

As the de facto leader of Slovenian Catholics, Vovk was carefully watched by the state; members of the secret police would attend his parish visitations and confirmations, search his office and read his letters. He was interrogated at least 90 times, questioned about his links to the Vatican and any attempt to work against the regime (and therefore act against 'the people'). He was encouraged on several occasions to create a 'national' church, more firmly under state control, but Vovk refused to compromise.

Pressure was put on him by targeting and imprisoning priests close to him, such as his trusty secretary, Božidar Slapšak. 'We know you would like to be put into prison', he was told on one occasion. 'That would please the Nuncio and the Vatican, who would write all about it and explain the reason another bishop had been locked up in Slovenia. We do not wish to give them this pleasure. Just be aware of the consequences of your own deeds'.

There were attempts on his life, most notably on 20 January 1952, as he travelled by train to bless a newly renovated organ in a church in the foothills of the mountains. As the train passed through a tunnel, a foul-smelling liquid was poured over him. Then, after alighting at his destination, he was surrounded by a mob, doused with petrol and set alight, to the chants of 'Burn, devil, burn!' It took hours for help to arrive and Vovk was left with serious burns and lifelong scars. The authorities presented it as an unfortunate incident, though evidence shows that it was carefully orchestrated by the secret police.

In 1959 Vovk was named Bishop of Ljubljana (elevated to archbishop two years later). When he met Pope St John XXIII shortly afterwards, he apologised for not being able to kneel due to his poor health. 'No', the pope replied, 'I should kneel before you'. He died four years later and many hope he will one day be honoured as a saint, a reminder of the dragons that have been fought in the city's recent past.

MARIJA BISTRICA (CROATIA)

'Queen of the Croats'

The Croatian shrine of Marija Bistrica is probably little known to most readers. I had never heard of it until I stumbled across it during a drive from Budapest to Zagreb. We thought that the shrine, located 23 miles from the capital, might constitute a useful stopping place and give a little taste of rural Croatia. Situated on the slopes of Mount Medvednica ('Bear Mountain'), the sat. nav. took us on a rather complex route through lush green fields, tiny villages and windy mountain tracks. Finally we reached a more substantial road and spotted the nineteenth-century pilgrimage church in the distance. On the square outside there were rows of stalls selling candles and gingerbread hearts; inside the basilica three pilgrims knelt singing a hymn to Our Lady in beautiful and moving harmony.

The little statue of Our Lady of Bistrica was probably made in the fifteenth century. Kept originally in a small wooden chapel near the site of the present shrine, the 'Black Madonna' had to be hidden by the parish priest in 1545 due to the constant threat from the Turks. Unfortunately the priest never revealed the location of the hiding place and his secret went with him to the grave. Those who had prayed before the statue searched for it to no avail. Then in 1588 a strange light was seen in the choir of the parish church and, on investigation, the image was finally discovered. Our Lady of Bistrica was once again given a place of honour.

The region continued to suffer from Turkish raids and in 1650 the statue had to again be safely stored away. It was placed behind the high altar and walled in, though with a window so that the Virgin's face could be seen. One Sunday, it is related, while the priest was preaching on the virtues of St Francis Xavier, a woman of noble appearance, dressed in blue garments and holding a lit candle, approached the pulpit and asked the priest to pray for her sight. The priest saw the same lady later that day as he travelled to a nearby house. When he tried speaking to her, she instantly disappeared. No one ever discovered who the mysterious lady was but some thought it was Our Lady herself, asking for her statue to be 'liberated' and her 'sight' restored.

With the turnover of successive priests and the violence and instability of the times, the 'Black Madonna' came to be forgotten until July 1684, when it was 'discovered' a second time and a local girl cured of paralysis. News quickly spread of the miracle and pilgrimages began to be promoted. A new church was constructed in the baroque style, as was a special road to accommodate the many pilgrims who came from Zagreb. One eighteenth-century chaplain, Petar Berke, produced a pilgrim's prayer book in the local dialect and a more weighty volume, *Miraculous Appearances and Graces* (1765), which told the history of the shrine. An indulgence granted to pilgrims by Benedict XIV in 1750 was a further boon.

Despite its popularity, the shrine has had to face the vicissitudes of history. A 1774 imperial decree of Joseph II forbade pilgrimages lasting more than a day in order to increase the productivity of the peasantry and avoid occasions for disorder. The bishop appealed and eventually an exception was made for Bistrica since pilgrims came not only from Croatia but from all around—from Slavonia, Stryia, Hungary, Bosnia and Illyria. Indeed, the shrine was a point of unity within the empire.

Disaster nearly struck on the Eve of the Assumption 1880, when fire broke out while important work was being done on the extension of the church. The whole interior was destroyed, although the statue survived the flames—many thought miraculously. The shrine was rebuilt; in 1923 it became a minor basilica and twelve years later Our Lady was solemnly crowned as 'Queen of the Croats'.

The twentieth century, of course, brought many further challenges, as the Croatians found themselves under Nazi and then Communist regimes. Under the latter, religious education was banned from schools, church property confiscated, pilgrimages restricted and at least 500 priests and religious executed. The Archbishop of Zagreb, Blessed Alozije Stepinac, was arrested and condemned to sixteen years hard labour. From the mid-1960s, however, conditions began to improve and in August 1971 an International Marian Congress was held at the shrine, attended by 126 theologians from 30 countries and some 150,000 pilgrims—a most uncommon spectacle in a Communist country! St Paul VI spoke to the crowds thanks to Vatican Radio; diplomatic relations had only recently been restored between the Holy See and Yugoslavia. It was a decisive moment in reasserting the region's Catholic identity. Appropriately enough, the Archbishop of Zagreb gave an address on 'The Tribulations of Croatia and the Virgin Mary'; just as she had protected the Croats from invasion in the past now she was interceding for their greater religious and personal freedom.

Shortly afterwards, Marija Bistrica was recognised by the local bishops as Croatia's National Marian shrine. The shrine complex was enlarged, with an outdoor Way of the Cross and a chapel with two floors of confessionals. Further red letter days were provided by the National Eucharistic Congress in 1984 and the visit of St John Paul II in 1998, on which occasion he beatified Cardinal Stepinac, who had been a great devotee of Our Lady of Bistrica.

The little image of Our Lady stands at the centre of this vibrant hillside shrine. She has guided the Croats through many tribulations and heard the muttered prayers of hundreds of thousands of pilgrims. As the inscription on one of the walls puts it: 'The soul of Croatia, the Mother of Jesus, the sun during our sufferings, do not stop shining!'

PERAST (MONTENEGRO)

Our Lady of the Rocks

Montenegro is 'the land of the Black Mountain'. Ever since watching the Bond film *Casino Royale* (2006), which was partly set there, I had wanted to see the stunning scenery for myself. The country is 4 % Catholic—religion in these parts depends more on ethnicity than geography; most Catholics are Croats and can be found (as one might expect) near the Croatian border. This is an area of great natural beauty. The Bay of Kotor (Boka Kotorska) contains nooks and crannies with delightful historic towns, all against the magnificent backdrop of mountains plummeting into the waters. Byron thought it was 'the most beautiful encounter between the land and the sea'.

Stopping for lunch at the village of Perast which, our guide book told us, resembled a little piece of Venice transplanted to the other side of the Adriatic, we noticed two islands with churches on them. One, it turned out, contained the local cemetery and was full of cypress trees, which in the Mediterranean fulfils the function of our yew. The other was man-made and housed the shrine of 'Our Lady of the Rocks'. A little boat made a regular voyage there and back. We decided to discover more.

According to tradition, a painting of Our Lady was found by some fishermen in 1452 on some rocks where the shrine now stands. The image was taken to one of their homes and miracles were soon attributed to Our Lady's intercession. Gradually, over time, the rock where the picture was found grew into an island thanks to the transportation of large stones and a church was built.

It is no surprise that devotion to 'Our Lady of the Rocks' is particularly fervent among seafarers in these parts. Ships were named after her and when passing by the island of her shrine would fire a gun salute and raise a flag three times, while the church's bells would ring. Even to this day vessels honk their horns when passing. One of the distinctive characteristics of the shrine is a unique collection of over two thousand *ex voto* images on silver plates, showing many examples of Mary's intercession when danger was faced at sea. There are ships tossing in violent storms, sailors being thrown aboard, vessels sinking and the constant danger of pirate raids. Many contain the inscription *Votum Feci Gratiam Accepi*, 'I made an oath and received the grace'.

Today the bay seems utterly peaceful but it was not always so. The Balkans constituted a frontier land between cultures and religions; from a Catholic point of view, it was where Western Christendom stopped and the lands of Orthodox Christianity and Islam began. For many centuries Perast—or 'Perasto'—was under the rule of Venice. Indeed, the town was the last to lower the Venetian flag in 1797 when the Serene Republic surrendered to Napoleon. This Italian legacy continues to this day in the wide range of pastas available at local restaurants, including the famous black risotto made from squid ink.

One of the more impressive *ex voto* images at the shrine involves the battle of Perast on 15 May 1654, when the Turks attacked the town and its outlying islands. The citizens were vastly outnumbered but, while about 72 Turks were killed and perhaps 300 injured, the defenders only suffered two casualties. The attackers eventually withdrew and the victory at Perast became the talk of Europe. It is commemorated each year by a procession of the image through the streets and then by boat to the shrine, accompanied by armed guard—a stark reminder that the peaceful waters can prove to be very dangerous indeed.

There were smaller naval skirmishes and constant raids by pirates—not of the Blackbeard or Captain Hook type but mostly corsairs from North Africa, in search of treasure and slaves ('white gold'). In June 1624, for example, sixteen galleys pillaged Perast and its churches and took much of the population into slavery. Such small-scale localised attacks were a problem across Europe until the eighteenth century, as we have already seen with regard to the Algarve.

Over the centuries, Mary's intercession has helped both individual believers in their fight against sin and Christians as a whole in their struggle for survival against external threats. Our Lady of the Rocks is one of many examples all over the Catholic world of this trust in Mary's protection, thanks to her closeness to her Son.

PRAGUE (CZECHIA)

Windows and Bridges

The Czech capital of Prague has so much to offer the tourist and pilgrim: the iconic Charles Bridge, the astronomical clock on the Old Town Hall, the numerous churches and the poignant Jewish Quarter, with Europe's oldest active synagogue. Catholics will try to visit the shrine of the Infant Jesus—tucked away on a side altar in Our Lady of Victories and yet famous across the world, including Ireland, where statues are often placed in windows and have a close connection with the weather.

Among the statues on the Charles Bridge is that of St John Nepomucene, who is greatly venerated in these parts—indeed, travelling around Central Europe one often sees his image on or near bridges. Typically, he is dressed in a cassock, cotta and biretta, carries a crucifix and sometimes holds a finger against his lips. Born in the 1340s he studied at the Universities of Prague and Padua and was ordained as a priest. He acted as Vicar General in Prague and, most famously, was murdered by King Wenceslaus (not to be confused with the saintly king of that name) on 20 March 1393. After being seized by the king's men and tortured, he was thrown off the Charles Bridge. Look carefully and you will see a cross marking the spot where this atrocity occurred. According to tradition, five stars appeared over the River Vltava that night and these have often been included by artists to form his halo.

There is some confusion about why exactly he was put to death so violently. The standard account explains that he acted as confessor to the king's wife. Wenceslaus suspected that the queen was having an affair and was enraged when St John refused to break the seal of the confessional. This may not have been the only reason why he got himself into the king's bad books. The late fourteenth century was a complex time politically, with Christendom divided between rival popes. The saint, along with his archbishop, supported Boniface IX in Rome, while Wenceslaus backed the anti-pope in Avignon, Clement VII.

Canonised in 1729, it is little surprise that he became such a popular saint. The Jesuits in particular promoted the cause since his witness tied in neatly with many of the concerns of the 'Counter-Reformation'—the stress on the sacrament of confession, for example, and papal authority. St John was also useful in countering interest in another Czech 'John': the heretic John Huss, burned at the stake in 1415, who had in fact been supported by King Wenceslaus. Many saw Huss not only as a proto-Protestant but as a national hero, as can be seen in the modern statue in the centre of Prague's Old Town Square. The omnipresence of Nepomuk's image, however, reveals that he too has become a true Czech hero.

One of the most significant sights in Prague from a historical point of view is an unassuming window in the Old Royal Palace. Just off the majestic Vladislav Hall, where kings were elected and presidents inducted, is the Chancellery. It was out of one of the windows here—there is some doubt as to which was the exact one—three men were thrown on 23 May 1618. Although they survived the 70-foot drop, this outrage precipitated the Thirty Years' War, one of the bloodiest conflicts of European history.

Curiously, the story of Prague is marked by at least two other 'defenestrations'. In July 1419 Jan Želivský, a radical Hussite (part of a reform movement that prefigured Protestantism), and his supporters raided the town hall after a stone was apparently thrown at them from a window. Several officials were consequently thrown to their deaths. Another Defenestration occurred centuries later, in March 1948, when the then Foreign Minister and former ambassador to the United Kingdom, Jan Masaryk, was found dead in the courtyard of the Černínský Palace, still dressed in his pyjamas and below his bathroom window. Explained away as suicide, many had their doubts and the joke made the rounds that 'Jan Masaryk was a very tidy man. He was such a tidy man that when he jumped he shut the window after himself'.

It is the Defenestration of 1618 that concerns us here. The events leading up to it are admittedly highly complex. Bohemia, of which Prague was the capital, formed part of the Holy Roman Empire, a network of kingdoms, principalities, counties, free cities and ecclesiastical territories stretching across Central Europe and owing allegiance ultimately to an elected emperor. Despite its name, not all of its subjects were Catholic; indeed, in Bohemia Protestants were in the majority. The Peace of Augsburg of 1555 granted some religious toleration but much depended on the faith of the local ruler: *cuius regio, eius religio* ('whose realm, his religion'). Despite this, tensions continued, especially in 'hotspots' such as Bohemia. In 1609 the Emperor, Rudolf II, was persuaded to issue a 'Letter of Majesty' granting religious toleration, but he was never fully trusted. His successor, Matthias, showed himself more progressive in his views, but being childless (like Rudolf) he chose a cousin, Ferdinand of Styria, to be his successor. Ferdinand was a zealous supporter of the Catholic Reformation and wanted to crush all religious dissent within the empire. In 1618 he used his influence to halt the construction of Lutheran churches in Catholic ecclesiastical territories. When the Bohemian Estates (or Parliament) protested, it was dissolved.

The meeting at Prague's Royal Palace that May morning in 1618 was thus highly fraught with tension. Protestant members of the Estates accused two of the emperor's representatives of masterminding this change in policy: 'you are enemies of us and of our religion, have desired to deprive us of our Letter of Majesty, have horribly plagued your Protestant subjects ... and have tried to force them to adopt your religion against their wills or have had them expelled for this reason'.

So it was that Jaroslav Borita von Martinitz, Vilém Slavata and Philipp Fabricius (a secretary) found themselves being thrown out of the window. Fabricius even managed to land on his feet. Supporters saw their survival as miraculous, especially since Martinitz was reported to have called on the blessed Virgin as he fell. Protestant propaganda quickly responded that they survived only because they landed on a dung heap and this version quickly became part of the accepted account. Modern historians have speculated that the cloaks worn by the three men may have played a role, for (as Peter H. Wilson writes) 'it had been a cool morning and with typical Habsburg parsimony the room had been unheated, obliging the Regents to retain their thick cloaks and hats'.

After the defenestration, war was perhaps an inevitability and both sides began to gather forces. The following year Matthias died and was finally succeeded by Ferdinand II, who gained the support of France, Spain and the Papacy. Ferdinand was already King of Bohemia—this was a title in its own right, though often held by the Holy Roman Emperor—but the Bohemian Estates now refused to recognise him as such. They elected their own 'king', a card-carrying Protestant: Frederick V of the Palatinate, one of the senior princes or 'Electors' of the Empire. He was known as the 'Winter King', since his sojourn in Bohemia only lasted one winter (1619–20), and he brought with him his British bride, Elizabeth Stuart, daughter of James I, and a growing family, including the young Prince Rupert. Another child, yet to be born, was Sophie, who would form the link between the Stuarts and the Hanoverians: her son would become George I.

On 8 November 1620 the Imperial army decisively defeated Frederick at Bílá Hora (White Mountain), now a suburb of Prague. A church dedicated to Our Lady of Victories was built on the battlefield, since the Catholic troops attributed their success to her intercession. Indeed, a Marian image seemingly desecrated by Calvinists was carried in front of the Catholic army. The battle was a decisive moment in Czech history. Ringleaders were executed, the majority of the nobility exiled, Protestant worship banned and Czech culture quickly overshadowed by the now-predominant German one.

However, the battle proved not to be decisive in the war, which dragged on until 1648. There were atrocities on both sides, whole regions were depopulated and it was not until the beginning of the eighteenth century that the population of the Holy Roman Empire recovered to its pre-war level. Peace allowed extensive rebuilding in the baroque and rococo styles—one reason why almost every town and village in Central Europe has a church dating from the period.

SOFIA (BULGARIA)

'Serdica is my Rome'

Bulgaria is a largely unknown country to most of us. Perhaps we have seen bottles of Bulgarian wine in the supermarkets, with exotic grape varieties such as Mavrud and Melnik. Perhaps we recall that several of its kings were called 'Boris' and that its last reigning monarch returned as Prime Minister in 2001, with the distinctively royal surname of 'Sakskobburggotski'. Perhaps as children we admired 'Uncle Bulgaria' of *Wombles* fame.

Thus, I set off to Sofia with an open-mind and an eagerness to learn something about this seemingly mysterious country. I was struck immediately by the capital's relaxed, unassuming atmosphere. How many countries have a presidential palace that shares its building with a Sheraton hotel?

All over the city centre there are also reminders of the past—not only the Soviet-era trams and architecture but the many 'pockets' of Roman ruins, some with underground underpasses arranged around them. Sofia is older than Athens and Rome. It was once a stronghold of the Thracians, who left us no written record but whose power and magnificence are obvious from the gold and silver vessels found in some of their burials.

Sofia is also a city of churches, both large and small. On my first evening I admired the splendour of the great Aleksandûr Nevski Memorial Church, honouring the Russians who liberated the country from Ottoman rule in 1877–8, and the cathedral, Sveta Nedelya, which was nearly destroyed by Communist terrorists in 1925. Vespers was being sung and a priest incensing the many icons dotted around the interior. A smaller church nearby, reached by descending time-worn steps, was holding the same service. The psalms were being recited alternatively by a priest in the sanctuary and a lady standing at a lectern—his wife, perhaps, or a faithful parishioner. They were hardly aware of my presence as I stood discreetly at the back, soaking in the atmosphere.

Sofia occupies a strategic location, near a natural spring and at the crossroads of two important roads. Although it only became the Bulgarian capital in 1878 and had long been a backwater under Turkish rule, it was a city of some importance in Roman times. Serdica, as it was then called, was a favourite residence of several Roman Emperors and the birthplace of Aurelian and Galerius. Constantine the Great famously said that 'Serdica is my Rome'. He moved his court there and even considered making it his capital, before deciding on Constantinople. Some have suggested that his mother, St Helena, was born in Serdica—a rival legend, of course, links her birthplace to the Essex town of Colchester.

Serdica played an important role in Christian history. In 344 some 170 bishops attended a Council there, including (if St Athanasius is to be believed) bishops from Britain. The meeting, which was held in the aftermath of the Council of Nicaea and aimed to resolve the Arian crisis, was dominated by tensions between East and West. Its canons (decrees) were largely about bishops: discouraging the translation of a bishop from one see to another, eliminating corruption and establishing norms for the right of appeal to Rome in disputes amongst the episcopate.

Some scholars suggest that a number of the fourth century churches that can still be traced in present-day Sofia were built at the time of the council to impress the visiting ecclesiastics, host the various liturgies and meetings, and house their retinues. One of the most important of these early churches is St Sophia. Beneath the sixth-century church, which for several centuries functioned as a mosque, can be found the remains of two fourth-century ones. There are some impressive decorative motifs, including a mosaic of the Garden of Eden, showing the confidence of the early Christian community.

Serdica's greatest moment came in April 311 when its distinguished son, the Emperor Galerius, came here to take the waters in the midst of his final illness. Just days before his death, he issued an edict that would change the course of Christian history. Eight years previously Diocletian had initiated a violent persecution of those who followed Christ, continued by Galerius when he succeeded him in 305. Churches were destroyed, property confiscated, privileges revoked and many Christians cruelly put to death; their names can be found in the martyrologies.

The reign of terror only ended when a dying Galerius passed an Edict of Toleration at Serdica. Why the change in policy? It may have been that the emperor thought his mortal illness was a sign of divine displeasure; Christian writers certainly thought as much and saw his death as a warning to those who persecuted the righteous. Perhaps he realised that his anti-Christian policy had failed to eliminate Christianity and that a different approach was needed. Galerius admitted that the persecutions had led to religious anarchy: 'we saw that they neither paid the reverence and awe due to the gods nor worshipped the God of the Christians'.

The Edict of Serdica permitted 'Christians to exist again and to hold their religious assemblies once more, providing that they do nothing disturbing to public order'. Those who had until recently been put to death were now encouraged to pray for the well-being and health of the emperor. The Edict not only put an end to persecution but was the first imperial document to formally recognise Christianity as a licit religion.

Galerius's Edict is often overshadowed by the Edict of Milan two years later, signed by the more popular Constantine and his co-emperor Licinius and considered a key moment in the conversion of the Roman Empire. However, Galerius's Edict was, in many ways, the decisive moment, putting an end to persecution and, for the first time, recognising Christianity as a 'licit' religion and encouraging toleration.

The Bulgarian capital, therefore, should occupy a special place in every Christian heart.

TIHANY (HUNGARY)

An Abbey on Lake Balaton

Down the ages monks have had an uncanny knack of choosing stunning locations for their monasteries. Beauty, after all, leads the mind and heart to God. I came across a prime example of this in Hungary: the Benedictine Abbey of Tihany. As even my ticket reminded me: 'Peace to those who come, and blessings on those who leave! … Take the experience of beauty with you that says in this place: the world is greater and more than what we can see'.

The twin towers with onion domes can be seen for miles around but it is only on reaching the monastery that you appreciate its astonishing setting, perched on a peninsula jutting out into Lake Balaton, the largest lake in Central Europe. From the abbey terrace you look across the blue waters to the opposite side several miles distant, the surrounding shores full of resorts and vineyards. The village at the foot of the abbey has thatched buildings and shops selling lavender, paprika and other local produce.

In former times much was made of Tihany's famous echo, said to be the cry of a proud princess who disappeared after being cursed by the king of the lake. However I saw no tourists trying it out: the echo has sadly diminished due to changes in the environment and the shoreline over the past century.

In a land-locked country it is little surprise that the lake is known as 'Hungary's Sea' and it is a popular destination at weekends; despite the lake's size it is surprisingly shallow, with an average depth of three metres. During the Communist era, the marginally more-lenient Hungarian regime meant that Balaton became a popular meeting place for East and West Germans, separated from each other by the Iron Curtain.

The abbey at Tihany goes back to 1055—and, one could say, even further beyond, for there were formerly Greek monks settled in the area. The monastery as we know it was founded by King Andrew I who had a key role in establishing Hungary as a Christian kingdom and still lies buried in the crypt. His wish was that the monks would pray 'for the salvation of the souls of himself and his wife, his sons and daughters and all of his relatives living or dead'. The Foundation Charter is regarded as a national treasure since it is the oldest-surviving document to include Hungarian words, including nearly a hundred place names.

Through his family connections—his wife's sister was married to the King of France—Andrew invited a small group of French monks to take up residence in this remote spot. They brought with them the relics of St Aignan (or Ananias) of Orleans, which explains why this obscure French saint is one of the abbey's patrons, appearing on the coat of arms beside a storm-tossed boat. As always there was a political point to all this: the king needed French support in countering the ever-present threat of the Holy Roman Empire.

Little remains of the medieval monastery; as with so many Hungarian churches and monasteries, the Turkish conquests of the sixteenth and seventeenth centuries led to much destruction. The abbey was eventually re-founded and rebuilt in the baroque style during the eighteenth century. Crammed full of paintings and statues, there are many charming details—such as the bearded figure of St Jerome on the pulpit, naked apart from his large brimmed cardinal's hat, or the cherubs playfully playing kettle drums and other instruments around the organ. This magnificent interior owes much to Sebestyen Stulhoff, a Viennese joiner who travelled to Tihany after the death of his beloved and served the community for the rest of his life. He is the only layman buried in the monks' crypt and tradition suggests that one of the adoring angels on the Lady Altar bears the features of his much-missed sweetheart.

This might suggest a new golden age in the monastery's history but there were further setbacks: Joseph II suppressed the community in 1787 as part of his religious reforms, leaving just one monk to act as parish priest (the one position that was deemed useful and productive) and once again the monks were expelled in 1950, the buildings being used as a poor house and museum and the church (at least) continuing to function. The community was only restored in 1990 though the visitor is hardly aware of this, such is the timelessness of the place.

One event in the twentieth century is still very much remembered. In November 1918 the last Austrian emperor and King of Hungary, Blessed Karl, was pressured to withdraw from state affairs at the end of the First World War. He refused to abdicate but was replaced by Admiral Miklos Horthy, elected as 'regent' in 1920. The king attempted a comeback in 1921 though he became distraught by the resulting violence and bloodshed. He was taken captive by the National Army and the last place he stayed on Hungarian soil was Tihany. Despite the challenging circumstances, he was given a dignified welcome by the monks, who were quietly impressed that he refused, as he had done previously, to abdicate, upholding all of his rights and duties 'under the Hungarian constitution as the Apostolic King of Hungary, crowned with the Crown of St Stephen'.

On 31 October 1921 the king and queen, accompanied by the abbot, went to the chapel to pray the *Itinerarium*, traditionally said before a long and possibly risky journey. He was then taken to a train that would hand them over to the British Navy and exile on the island of Madeira. The saintly king, dedicated to the cause of peace and to his family, died the following year, aged only 34, and was beatified in 2004. The abbey subsequently erected a marble plaque in his honour as well as a Calvary, brutally destroyed by the Communists in 1960 but recently restored. Thus, as the guide book puts it, at this beautiful monastery on Lake Balaton 'one of the first Hungarian kings, Andrew I, meets with the very last', encapsulating the great drama of the country's history.

NORTHERN EUROPE

Denmark, Finland, Norway, Sweden

HELSINKI (FINLAND)

In Search of St Henry

It was well below zero as we crossed the waters of the Baltic Sea on a little ferry. We insisted on sitting on the top deck to take photos of the little islands that passed by, with their snow-topped buildings that looked as if we were moving through a three-dimensional Christmas card, but we could hardly move since the floor was covered in ice. Behind us was the Helsinki skyline, dominated by the Lutheran and Orthodox cathedrals. Helsinki's little Catholic cathedral could not be seen; tucked away in a side street, it is not much bigger than my parish church. Finland must be one of the least Catholic countries in western Europe—it was one of the last to receive the Catholic Faith and one of the first to turn to Protestantism in the sixteenth century. Today, out of a population of 5.1 million, there are around 8,000 Catholics and the country's only diocese consists of just seven parishes, each of which spans a huge area.

In front of us is the vast sea fortress of Suomenlinna, one of Finland's top tourist attractions. Built in the eighteenth century, while Finland was still part of Sweden, the fortress spans six interconnected islands. Such was its size that it became known as the 'Gibraltar of the North'. The Swedes who built Suomenlinna regarded as it as a key defence in these strategically important waters, so close to St Petersburg, and the Russians also saw it as valuable when they gained control of the 'Grand Duchy of Finland' in 1809.

It was a surprise to discover that the Royal Navy bombarded this picturesque fortress in August 1855 during the Crimean War, along with French ships. As the inhabitants of Helsinki rather nervously watched the spectacle from the safety of the Finnish shore, the fortress was badly damaged. Although most of the Crimean War was fought out on the Black Sea, with famous battles such as the Alma and Balaclava, the Baltic campaign attacked Russia on its western flank. Historians now see the 'Battle of Suomenlinna' as little more than a gesture showing the might of the Anglo-French fleet at a time when things were not going so well in the Crimea. It also demonstrated that naval warfare was fast developing: for the first time in history the British had to sweep the waters for thousands of mines laid by the Russians.

I wonder how many of the seamen who attacked Helsinki knew that the patron saint of Finland was an Englishman: St Henry. Although

Helsinki was founded in 1550 and would not have been known by the saint, the Catholic cathedral is dedicated to him. His story takes us back to 1148, when Cardinal Nicholas Breakspear—soon to become England's only pope, Adrian IV—was sent as papal representative to Sweden and Norway. Here he did much to organise and reform the Scandinavian church. One of his *entourage* was St Henry.

Little is known of his early life. He may have spent some time in Rome, as part of Breakspear's household, before travelling to Scandinavia and being consecrated Bishop of Uppsala (Sweden) in 1152.

In 1154, the Swedish king, St Eric IX, mounted a 'crusade' against pagan Finland, partly as a response to raids on his territory. The king was said to have been encouraged in this by the English cardinal and bishop, Henry, although it undoubtedly involved a strong political motive: thanks to St Eric, Sweden would dominate Finland until 1809. According to tradition, the Swedes offered peace on condition that the Finns converted to Christianity. This offer was refused and so a bloody battle ensued, which was won by St Eric. Although there is evidence that Christianity had already reached the Finns from Sweden and Russia in the eleventh century, there was still much evangelisation to be done and St Henry baptised many of the defeated Finns.

St Henry stayed on in Finland after St Eric returned to Sweden, established the first Finnish see at Nousiainen and travelled extensively around the south-west coast. The bishop's travels, however, only lasted six months and were ended by his murder on 19 January 1156 on Kirkkosaari in the middle of a frozen Lake Köyliö. His assassin was a peasant called Lalli, a murderer the saint had previously excommunicated. The story goes that, having hacked St Henry to death, Lalli put on the mitre as a jest, but when he took it off, he found that his own scalp had been torn off! The murderer also tried to take the saint's Episcopal ring but could not remove it. Finally, in desperation, Lalli cut off the bishop's finger, but the ring fell into the snow and could not be found. He eventually drowned himself in the lake.

A blind man and his son, who were walking nearby, found the ring the following spring. The thaw had set in and the boy saw a raven pecking at something in the ice. They approached and found a human finger, with a gold ring upon it. Thinking it was a relic of the saint, the blind man held the finger to his eyes and immediately regained his sight. Another tradition states that the ring can be seen shimmering through the waters of Lake Köyliö to this day, although it can never be reached.

The story of St Henry has been dismissed as 'crusade propaganda, not fact'. Others have questioned whether the saint's origins were really English. However, it cannot be discounted that St Henry was widely venerated as a saint and martyr during the Middle Ages. His body was buried at Nousiainen and later moved to the cathedral at Turku, the old capital. He was never formally canonised, but soon became considered the Apostle of Finland, a saint especially invoked by seafarers during storms. A pilgrimage is still made in his honour to Kirkkosaari island. Meanwhile St Henry's fame spread to his native land. A chapel was dedicated to him at the Carmelite priory of Great Yarmouth. He was also included in Pomerancio's series of frescoes of English saints and martyrs at the Venerable English College, Rome.

Interestingly, the saint's murderer, Lalli, became something of a national hero following the Reformation—a 'freedom fighter' who opposed the foreign influence of Sweden and Rome and stood for Finland's long journey to independence. There is now even a statue of him near the site of the saint's martyrdom.

Despite the efforts of St Henry and other later missionaries, such as the English Bishop Thomas, the conversion of Finland was a gradual process. In fact, burial practices in Karelia (around the Russian border) remained pagan until the beginning of the fourteenth century. In the 1830s the folklorist Elias Lönnrot collected tales, songs and poems from this region to form the *Kalevala*, Finland's equivalent of the *Iliad*, which would inspire the music of Sibelius. The final section treats the story of the 'Newborn King', in which a virgin called Marjatta (or Mary) falls pregnant after eating a berry, is rejected by her family and gives birth to a boy who is worshipped by the sun and moon as their Creator. In a charmingly Finnish adaptation of the Nativity story, Jesus is born in a stable because there was no room for them in the ... sauna. This was considered a perfect place for giving birth, given its sterile nature and the pain-reducing qualities of the steam. Thus, Christianity came to the far north and became intertwined with folk beliefs and a distinctive way of life.

St Henry's feast day (19 January) marks the half-way point in the long and severe winter. As the saying goes, around the saint's feast 'the bear rolls over to the other side'.

ROSKILDE (DENMARK)

The Christian Origins of Bluetooth

Wandering around museums and ancient sites, we sometimes find ourselves face to face with the mysterious world of runes. These inscriptions, using bizarre-looking characters, were an important means of written communication for the peoples of northern Europe during the first millennium AD. They are of obvious interest to historians but also summon up images of codes waiting to be broken and the casting of magical spells.

Only a handful of people can read them but there is one runic inscription familiar to most people. Look at your mobile or tablet and notice the familiar Bluetooth device in a blue oval. It may look very modern but it is actually the initials of a tenth-century Danish king, Harald Bluetooth, adopted from Scandinavian runes of the time. One of its developers, Jim Kardach, explained that the king was 'famous for uniting Scandinavia just as we intended to unite the PC and cellular industries with a short-range wireless link'.

Harald Bluetooth probably got his unusual name because he had a bad dark-coloured tooth that became something of a personal trademark. It was not unusual for rulers to gain such names: his son was Sweyn Forkbeard (briefly King of Denmark but also of England) and his father Gorm the Old (making him sound rather like a character from Tolkein). It seems that Harald at first ruled jointly with Gorm and then alone after his death. He was clearly an able leader, building a series of ring forts at strategic locations, gaining power over Norway and attempting to counter the threat from across the German border.

But the king who is memorialised in our cars and electronic devices is best remembered for establishing Denmark as a Christian kingdom. Missionaries had long been present among the Danes; in 720 the English St Willibrord had tried to convert King Ongendus, who had been described as 'more savage than any beast and harder than stone'. A Christian bishop called Poppo was present at Bluetooth's court. According to an almost contemporary chronicler, he claimed that the Christian God was the one true god while Odin, Thor and the other Norse deities were actually demonic. Harald was startled at this bold teaching. He was happy to recognise that the Lord Jesus had a place in the divine pantheon but not as the one and only Saviour. And so he challenged Poppo to put his claims to a test. As often happened in legal cases, he was put to the ordeal. This could take a number of forms: in Poppo's case, he was told to pick up a red-hot iron, walk with it for several paces and then throw it. His hand was then bandaged and examined four days later; it was found to be free of any scars. This, combined with the bishop's courage and conviction, made a deep impression on the king, who was quickly baptised.

As a sign of his new faith, Harald reburied his parents in the Christian manner at Jelling. The stones still stand, with a distinctive depiction of Christ Crucified (the earliest in Scandinavia) and a runic inscription saying 'King Harald bade this monument be made in memory of Gorm his father and Thyra his mother, that Harald who won for himself all Denmark and Norway and made the Danes Christians'. It has been described as 'Denmark's baptism certificate'.

Denmark was now Christian. The new-found faith brought the kings not only the promise of personal salvation but political benefits, especially in the on-going struggles with the German emperor. Indeed, it was a German archbishop, based in Hamburg-Bremen, who claimed jurisdiction over Scandinavia and subsequent Danish kings tried to counter this by forging a link with Canterbury, especially during the brief period that England and Denmark were one. King Canute—famous to countless school children for trying to command the sea tide and thus demonstrate the limits of earthly power—appointed Englishmen to four Danish bishoprics to lessen German influence and this helped lead the way to a more independent Danish Church.

Despite Bluetooth's achievement, his life ended violently, the victim, it seems, of a rebellion led by his son, Sweyn, around 986. He was buried at Roskilde, about 20 miles west of Copenhagen, though his remains have never been discovered. He had established his capital here and erected a church in honour of the Holy Trinity. It was later replaced by a brick cathedral built in the French gothic style, one of the gems of northern Europe and the final resting place of Denmark's kings and queens. Here lies Margrete I, Queen of Denmark, Sweden and Norway, in a beautifully delicate alabaster tomb behind the high altar, and that most Renaissance of princes, Christian IV, in a large chapel, surrounded by his family.

Spare a thought for Harald Bluetooth next time you take a call in the privacy of your car or stream music to a loudspeaker. Even the emblem that bears his name attests to the great changes he presided over, for with the coming of Christianity the old runic script was replaced by the Latin alphabet. He tried to unite his people not only as a polity but before God.

TRONDHEIM (NORWAY)

The Seat of Norway

Trondheim may be Norway's third largest city but it has a decidedly provincial air and is dominated by the world's most northerly medieval cathedral: the Nidarosdomen. The impressive grey-stoned west front and green spire are perhaps a surprising sight in this land of blue-black fjords, vast seascapes and ragged mountains. The cathedral has experienced several fires in its long history and been restored numerous times; nevertheless, it bears witness to Norway's honoured status in medieval Christendom.

A walk around the city provide a crash course in Norway's sacred history. In the main square is a statue of its founding father, King Olav (Olaf) Tryggvason. A tough Norse raider, he had been born in Orkney and spent some years at the court of Kyiv. He is said to have been influenced by a hermit he had encountered on the Isles of Scilly (possibly the obscure St Lide). In 994 there was some sort of ceremony, often described as a baptism, at—of all places—Andover (Hampshire), which may have been part of a broader political treaty. Nevertheless, he is credited as building Norway's first church and converting his subjects, though often through brutal means. The process of Christianisation had begun earlier in the reign of Haakon the Good, who had come to know the Church in his youth at the English court of Athelstan.

These short biographies remind us of the cosmopolitan character of these Northmen. Forget our modern national borders; what mattered then was the ease of access provided by the sea. What we call the Atlantic Ocean, North Sea and Irish Sea were express highways for these skilled sailors and navigators, who gradually built up a far-flung, informal empire. Indeed, for much of the early eleventh century Norway, Denmark and England were joined together in personal rule.

It is another Olaf that Trondheim chiefly remembers: Olaf Haraldsson—St Olaf, the country's *Rex Perpetuus* (Perpetual King). His sanctity rests upon his support for the Church, his loss of throne and subsequent 'martyrdom' at a battle fought at nearby Stiklestad (1030), and the many miracles claimed at his tomb. He was as fearsome as any other Viking; his means of evangelisation were not always peaceful and one poem commemorates his successful attack on London Bridge in 1014. Folk tales record his slaying of dragons and trolls. His saintly status was officially recognised by Pope Alexander III in 1164 and pilgrims flocked to Trondheim, despite the long distances involved. A number of churches were dedicated to him in England, including London's St Olave Hart Street, where Samuel Pepys was buried.

The episcopal see of Nidaros at what is now Trondheim dates from the twelfth-century legatine mission of the English Nicholas Breakspear, later to become Pope Adrian IV. The cathedral became the seat of a huge archdiocese, with its Metropolitan jurisdiction spreading to Greenland, Iceland, Orkney, the Faroes and the Isle of Man (which was under Norwegian control until 1266). The 1100s were a golden age, in many ways, for Christian Norway: King Sigurd I may hardly be a household name but he was the first European monarch to directly participate in a crusade to the Holy Land, between 1107 and 1111. It was a largely successful campaign; he sailed with 60 ships via England, Santiago, Lisbon, the Balearics and Sicily, and spent time with the Byzantine emperor at Constantinople. He helped capture Sidon and brought back to Trondheim a relic of the True Cross.

Norway today has a tiny Catholic population, many of whom have a migrant background. The country has one diocese, based in Oslo, and two territorial prelatures in the north (Tromsø) and centre (Trondheim)—a reflection of its missionary status. At the turn of the third millennium, there has been a revival of religious life, particularly from the Cistercian tradition. Trappistine nuns from Iowa opened a house at Tautra in 1999 and their male counterparts from Cîteaux established a monastery about a mile from the ruins of the medieval Munkaby Abbey in 2007. In 2020 the Norwegian-born Abbot of Mount St Bernards (Leicestershire), Erik von Varden, was consecrated bishop (or, more correctly, prelate) of Trondheim in an impressive ceremony at Nidaros Cathedral. Once again, the Catholic community in Norway received support from across the North Sea.

VADSTENA (SWEDEN)

Sibyl of the North

Situated on Lake Vattern, Vadstena boasts a castle and a narrow-gauge railway, and despite its population of roughly 6,000, has the status of a city. It is the old abbey, with its large church, which is of particular interest—the resting place of St Bridget (Birgitta), a towering figure of the medieval church. She has been given lots of impressive titles: 'Ambassadress of God', 'Co-Patroness of Europe', 'Sibyl of the North', 'Pilgrim of Unity', even 'the first emancipated woman'. Certainly, she reminds us that women did have a voice in the Middle Ages and an important part to play in society and in the Church, though obviously this was partly due to her privileged background, which opened many doors. She was a new sort of saint—a widowed mother of eight who was neither a martyr nor (technically) a nun; the foundress of a religious order who travelled widely, from Sweden to Rome, Santiago and Jerusalem; a visionary who influenced kings and popes; a proud Swede who spent the last 24 years of her life on the other side of Europe.

St Bridget was born on or around 14 June 1303. Sweden, of course, was at the edge of civilisation—a frontier territory rather like Ireland or Scotland. It seems that the Gospel reached the region from the eighth century, thanks largely to the labours of St Ansgar, 'Apostle of the North', and various English and Irish missionaries. Here we could mention St Sigfrid, an eminent priest of York who is known as 'Apostle of Sweden', St David, an English-born abbot, and the martyr St Eskil. There was St Botvid, too, who though born in Sweden was converted to Christianity after visiting England and returned to his home country as a missionary.

St Bridget was the daughter of a prominent Swede, Birger Persson, governor of the province of Uppland (on the eastern coast, just north of Stockholm), a major landowner and lawyer. Given her high birth and wealth, it is little wonder that some sources (mistakenly) describe her as a 'princess', though it seems that through her mother she was related to the royal family.

It was clear from the very start that the little girl was close to God and had been given a particular vocation. Indeed, on the day of her birth a neighbouring priest was told by a virgin sitting on a cloud that the baby's 'wondrous voice shall be heard all over the world'. In

1316, aged thirteen or fourteen, she married Ulf Gudmarsson, a man described as 'rich, noble and wise', who was five years her senior. Like her father, he became a figure of some importance—a lawyer and a member of the King's Privy Council. St Bridget, it seems, would have preferred to dedicate her life to God in the cloister but eventually came to love him like 'her own heart'. They were married for twenty-eight years and had eight children together: four sons and four daughters, one of whom (Catherine) is also recognised as a saint. The couple attended daily Mass, became Franciscan Tertiaries, were lavish in giving alms to the poor and, we read, 'caused a large house to be built for the needs of sick and poor people, and often she served them herself very humbly, and washed their feet and kissed them'.

St Bridget, then, is a very accessible figure—no distant mystic or 'holier-than-thou' Foundress but a wife and mother, who was able to pursue a life of holiness amid all the distractions of the world; a woman of action. She was well known at the Court and spent a period in the household of Blanche of Namur, who had married King Magnus in 1335. The saint acted as a lady-in-waiting, helping introduce her to Swedish ways; she also (perhaps less successfully) tried to lead the royal couple closer to God.

St Bridget and her husband were keen pilgrims—reminding us that Sweden was very much part of Catholic Christendom, despite its remote location. Indeed, the saint's father, grandfather and great-grandfather are said to have made pilgrimages to the Holy Land and Santiago de Compostela—an epic journey in those days before air travel! The saintly couple visited the relatively local shrines of St Olaf in Trondheim and St Botvid in Salem (not far from Stockholm).

Having had their appetites wetted, they then planned a pilgrimage to Compostela in 1341. The journey, which they made with a small group of relatives, friends and priests, seems to have been life-changing. It made her aware of two major themes that would constantly reappear in her later life. They passed through a France that was torn apart by the so-called Hundred Years' War. She may well have passed close to the city of Avignon, where the pope was currently residing, due to various complex political issues. This would be another key concern for her: to persuade the pope to return to Rome, the centre of unity.

Back in Sweden, Ulf retired to the Cistercian monastery at Alvastra, where one of their sons was a student. He had fallen ill on the pilgrimage and his health was still weak; he died on 12 February 1344. St Bridget decided to give herself completely to God and received many visions.

She dictated her experiences to her confessors-secretaries, who translated them from Swedish into Latin and gathered them in eight volumes entitled *Revelations*. Later on a further collection was produced, *Revelationes extravagantes* (supplementary revelations). These belong to our rich Catholic tradition; as St John Paul II commented, 'the Church, which recognised Bridget's holiness without ever pronouncing on her individual revelations, has accepted the overall authenticity of her interior experience'.

Slowly, over time, she discerned that these visions concerned the personalities and issues of the day. She sent envoys to the kings of England and France in 1348 urging them to make peace. She thought they were like 'two wild beasts! One of them is greedy to swallow everything it can get. The more it eats the hungrier it gets ... The other animal wants to exalt itself above all men and to rule over them. Each of the two animals tries to swallow the heart of the other'. She sent messengers to the pope, too, that same year, telling him to return to Rome, preach the word of God and announce the year of jubilee. In this, of course, she resembles her contemporary and fellow Patroness of Europe, St Catherine of Siena.

One of the most important visions that she received concerned a new religious order that she should establish. This happened at Vadstena, while she was visiting the king's palace there. Christ Himself told her that many religious Orders were in decline:

> I lament that the fences around the vineyards have fallen down, the watchmen sleep and robbers break in, the roots are being dug up by moles, the branches are withered by drought and the grapes blown down by the wind and trodden under foot. But, so that the wine shall not entirely disappear I shall plant for myself a new vineyard, and to it you shall bear the vine branches of my words and there they shall take root.

And so began the Order of the Most Holy Saviour—the Bridgettines. King Magnus was still sufficiently supportive of the saint to grant her use of his house at Vadstena, though the foundation took decades to be consolidated as St Bridget waited for papal approval and faced much opposition in Sweden.

The Rule envisaged a double monastery of men and women, similar to the ones that existed in Saxon England (such as St Hilda's Whitby) or were run at a later date by the Gilbertines (also largely in England) or the French Order of Fontevrault. The abbess was in charge of temporal affairs; all deeds were in her name and all charters addressed to her, while the superior of the monks (the 'Confessor General') directed the spiritual life of both branches. There were supposed to be 60 nuns, thirteen priests (symbolising the twelve apostles and St Paul), four deacons (calling to mind the Latin Doctors of the Church) and eight lay brothers—coming to a total of 85 (the thirteen apostles plus the 72 disciples). The sisters wore on their heads, then as now, the distinctive 'Crown of the Five Precious Wounds'. The brothers led a less enclosed life than the sisters and were able not only to look after the spiritual needs of the nuns but to preach to the faithful and undertake pastoral work. The spirituality of the Order was based on the Lord's Passion and a devotion to Our Lady.

In 1349 St Bridget left Sweden for good and travelled to Rome. She was, it seems, frustrated with her largely unsuccessful efforts to 'convert' the royal court in Sweden. She wanted to win papal approval for her Order and also persuade the pope to return to Rome and mediate a peace between France and England. She settled first into first a room which had a window looking into the church of San Lorenzo in Damaso and then a house on what is now the Piazza Farnese (where the Bridgettine convent is today). She lived here with several companions (including her daughter St Catherine) and became a familiar figure at the many shrines of the city and beyond; indeed, she visited Milan, Pavia, Assisi, Bari, Naples and Monte Gargano, to name just a few. She did much work with the poor and with pilgrims (who often stayed at her house), and was well known for her visions and prophecies (even though they were often manipulated by the various factions in the Church to support their agenda). Such was her generosity that she got into debt and had to beg for survival. On one occasion, when a mob threatened to break into her house, Our Lady appeared and assured her of her protection. As a result, the Bridgettine started singing the hymn *Ave Maris Stella* at the end of Vespers.

In 1367 Urban V became the first pope to set foot in Rome for some 60 years, thanks partly to the protestations of St Bridget. There was much business to complete, including the approval of the Bridgettine Rule—modifications were made and the Rule, which St Bridget believed she had received from Christ Himself, technically acted as a 'supplement' to the Rule of St Augustine. This was because the Fourth Lateran Council of 1215 had said that any new Orders should follow one of the tried and tested Rules.

With her Order approved, work resuming on the mother house at Vadstena and the pope back in Rome (although, as it turned out, only temporarily), St Bridget was able to set out on one last pilgrimage: to the Holy Land. This was a difficult journey for a 68 year-old to undertake and was not without drama: they were nearly shipwrecked near Jaffa. She stayed in the Holy Land for four and a half months and received many insights into the life and passion of the Lord.

Those who accompanied her included an English knight, William Williamson, and her son, Karl, who died *en route* in Naples. He seems to have been the black sheep of the family and after his death St Bridget had a vision of his particular judgement. The Virgin Mary was his advocate, Satan his chief accuser. Despite his many sins, Karl was at last acquitted and admitted to eternal glory largely because of the virtues, prayers and hardships borne by his mother!

The journey back to Rome would be her last: her health was failing. But she continued to act as God's mouthpiece. Stopping off at Cyprus, she denounced the sinfulness that she saw at court and in society at large, and in Naples she spoke out for the non-Christian slaves who were often mistreated. Back in the Eternal City, she died on 23 July; her body was buried in Rome and eventually taken back to Vadstena by her daughter.

The saint's granddaughter, Ingegerd Knutsdotter, was the first recognised abbess of this important abbey, that attracted benefactors and pilgrims over the next 200 years. There were close links to the Crown and two fifteenth-century queens chose to be buried there. At the Reformation, the double community lingered on—novices were still received, though monks and nuns free to leave at any point to get married. When attempts were made to introduce Protestant services in 1540, it is reported that the nuns plugged their ears during the sermon. There was a Catholic revival later in the sixteenth century—a seminary was even established in 1592—but the foundation was ultimately dissolved in 1595 and the surviving nuns moved to Marienbrunn Abbey in Gdansk. The buildings have since variously served as a home for veterans, school, hospital, prison, asylum, hotel and museum.

A Bridgettine community was established in Vadstena from 1963 with a community of Dutch sisters; in 1991 Pax Mariae became an autonomous abbey. St Bridget, described by Margery Kempe as being 'kind and meek to every creature' and with 'a laughing face', once again is present in her beloved homeland.

www.ingramcontent.com/pod-product-compliance
Ingram Content Group UK Ltd.
Pitfield, Milton Keynes, MK11 3LW, UK
UKHW041858190726
13854UKWH00002B/970